DIVIDED HOUSES

DIVIDED HOUSES

RELIGION AND GENDER IN MODERN FRANCE

CAROLINE FORD

CORNELL UNIVERSITY PRESS

Ithaca and London

First published 2005 by Cornell University Press

Printed in the United States of America

Design by Scott Levine

Library of Congress Cataloging–in–Publication Data

Ford, Caroline C., 1956–
   Divided houses : religion and gender in modern France / Caroline Ford.
      p. cm.
   Includes bibliographical references and index.
   ISBN 0–8014–4367–9 (cloth : alk. paper)
   1. Women—France—19th century. 2. Women—France—
Religious life. 3. Sex role—France. I. Title.
   HQ1613.F67 2005
   282'.44'082—dc22

                          2004030953

Cornell University Press strives to use environmentally responsible suppliers and materials to the fullest extent possible in the publishing of its books. Such materials include vegetable-based, low-VOC inks and acid-free papers that are recycled, totally chlorine-free, or partly composed of nonwood fibers. For further information, visit our website at www.cornellpress.cornell.edu.

Cloth printing   10 9 8 7 6 5 4 3 2 1

FOR SANJAY

CONTENTS

PREFACE

This book emerged out of a long-standing interest in how France confronted issues posed by cultural difference in the nineteenth and twentieth centuries. This difference expressed itself in the assertion of religious claims, expressions of local or regional identities, and calls for linguistic pluralism since the French Revolution. That revolution left France with a conception of nationhood based on cultural assimilation, which underpinned France's *mission civilisatrice*, its attempt to integrate the various regions of metropolitan France and the far-flung corners of the French empire into a common culture. Central to the project of cultural assimilation is the principle of *laïcité*, which was forged only slowly as an operative ideological justification for republican campaigns to secularize public education and the public sector more generally by the late nineteenth century. I wished to understand how and why this principle came into being and how it related to developments within the dominant religion of Catholicism in the nineteenth century. The laicizing initiatives that had begun during the French Revolution culminated in the Separation of Church and State in 1905, but the issues raised by religious and cultural difference have not been resolved. While this book focuses on the history of French Catholicism in the nineteenth century, it was written as the French once again debate the issues surrounding the republican principle of *laïcité* in the state's opposition to young Muslim women's wearing headscarves in public schools. It is my hope that this study will put these contemporary debates in a broader historical perspective.

This book owes a great deal to historians of gender, religion, and France, and it is a pleasure for me to acknowledge them here. This project can be traced to discussions that I had with Olwen Hufton while I was a beginning assistant professor at Harvard—and finishing another book— in the early 1990s. She has generously given her time, insights, and solid support ever since. I benefited from conversations that I had at various moments with David Blackbourn, Rachel Fuchs, Sima Godfrey, Ruth Harris, Lynn Hunt, Colin Jones, Thomas Kselman, Peter McPhee, John Merriman, Alex Owen, Tim Tackett, and Peter Ward. Laura Lee Downs has been a subtle critic and interlocutor since I first met her in Paris almost ten years ago. My sister, Marjorie, and my brother-in-law, Matthew Huntley, have always provided a wonderful home away from home, and Jocelyne Baverel has been an incomparable friend.

Parts of these chapters were presented at the University of Reading, Cornell University, Oxford, Harvard, the University of Chicago, the Ecole des Hautes Etudes en Sciences Sociales in Paris, and at the University of California at Los Angeles. I appreciate the comments that were offered to me in these various venues. I am very grateful to John Ackerman for his interest in this project and for skillfully shepherding the manuscript through the publication process. Elizabeth Loving was very instrumental in locating some of the illustrations for this book. The staff of the Bibliothèque Nationale de France were unfailingly helpful, and I was glad that I was able to complete the necessary archival research before the Archives Nationales in Paris closed its doors to scholars for several years. Some of the material for chapters 2, 3, and 4 appeared in a different form in "Private Lives and Public Order in Restoration France: The Seduction of Emily Loveday," *American Historical Review* 99, no. 1 (February 1994); in "Female Martyrdom and the Politics of Sainthood in Nineteenth-Century France: The Cult of Sainte Philomène" in *Catholicism in Britain and France since 1789*, ed. Nicholas Atkin and Frank Tallett (London, 1996); and in "Story-Telling and the Social Imagery of Religious Conflict in Nineteenth-Century France: The Case of Jeanne Françoise Le Monnier," in *The Moral World of the Law*, ed. Chris Wickham and Peter Coss, Past and Present Publications (Cambridge University Press, 2000). All translations from French are my own, unless otherwise indicated. Research for this project was generously supported by the Georges Lurcy Educational Trust, a Minton Faculty Fellowship from Harvard University, a fellowship from the Women's Studies in Religion Program at the Harvard Divinity School, a Fulbright Fellowship to France, and a Humanities and Social Sciences Grant from the University of British Columbia.

Finally, Sanjay Subrahmanyam kindly commented on the entire manuscript, but it was his marvelous cooking—with its red chilies, mustard seed, and tamarind—that sustained me as this project neared completion. His warm affection, intelligence, and wicked humor have made my life richer in every conceivable way. I dedicate this book to him.

Oxford, July 2004

DIVIDED HOUSES

INTRODUCTION

This book explores the phenomenon of the "feminization of Catholicism" in France from the French Revolution to the First World War, and focuses on two broad themes. First, it examines the impact of the feminization of Catholicism on the civil and social status of women, which gave rise to heated debates about the limits of female agency, paternal authority, women's property rights, and women's role in the family and in society. Second, it shows the way in which conflicts surrounding these issues contributed to the formation of a distinctive kind of *laïc* or secular political language that came to be associated with French republicanism in the nineteenth and twentieth centuries. French republicanism is uncompromisingly secular and is predicated on the principle of *laïcité*, which was inspired by a deep-seated anticlericalism. It continues to shape controversies about cultural difference, which have been reignited in Europe in recent years by the "retour du religieux" (or return of religion to public life), immigration, and identity politics in Muslim communities in the 1980s and 1990s.[1] The sound and fury occasioned by the so-called "affaire des foulards" or "scarf affair" of 1989, which blew up when three Muslim

---

[1] For an overview of some of the parameters of this debate, see *Religions, laïcité, intégration: Actes du colloque organisé au Centre Georges Pompidou, 25 mai 1991* (Paris, 1993); Françoise Gaspard and Farhad Khosrokhavar, *Le foulard et la République* (Paris, 1995); David Beriss, "Scarves, Schools and Segregation: The Foulard Affair" *French Politics and Society* 8, no. 1 (Winter 1990): 1–13; Guy Coq, *Laïcité et république: Le lien nécessaire* (Paris, 1995).

girls were expelled from a school for wearing religious symbols in the form of headscarves, demonstrated the depth of the passions engendered by expressions of religious and cultural difference in France's school system, which had been secularized since the late nineteenth century. The passions that the explosive and emotionally charged "affaire des foulards" aroused were rooted in a long-standing struggle to establish a nation predicated on the principle of *laïcité* from the French Revolution onwards.

While anticlericalism has been linked to the alleged role that religion played in the lives of women, this book assesses how it came to constitute and consolidate *laïc* political culture in the century following the French Revolution. *Laïcité* has become an inherent part of twentieth-century republican universalism, and debates about the nature and meaning of female religiosity have been central to the way in which it was articulated and defined. This book is therefore intended to provide a historical and gendered dimension to current conflicts in France surrounding religious difference and the principle of *laïcité*.

The term "feminization," when applied to religion, requires some explanation. Historians and contemporaries have employed it to describe changes in the nature and practice of Protestantism and Catholicism in both Europe and America toward the end of the eighteenth century, but it has been used rather loosely and has been accorded varying meanings in different national and denominational contexts. Ann Douglas gave currency to the concept in her book *The Feminization of American Culture* where she defined the "feminization" of Protestantism in America in terms of the preponderance of women in congregations; the growing role that women exercised over religious life; and the resulting "feminization" and "softening" of theology and religious practices.[2] Ann Douglas's thesis has been the subject of considerable controversy and critique. While not denying the conspicuousness of women in the formal practice of religion during the nineteenth century, these critiques have centered on the equation of "feminization" with sentimentalization and the strength of the role that the Church gave women in the sphere of religion. Other historians have explored the origins of the important presence of women within congregations, linking this phenomenon to their exclusion from the public sphere of the Republic, and its consequences for the development of American and French political culture.[3]

---

[2] Ann Douglas, *The Feminization of American Culture* (New York, 1977).

[3] "Arguably, therefore, the discourse of the Revolution succeeded perfectly in carrying out its 'hidden agenda' of the exclusion of women from a public role, leaving for them recourse to the surviving universalistic language of the Church." Dorinda Outram, "*Le langage mâle de la vertu*: Women and the Discourse of the French Revolution," in *The Social History of Language*,

Like historians of America, historians of Britain have also noted the importance of women in nineteenth-century religious life. For example, Leonore Davidoff and Catherine Hall, Deborah Valenze, and Alex Owen have shown in varying ways the prominence of women in the practice of religion—both formal and informal—and have linked this prominence to broader changes in British society.[4] These historians have focused some attention on the consequences of the conspicuous presence of women in the practice of religion, arguing that it often made a direct contribution to the development of modern feminism.

Religious sociologists and historians of religion in modern France have long observed the centrality of Catholicism in the lives of French women following the French Revolution.[5] Madeleine Rébérioux has asserted that "women incontestably resisted better than men the sirens of *laïcité*" and "those of science" in a country whose "cultural exceptionalism" resides in its virulent anticlericalism and in its institutional and cultural *laïcisation*.[6] Indeed, in recent years historians have shown that nineteenth-century religious revivals, the emergence of new cults and pilgrimages, the development of new forms of Catholic devotion, and most especially women's strong attachment to religion, call into question a once stereotyped image of the nineteenth century as a secular age.[7]

The feminization of Catholicism in France has been defined by historians in the following terms: first, in the discrepancy between the formal practice of religion among men and women; second, in the "feminiza-

---

ed. Peter Burke and Roy Porter (Cambridge, 1987), p. 133. Also see Joan Landes, *Women and the Public Sphere in the Age of the French Revolution* (Ithaca, N.Y., 1988).

[4] Deborah Valenze, *Prophetic Sons and Daughters: Female Preaching and Popular Religion in Industrial England* (Princeton, N.J., 1985); Lenore Davidoff and Catherine Hall, *Family Fortunes: Men and Women of the English Middle Class* (Chicago, 1987); Alex Owen, *The Darkened Room: Women, Power and Spiritualism in Late Victorian England* (Philadelphia, 1987).

[5] Claude Langlois, *Le catholicisme au féminin: Les congrégations françaises à supérieure générale au XIXe siècle* (Paris, 1984); Jacques Léonard, "Femmes, religion et médecine: Les religieuses qui soignent en France au XIX siècle," *Annales, économies, sociétés, civilisations* 32 (1977):887–907. For studies of spiritual life within religious communities, see Odile Arnold, *Le corps et l'âme: La vie des religieuses au XIXe siècle* (Paris, 1984); Yvonne Turin, *Femmes et religieuses au XIXe siècle: Le féminisme "en religion"* (Paris, 1989); and Rebecca Rogers, "Retrograde or Modern? Unveiling the Teaching Nun in Nineteenth-Century France," *Social History* 23 (May 1998): 146–64. Women were also prominent in the pilgrimage movement that emerged at Lourdes. See Ruth Harris's *Lourdes: Body and Spirit in the Secular Age* (London, 1999).

[6] Madeleine Rebérioux, "Ruptures et figures contemporaines: L'héritage révolutionnaire," in *Histoire de la France: Les formes de la culture*, vol. 4, ed. André Burguière and Jacques Revel (Paris, 1993), p. 414, 416.

[7] See, for example, Owen Chadwick, *The Secularization of the European Mind* (Cambridge, 1975).

tion" of religious personnel as manifested in the explosion of female religious communities and the sharp rise in the number of women who
joined them; and third, in terms of the "feminization"—read sentimentalization—of forms of devotion. This phenomenon was commented on frequently in legislative chambers, memoirs, novels, and plays, among religious and anticlerical commentators alike. Davidoff and Hall, among
others, have also suggested that religion was embraced actively by Protestant middle-class men and played an important role in defining certain
conceptions of English bourgeois masculine identity. While religious re-
vivalism in France was not solely a feminine phenomenon and religious
practices differed according to region and class, the religious bifurcation
between men and women was quite pronounced in France, and it was one
to which Catholics and unbelievers frequently alluded.[8] Monseigneur
Félix Antoine Philbert Dupanloup (1802–78), the influential bishop of
Orléans, saw in women an instrument through which to rechristianize society and to bring men, who had largely deserted the Church in the aftermath of the French Revolution, back into the fold.[9] He claimed that
"everywhere the Christian religion has passed, it has created religious
women. Catholic women populate our churches, Protestant women,
Protestant churches, Jewish women, Jewish temples. It is the honor of
woman everywhere to place their weakness and modesty at the foot of the
altar."[10] Anticlerical commentators, associating the Catholic Church with
political conservatism, also recognized a "natural" religiosity in women,
and argued against their participation in public affairs precisely because
they could serve as an instrument of political reaction. Historians have
suggested that fears about clerical meddling in part explains why women
received the vote so late in France—following the Second World War.[11]
There has, however, been no extensive analysis of the larger cultural and
social meaning of the prevalent discourses regarding the natural religiosity of women for the development of French political culture, for the civil
status of women, and for the way gender relationships came to be perceived in postrevolutionary French society.

---

[8] For the role of religion in the lives of Catholic men in the nineteenth century, see Paul Seeley, "*O Sainte Mère*: Liberalism and the Socialization of Catholic men in Nineteenth-Century
France," *Journal of Modern History* 70, no. 4 (December 1998): 862–91.
[9] Mgr. Dupanloup, *La femme chrétienne et française: Dernière réponse à M. Duruy et à ses défenseurs*
(Paris, 1868).
[10] Ibid., p. 119.
[11] Steven Hause and Anne R. Kenney, *Women's Suffrage and Social Politics in the French Third Republic* (Princeton, N.J., 1984), p. 238.

Olwen Hufton and Suzanne Desan have posited that the French Revolution played a major role in accelerating the process by which French Catholicism became feminized, but the ramifications of their study for the Revolutionary period have not been carried into the nineteenth century.[12] One of the few forays into this subject, Claude Langlois's magisterial *Le Catholicisme au féminin*,[13] ably documents the extraordinary growth in female Catholic religious communities and observes that the overwhelming majority of women who chose the religious life entered active religious congregations rather than religious orders requiring formal vows. They were not cloistered nuns, separated from society. They lived and worked in the world. Langlois's work is more one that explores the social history of this phenomenon than one that investigates how it was perceived and what impact it had. Similarly, Bonnie Smith's study of the women of the bourgeoisie in northern France[14] points to the importance of religion in the lives of bourgeois women and shows how religion created a kind of cultural barrier between the sexes. Yet Smith does not move beyond the confines of the region or the bourgeoisie to explore the broader significance of a marked female religiosity for the development of the family, political culture, and the law from the French Revolution to the First World War.

This book employs the term "feminization of religion" in two ways. First it refers to the general association of Catholicism and religious practice (attendance at mass and religious devotion) with the sphere of the feminine. Second, it denotes the massive numbers of women who entered Catholic religious orders and congregations during the nineteenth century, in contrast to men. My purpose is not to write a social history of this latter phenomenon, which has been very ably explored by others. In other words, I do not seek to show how and why women entered the Church in unprecedented numbers, though I will suggest reasons for this trend.[15] Rather I explore the political and cultural significance of nineteenth-century understandings of female religiosity, the meanings with which fe-

---

[12] Olwen Hufton, "The Reconstruction of the Church, 1796–1801," in *Beyond the Terror: Essays in French Regional History, 1794–1815*, ed. Gwynne Lewis and Colin Lucas (Cambridge, 1983), pp. 21–52; and Suzanne Desan, *Reclaiming the Sacred: Lay Religion and Popular Politics in Revolutionary France* (Ithaca, N.Y., 1990), esp. pp. 197–216.

[13] See above, note 5.

[14] Bonnie Smith, *Ladies of the Leisure Class: Bourgeoises of Northern France* (Princeton, N.J., 1981).

[15] In addition to Langlois and Smith, see Sarah Curtis's more recent *Educating the Faithful: Religion, Schooling, and Society in Nineteenth-Century France* (DeKalb, Ill., 2000).

male devotion was invested, and how it came to be represented and con-tested in French politics, society, and culture.[16] I will argue that the femi-nization of religion was in part a nineteenth-century construction and that the phenomenon was also a reflection of a perceived rejection of Catholicism by men, which threw women's religiosity into sharp relief. I focus specifically, however, on one aspect of the feminization of reli-gion—not the phenomenon as a whole—namely, women's embrace of the religious vocation. I explore the fears and conflicts that it engendered and how it contributed to the principle of *laïcité* that came to be enshrined in the French secular culture.

The term *laïcisme* first appeared in 1842 to designate "a doctrine which tends to give institutions a nonreligious character," and according to Emile Littré's dictionary, *laïcité* was first coined in 1871 during debates over the removal of religious personnel and religious teachings from pri-mary schools.[17] *Laïcité* was a political and moral concept, implying the sep-aration of civil society from religious society, even though, as Philip Nord has suggested, it also represented "a blend of rationalism, moral purpose-fulness, and humanitarian vision," retaining characteristics of a kind of re-ligious mystique, as Ferdinand Buisson's *foi laïque* implies.[18] It gradually emerged as a political ideal espoused by the *libre pensée* movement follow-ing the Revolution of 1848.[19] In practical terms it represented a refusal to allow particularistic religious institutions or beliefs to intrude upon the public domain or to allow their claims to supersede those of a secular state or nation.

Historians have traced the concept of *laïcité* to a variety of sources—to Comtean positivism, to doctrines of philosophical materialism, and to lib-eral Protestantism, with its emphasis on reconciling, in the words of Philip Nord, the "demands of science and moral conscience."[20] To this extent, they have chiefly emphasized the intellectual roots of *la foi laïque*. Laic

---

[16] For recent perspectives on the problems of narrative and representation in history, see Karen Haltunnen, "Cultural History and the Challenge of Narrativity" in *Beyond the Cultural Turn*, ed. Victoria Bonnell and Lynn Hunt (Berkeley, 1999), pp. 165–81; William Cronon, "A Place for Stories: Nature, History and Narrative," *Journal of American History* 78 (1992); Sarah Maza, "Stories in History: Cultural Narratives in Recent Works in European History," *American Historical Review* 101 (December 1996): 1493–1515.

[17] Guy Bedouelle and Jean-Paul Costa, *Les laïcités à la française* (Paris, 1998), p. 10.

[18] Philip Nord, *The Republican Moment: Struggles for Democracy in Nineteenth-Century France* (Cambridge, Mass., 1995), p. 109.

[19] For a discussion of the political dimensions of laic thought see Jacqueline Lalouette, *La libre pensée en France, 1848–1940* (Paris, 1997), p. 143; John Eros, "The Positivist Generation of French Republicanism," *Sociological Review* 3 (1955): 255–73; and Bedouelle and Costa, *Les laïcités à la française*.

[20] Nord, *The Republican Moment*, p. 91.

faith certainly guided republican policy throughout the thirty years that preceded the First World War and manifested itself in the purge of religious personnel from hospitals and state schools; the dissolution of unauthorized religious congregations; the removal of classroom crucifixes; the banishment of religious instruction from state schools and its replacement by civic instruction; and civil marriages and funerals. And these initiatives culminated, of course, in the Separation of Church and State in 1905. While there is an enormous literature on *laïcité* in France,[21] the central role that the feminization of religion played in the formation of a laic political discourse has remained unacknowledged.[22] Yet, women's entry into religious orders, in particular, challenged the principle of paternal authority, the integrity of the family, and property relations in ways that contributed to debates about the necessity of incorporating the principle of *laïcité* into French law and public institutions by the end of the nineteenth century.

The intense conflict that female religiosity inspired in public and private life in nineteenth-century France stands at the center of the Nobel Prize–winning author Roger Martin du Gard's 1914 novel *Jean Barois*. The novel centers both on the political debacles surrounding the Dreyfus affair, on which the novel is based, but also, more poignantly, on Barois's private life as well. As Barois, the freethinker, lost his faith, he became estranged from his highly devout wife. He also eventually lost his daughter, who took her vows as a nun, to the Church. Jean Barois's alienation from his family bears out what nineteenth-century commentators observed throughout the century: the "intellectual divorce" between men and women, which was created by women's continued attachment to Catholicism and men's desertion of the Church. The consequences for many were dire. Jules Michelet argued in 1845 that at any family table, mother, wife, and daughter shared the same opinions, and if the husband tried to express his views on religion or other serious and profound issues, his own mother would shake her head sadly, his wife would contradict him, and his

[21] See, for example, Louis Capéran, *La laïcité en marche: Histoire de la laïcité républicaine* (Paris, 1961); Coq, *Laïcité et république*; Bedouelle and Costa, *Les laïcités à la française*; Marcel Gauchet, *La religion dans la démocratie: Parcours de la laïcité* (Paris, 1998); and Jacqueline Lalouette, *La république anticléricale, XIXe–XXe siècles* (Paris, 2002).
[22] The relationship between the "private" dimension of anticlericalism and its links to female religiosity has been examined in an important, but largely isolated article on the subject, in which Theodore Zeldin argues that men's resentment of the prying eyes of the priest in the confessional contributed to an almost visceral hatred of the clergy. Zeldin, "A Conflict of Moralities: Confession, Sin and Pleasure in the Nineteenth Century," in *Conflicts in French Society: Anticlericalism, Education and Morals in the Nineteenth Century* (London, 1970), pp. 13–50.

daughter, without saying anything would disapprove: "They are on one side of the table, you on the other, and alone."[23] He went on to suggest that the wives and daughters of French men and women were "governed by our enemies [priests]," as they were "naturally envious of marriage and family life."[24] Similarly, Jules Simon observed in 1864 that there was a deep discord in the relationship between men and women, a lack of accord which threatened the unity of the family, and he advocated secular education for women to create a new harmony between the sexes.[25] This sentiment inspired the vast scheme to secularize primary education and to make it available to women. One of its chief architects, Jules Ferry, argued as early as 1870, "Equality of education is unity reconstituted in the family" for the reason that "today there is a barrier between woman and man, between wife and husband, which makes many marriages, while outwardly harmonious, result in the most profound differences of opinions, of tastes, of feelings."[26] The result was catastrophic, Ferry believed, because in his view "there is no longer a marriage, for real marriage, gentlemen, is the marriage of souls."[27]

My approach to understanding the significance of female religiosity, and more specifically the rise in the number of female religious in nineteenth-century France, departs from those that have been used in recent religious histories of France. Historians of religion in France have been pioneers in the field of religious sociology and have produced an impressive amount of quantitative data on clerical recruitment as well as attendance at mass and the performance of Easter duties. These data have served as barometers of religious feeling and indices of popular mentalities. While this serial approach to the study of religious phenomena has been very fruitful, and has helped historians to identify the striking divergence in male and female religious practice, the meaning attached to these impressive figures has often been neglected. The faces and identity of the individual women who occupied church pews on Sunday, who joined confraternities, and who entered female religious congregations in massive numbers have been obscured. This book's primary concern is to

---

[23] "Votre mère secoue tristement la tête; votre femme contredit, votre fille, tout en taisant, désapprouve. . . . Elles sont d'un côté de la table, vous à l'autre, et seul." Jules Michelet, *Du prêtre, de la femme, de la famille* (Paris, 1861), p. 2.
[24] Quoted in McMillan, "Religion and Gender in Modern France: Some Reflections," in *Religion, Society and Politics in France since 1789,* ed. Frank Tallett and Nicholas Atkin (London, 1991), p. 55.
[25] Jules Simon, *Revue des deux mondes,* 15 August 1864, pp. 21–22.
[26] Quoted in McMillan, "Religion and Gender in Modern France," p. 55.
[27] Ibid.

explore the impact of the feminization of Catholicism on the development of French republican secular culture, but I hope that the men and
women who inhabit this book will also come alive.

This book is based on a wide variety of sources, including parliamentary debates, memoirs, novels, legal cases, and dozens of dusty files in the
F19 series (*Cultes* or Religious Affairs) in the National Archives. Much of
the printed primary material that I rely on was published in pamphlet
form and is only available in archives concerning religious congregations
preserved in the Archives Nationales. Some of it has also been preserved
in the Bibliothèque Nationale in Paris, but many sources have undoubtedly disappeared because of the form in which they were published. I was
fortunate that the Widener Library of Harvard University purchased the
private library of one of the great political figures of the nineteenth century, comte Boulay de la Meurthe (1761–1840), who collected much of
this pamphlet literature, which was subsequently bound together in book
form. This material serves as a basis for some of the *microhistoires* around
which this book is constructed.[28]

A book based on microhistories necessarily begs the question of the
"representativeness" of the cases at hand. While many of the women who
populate this book are unusual in their powerful defiance of family, state,
and the Catholic Church, public response to these cases and the issues
that they raised were representative of broader social anxieties, fears, and
concerns that came to the fore in similar cases time and time again during
the course of the nineteenth century. Microhistories thus provide a window onto social and political processes at particular moments in time,
while revealing the ways in which specific individuals both asserted their
own unique agency and were also constrained by their position in time.[29]
It is my intention to show through these individual case studies how the
concerns of a particular society at a given historical moment came to be

[28] For a discussion of microhistory and its contributions to the reconceptualization of social
and cultural history, see Jacques Revel, ed., *Jeux d'échelles: La micro-analyse à l'expérience* (Paris,
1996); Gregory Brad, "Is Small Beautiful? Microhistory and the History of Everyday Life,"
History and Theory 38, no. 1 (Fall 1999): 100–110; and Carlo Ginzburg, "Microhistory: Two or
Three Things I Know about It," *Critical Inquiry* 20 (Autumn 1993): 10–35.
[29] As Caroline Walker Bynum has argued, "we also learn from texts, and the events they describe and incite, because we find in them the ignoble, the insignificant, the self-
contradictory and paradoxical. In the inconsistencies and ironies of texts—judged as such by
our standards—we learn things the past did not understand about itself." Bynum, *Fragmentation and Redemption: Essays on Gender and the Human Body in Medieval Religion* (New York,
1992), p. 23. Joan Scott makes much the same point in *Only Paradoxes to Offer: French Feminists
and the Rights of Man* (Cambridge, Mass., 1996), which is also based on a set of individual case
studies.

articulated, and to highlight the contradictions within individuals driven by competing allegiances and impulses. Microhistorical approaches often demonstrate the extent to which history can never be a seamless web.[30]

The chapters in this book are organized both chronologically and thematically, spanning a period from the French Revolution to the beginning of the Third Republic. The case studies form a series of episodes located in the Napoleonic period, Restoration, July Monarchy and Second Empire. Their coherence lies in the way in which each illuminates an aspect of the feminization of the Catholic religious vocation throughout the nineteenth century, and each shows the way in which these cases found resonance in French society and helped to propel the drive toward limiting the role of religion in French public life. They are linked by a "ramifying chain of historical concerns," to use Natalie Davis's turn of phrase.[31] Each case explores, in particular, the ways in which the female religious vocation challenged first, the principle of paternal authority; second, property relations; third, the status of women enshrined in French civil law; and fourth, the role of women in marriage and the family, contributing to a form of secular anticlericalism that has been one of the central aspects in a *laïc* political culture.

The first chapter explores the origins of the feminization of Catholicism in the Old Regime and the changing discourses regarding its meaning. I go on to consider the discourse surrounding the "feminization of religion" and how language regarding the "natural" religiosity of women both constituted and gave meaning to the phenomenon. This chapter shows how and why the association of religion with the realm of the feminine during the revolutionary decade was given a new political significance, and the ramifications of this new association. I will examine the ways in which revolutionary rhetoric came to shape revolutionary and postrevolutionary political and religious culture at a moment when reli-

[30] For a discussion of the challenge to the historian of placing the reader "in some relationship of closeness or distance to the events and experiences" he or she is recounting, see Mark Salber Phillips, "Historical Distance and the Historiography of Eighteenth-Century Britain," in *Economy, Polity, and Society: Essays in British Intellectual History, 1750–1950*, ed. Stefan Collini, Richard Whatmore, and Brian Young (Cambridge, 2000), p. 33.

[31] Natalie Z. Davis, *Society and Culture in Early Modern France* (Stanford, Calif., 1975), p. xvii. My approach has been influenced by a number of historians of early modern Europe, who have attempted to illuminate a larger theme through a collective analysis of particular episodes or case studies. See, in addition to the work of Davis, David Warren Sabean, *Power in the Blood: Popular Culture and Village Discourse in Early Modern Germany* (Cambridge, 1984); Robert Darnton, *The Great Cat Massacre and Other Episodes in French Cultural History* (New York, 1985); and Sarah Maza, *Private Lives and Public Affairs: The Causes Célèbres of Prerevolutionary France* (Berkeley, Calif., 1993).

gion was relegated to the "private" sphere of the family and the nation was endowed with a new sacrality. Subsequent chapters of the book will explore the consequences of the "feminization" of religious personnel and the alleged "feminization" of popular devotion in the nineteenth century for women's civil status, the development of republicanism, anticlericalism, and French politics and culture more generally.

As the numbers of women religious grew by leaps and bounds during the nineteenth century, so did the number of complaints that were filed by and against them with the Ministry of Religious Affairs and in legal courts. These complaints and suits ranged over the period between the 1820s and 1880s, but they were particularly numerous during the Bourbon Restoration (1820s), the July Monarchy (1840s) and the Second Empire (1850s and 1860s). They can be divided into two general types, and I will examine each in turn through the lens of cases that became particularly significant in French public life. The first type of complaint alleged that orders accepted young novices and allowed them to take holy vows without parental consent, raising questions about women's civil status and civil rights. This is the focus of chapter 2, which centers on an 1822 appeal to the French government by Douglas Loveday, an English Protestant businessman residing in France, who demanded custody of a daughter who had converted to Catholicism and fled the paternal home for a French convent. The debate that the affair engendered in the press and the Chambers of Peers and Deputies generated highly charged discussions about the rise in the number of "women religious,"[32] their influence in French society, and rights to challenge the principle of paternal authority, which was enshrined in postrevolutionary law. I will attempt to assess the kinds of contradictions that the affair revealed in political circles, and among the Right and Left, both of whom agreed that paternal authority should serve as a basis for public order in postrevolutionary civil society.

The second major complaint came from those who charged religious orders with kidnapping, religious "seduction," and incarceration. Chapter 3 explores the structure and function of these narratives of seduction—within the context of a rich novelistic literature on the subject—written primarily by anticlerical men in the 1840s. It will be further explored through an 1845 complaint lodged by a nun against her own order. Jeanne Le Monnier of the Saint Sacrement of Bayeux alleged that she had

---

[32] I use the term "women religious" throughout this book to designate women who joined a number of different kinds of female religious communities and who took vows. Not all of these women were cloistered and not all of them can strictly be defined as "nuns."

been incarcerated and held against her will first in a convent and then in an asylum. Added to cases of this kind were those that involved the forced conversion of Protestant or Jewish children to the Catholic faith. Among the latter, the most famous international case was the Mortara affair, the forced conversion of a young Jewish boy from Bologna and his subsequent sequestration, which sent shock waves through France and which ultimately contributed to the founding of the Alliance Israélite Universelle in Paris in 1860.[33] The most spectacular French case of forced conversion, which held the attention of the press and public, was the so-called Bluth or Mallet case of 1860, which involved the conversion of three young Jewish girls to Catholicism—a case which led to the charge of *détournement des mineurs* or corruption of minors.

Chapter 4 assesses some of the ramifications of the alleged "feminization" of Catholic devotion, which was manifested in changing devotional practices of the nineteenth century. This chapter will analyze how both anticlericals and the Church invoked the growing "sentimentalization"—read feminization—of female piety in a rhetorical emphasis placed on the "natural religiosity" of women. While one of the central characteristics of nineteenth-century Catholic piety was the rise of Marianism, this study will focus on less studied forms of female devotion.[34] It examines a specific cult of a female saint, that of Sainte Philomène, an adolescent Christian martyr who allegedly died at the hands of the Emperor Diocletian. I assess the religious representations of her martyred body, which was the subject of many paintings—some of which were executed by female artists—in the 1830s, 1840s, and 1850s. I will place women's involvement in Philomène's cult within the wider context of the devotional changes of the nineteenth century, and how she came to be supplanted by the cults of Joan of Arc and Thérèse de Lisieux by the end of the century. I wish to understand how and why the cult of Sainte Philomène came to be defined as "feminine," and the larger significance of the identification of religion with the sphere of the feminine for the Church itself.

Anticlerical sentiment came to a head in the years following the Revolution of 1848 and by then, the government was besieged by complaints that contested a daughter's or a sister's right to bequeath or take her inheritance and family patrimony to a religious order. In cases in which the property rights of women religious were at issue, the Catholic Church gen-

[33] David Kertzer, *The Kidnapping of Edgardo Mortara* (New York, 1997).
[34] For a recent study of the phenomenon of Lourdes, see Harris, *Lourdes.* For Marianism in Germany, see David Blackbourn, *Marpingen: Apparitions of the Virgin Mary in Bismarckian Germany* (Oxford, 1993).

erally sought to protect the assets brought to the Church by women, but it defended the right of religious communities to possess such property rather than defending the property rights of women religious per se. As fathers, brothers, and uncles challenged the property rights of women religious and those of religious communities in the name of family and patrimony, the state was frequently asked to adjudicate family disputes. Church and state were more often than not the bitterest of political enemies during the nineteenth century, and the family became the cultural battleground on which their struggle was played out. As women religious were not covered by the Napoleonic civil code, for example, the state and courts were frequently confused about the legal disposition of their property and the corporate claims to property by religious communities themselves.

Chapter 5 examines the legal ramifications of the "feminization of religion" in the realm of women's property rights through an 1864 civil suit brought by the marquise de Guerry, a seventy-four-year old noblewoman, who had been a member of a convent for thirty years and who, upon deciding to leave her convent following a conflict with the clerical hierarchy, demanded the return of the considerable property that she had brought to it many years before. After having taken her case to the Vatican, where it was dismissed, she took it before the civil courts in France. This unusual and dramatic case highlighted the ambiguities regarding the property rights of women religious and will provide a different perspective on the now significant work that has been done by labor historians on the transformation in the legal disposition and political/cultural conceptions of individual and corporate property in the nineteenth century.[35] This chapter will provide new perspectives on the nineteenth-century Ultramontane and Gallican divide in French Catholicism. Ultramontanes supported the ultimate authority of the pope and papal courts over national or diocesan authority within France, while Gallicans favored limiting papal authority and supported the notion of a French national church. While the origins of this divide can be traced to the seventeenth and eighteenth centuries, it became more pronounced in the nineteenth century. For many, Ultramontanism also represented a new form of piety, associated, for example, with intense devotion to the Virgin Mary, to cults such as those of Sainte Philomène, and to the Eucharist, as well as with sentimental and "kitsch" forms of religious practice that were reflected in "Saint-Sulpice art" and in the commercialization of religious objects. For one historian, this form of piety perhaps "appealed particularly to women, and may have been both

---

[35] Cf. William Sewell, *Work and Revolution in France: The Language of Labor from the Old Regime to 1948* (Cambridge, 1980).

the cause and consequence of their growing dominance in religious practice."[36]

One must understand the feminization of religion in France, of course,
within the context of an alleged feminization of religion in Western Europe and the United States. Historians have argued, for example, that the
phenomenon had a different impact on Protestant and Catholic women:
among Protestants it led to a kind of dissolution of alleged boundaries between the public and private, particularly through women's involvement in
charitable organizations, contributing in important ways to the development of feminism. Historians have argued that among Catholics the feminization of religion was an inherently conservative force in French society,
contributing to the relegation of women to the domestic sphere. Contemporaries like the historian Jules Michelet in *Du prêtre, de la femme, de la
famille* (1845) argued that a largely feminized church and laity became
pawns of a politically reactionary church, and the family a private political
battleground. This book takes issue with this shibboleth and also illustrates
the surprising paradoxes inherent in the relationship between women and
the Catholic Church. The Catholic hierarchy and secular republicans assumed a "natural" religiosity among women, but this religiosity, and the
religious vocation, more particularly, could and did come to threaten the
family, marital relations, and the Catholic hierarchy itself. Nuns took on
charitable and educational tasks that the French state did not begin to provide for society until the end of the nineteenth century, which gave these
women an autonomy over their individual lives that was unimaginable to
their secular counterparts. While I do not argue that this constituted a
kind of black-garbed feminism, I do suggest that it is at best problematic to
equate female religiosity with the survival of a kind of traditional "pre-
modern" Catholicism that subjugated women in a modern age.

I will argue that two contradictory models of the "femme chrétienne"
emerged during the course of the nineteenth century. One legitimized
the subordination of women, and the other effectively challenged gender
relationships set out, for example, in the Napoleonic civil code. While
much of the normative and prescriptive literature concerning the "femme
chrétienne" valorized the role of women in the family, the considerable
freedom that women religious exercised in disposing of their property
and persons meant that they implicitly challenged that role.

---

[36] Ralph Gibson, *A Social History of French Catholicism, 1789–1914* (London, 1989), p. 265. For
a discussion of Ultramontane piety, see Gérard Cholvy and Yves-Marie Hilaire, *Histoire religieuse de la France contemporaine, 1800–1880* (Paris, 1990), pp. 153–96. For a survey of Ultramontane art, see Michael Paul Driskel, *Representing Belief: Religion, Art, and Society in
Nineteenth-Century France* (University Park, Pa., 1992).

The popularity of the religious vocation can be attributed to the religiosity of women as well as to the fact that active, noncloistered communities—the form favored in the nineteenth century—offered women opportunities denied to them elsewhere. Mrs. Anna Jameson remarked in 1855, "Why is it that we see so many women carefully educated going over to the Roman Catholic Church? For no other reason but that for the power it gives them to throw their energies into a sphere of definite utility under the control of a higher religious responsibility."[37] In other cases women fled poverty, abuse, or a troubled past. Whatever may have been the sources of the proliferation of female religious communities, it had important consequences for property relations, women's legal position in society, and the development of the family in the nineteenth century. For this reason it is somewhat striking that historians of gender in France, in contrast to those in Britain, have, with very few exceptions, shied away from the study of women's relationship to religion, given its importance in women's lives in the nineteenth century. They have tended to focus more on the origins of French feminism–which was a minority movement in France–on the family, or on women in the labor movement, social reform, and education.[38] Sylvie Fayet-Scribe suggests that historians of gender have preferred not to explore women's religiosity because it appears to be some kind of archaic throwback.[39] I hope that this book will contribute to an understanding of a very important moment in the history of gender in France by showing the complicated role that religion played in French society in the postrevolutionary period.[40] Finally, I will indicate how the em-

---

[37] Jameson, *Sisters of Charity: Catholic and Protestant, Abroad and at Home* (London, 1855), pp. 101–2.

[38] Among many others, see, for example, Joan Scott's recent *Only Paradoxes to Offer;* Christine Bard, *Les Filles de Marianne: Histoire des féminismes, 1914–40* (Paris, 1995); Elinor A. Accampo, Rachel G. Fuchs and Mary Lynn Stewart, ed. *Gender and the Politics of Social Reform in France, 1870–1914* (Baltimore, 1995); Françoise Mayeur, *Enseignement secondaire des jeunes filles sous la Troisième République* (Paris, 1977); Rebecca Rogers, *Les demoiselles de la Légion d'Honneur* (Paris, 1996); and the voluminous work of Michelle Perrot, including her recent *Femmes Publiques* (Paris, 1997).

[39] "Catholic women have not been a preferred subject among researchers, and seem to have had a bad press," because they are considered "a priori 'nonfeminist.'" The subject represents "a reservoir of archaisms with little interest." Sylvie Fayet-Scribe, *Associations féminines et catholicisme, XIXe–XXe siècle* (Paris, 1990), p. 15.

[40] There have been a growing number of studies that focus on women and religion in France. Other than the works cited above see, for example, Nicole Edelman, *Voyantes, guérisseuses et visionnaires en France 1785–1914* (Paris, 1995); a special 1995 issue of *Clio: histoires, femmes et sociétés* entitled *Femmes et religions* and edited by Claudine Leduc and Agnès Fine; Odile Sarti, *The Ligue Patriotique des Françaises* (Hamden, Conn., 1992); and Ann Cova, *Au Service de l'Eglise, de la Patrie et de la famille—Femmes catholiques et maternité sous la IIIe République* (Paris, 2000).

brace of the religious vocation could often be an expression of volition and agency rather than of subjection. These cases suggest that not all independent and assertive women were necessarily associated with a secular feminist movement in the nineteenth century.

This study emerged out of a long-standing interest in the relationship between religion, secularism, and political culture in France.[41] These microhistories provide a window onto the individual lives of women in religious communities and the issues that they raised for both the Catholic Church, the French state, and society at large. The gendered characteristics of Catholic religious practice in France since the French Revolution have profoundly shaped the form that anticlerical republicanism has assumed in the nineteenth and twentieth centuries. The most dramatic manifestation of this anticlericalism in the nineteenth century was the great secular crusade, which led to the dismantling of female religious congregations, the creation of a secular educational system, and the foundation of L'Etat laïque in the thirty-five years before the First World War. While the force of that crusade was largely spent by 1918, the spirit that pervaded it has continued to inspire ongoing debates about cultural difference and the place of religion—originally Catholicism and more recently Islam—in French civil society from the nineteenth right through to the twenty-first century.

---

[41] See my *Creating the Nation in Provincial France: Religion and Political Identity in Brittany* (Princeton, N.J., 1993).

CHAPTER 1

"Fanatiques et Dévotes Imbéciles"

In 1792 the revolutionary Montagnard deputy Joseph Marie Lequinio (1740–1813) published a twelve-page pamphlet, entitled *Les préjugés détruits*, on the future and fate of women in French society. Two of those twelve pages were devoted to the subject of religion. There he claimed that women were by their nature religious and that this natural religiosity could be attributed to their "sensibilité": "women are devout because they have a great need to love that is particularly noticeable at the end of their life" when time had served to diminish their physical charms.[1] Lequinio's observation concerning religious belief and prejudice among women in their advancing years is not very different from that of a far more influential prerevolutionary writer on the subject, Denis Diderot: "Neglected by her spouse, abandoned by her children, a nonentity in society, religion is her last and sole recourse." Alongside this interpretation, Diderot espoused more essentialist views regarding women's "natural" religiosity: "Woman carries within her frame an organ subject to terrible spasms which dominate her and arouse fierce phantoms of all kinds in her imagination. . . . Nothing is nearer to her than ecstasy, vision, prophecy, revelation, fiery poetry and hystericism. . . . The woman dominated by hysteria feels celestial powers I cannot know. . . . It was a woman who walked out into the streets of Alexandria with bare feet, her hair unkempt, a torch in

[1] Cited in Dominique Godineau, *Citoyennes tricoteuses: Les femmes du peuple à Paris pendant la Révolution française* (Paris, 1988), p. 253.

one hand and a ewer in the other, proclaiming,'I want to burn the heavens with a torch, and extinguish hell with this water, so that man may love
God for his sake alone!' "[2]

The view that women were by their very nature prone to irrationality,
disorderliness, emotional excess, superstition, hysteria, and religion is by no
means specific to eighteenth-century France.[3] Arguments to this effect can
be found in David Hume's *Natural History of Religion*, in which he asserted:
"What age or period of life is most addicted to superstition? The weakest
and the most timid. What sex? The same answer must be given. The leaders
of every kind of superstition, says Strabo, are the women. These excite men
to devotions and supplications, and the observance of religious days."[4] Such
appraisals can also be found in twentieth-century Russia where in the first
decade of Soviet power the dominant image of peasant women among Bol-
sheviks was that of an ignorant and superstitious *baba*.[5] The association of
women with the sphere of the religious has had a long history, but it came
to take on a very specific and powerful political and cultural significance in
France during the revolutionary decade (1789–99). Indeed, historians have
argued that the French Revolution marked the beginning of a feminization
of the dominant religion of Catholicism in France, a phenomenon that was
to persist throughout the nineteenth century.[6]

Yet as early as the seventeenth century, women were already "the execu-
tive arm of the social policy of the Counter-Reformation in spite of the
church hierarchy, which concerned itself largely with controlling their activities."[7] François de Sales praised the feminine qualities which drew women to
the Church and lauded in no uncertain terms "le sexe dévot."[8] Women

[2] Denis Diderot, *Des Femmes, Oeuvres complètes*, vol. 10 (Paris, 1971), 41–43.
[3] See, for example, Natalie Z. Davis, "Women on Top," in *Society and Culture in Early Modern France*,), pp. 124–25; and Barbara Alpern Engel, "Women, Men and the Languages of Peasant Resistance, 1870–1907" in *Cultures in Flux: Lower-Class Values, Practices, and Resistance in Late Imperial Russia*, ed. Stephen P. Frank and Mark D. Steinberg (Princeton, N.J., 1994), pp. 34–53, esp. pp. 41–42.
[4] Cited in Peter Brown, "Learning and Imagination," in his *Society and the Holy in Late Antiquity* (Berkeley, Calif., 1982), pp. 11–12.
[5] Beatrice Farnsworth, "Village Women Experience Revolution," in *Russian Peasant Women*, ed. Beatrice Farnsworth and Lynne Viola (New York, 1992), pp. 145–66.
[6] Langlois, *Le catholicisme au feminin*; Hufton, "The Reconstruction of the Church"; Hufton, *Women and the Limits of Citizenship* (Toronto, 1994); Desan, *Reclaiming the Sacred*; Desan, "The Family as a Cultural Battleground: Religion vs. the Republic under the Terror" in *The French Revolution and the Creation of Modern Political Culture*, vol. 4: *The Terror*, ed. Keith Michael Baker (New York, 1994), pp. 177–93.
[7] Olwen Hufton and Frank Tallett, "Communities of Women, the Religious Life, and Public Service in Eighteenth-Century France," in *Connecting Spheres: Women in the Western World, 1500 to the Present*, ed. Marilyn Boxer and Jean Quaetert (Oxford, 1987), p. 75.
[8] Linda Timmermans, *L'accès des femmes à la culture (1598–1715)* (Paris, 1993), p. 623.

drawn to religious life during this period assumed the veil, embraced monastic life, and accepted strict enclosure and the celibate life. Indeed, entry into a recognized religious order required the taking of solemn vows before witnesses and an ecclesiastical representative. It was, in effect, a public, permanent, and lifelong commitment. An office of the dead was frequently recited after an aspirant's public declaration because, in taking her vows, she in effect "died to the world." She no longer existed as a person in civil law, but was rather, accepted into the Catholic community and was henceforth subject to its jurisdiction. Whatever property she brought to the order became the collective property of the community.[9]

However, the seventeenth century witnessed the emergence of entirely new and very different kinds of female religious communities, alongside preexisting cloistered and contemplative orders which could trace their origins to early Christianity. These included the Ursulines, a congregation devoted to teaching; the Visitandines, who devoted themselves to the sick; and the Filles de Notre Dame de Charité, whose task was to rehabilitate "fallen women." The seventeenth century also gave rise to forms of female mysticism and visionaries that were both praised and feared by the clerical hierarchy. In short, the seventeenth century saw the beginnings of new kinds of religious and social commitment with the emergence of the active, secular sister, who shunned the contemplative, cloistered life in favor of service to society in the form of teaching, nursing or charitable work. Whereas the *religieuse* assumed solemn vows, led a cloistered existence in a religious community, and devoted herself to prayer and meditation, the new *congréganiste* was a visible and active member of society. The *congréganiste*, moreover, took simple, private vows of poverty, chastity, and obedience, though the nature of these vows varied enormously from religious community to religious community. These communities represented a clear break with forms of community and female religiosity prior to the Counter-Reformation, thereby creating new consequences. A new active, secular, female apostolate, as opposed to one based on the contemplative life, became another model for female aspirants by the French Revolution. The religious vocation also gradually came to be democratized as more and more women from humbler strata of society embraced the religious life.

By 1790 the number of female religious communities, comprising *congréganistes* and *religieuses*, outstripped that of male religious communities,

---

[9] Elizabeth Rapley, *The Dévotes: Women and the Church in Seventeenth-Century France* (Montreal, 1990), p. 175.

suggesting that the beginnings of the feminization—or it might alternatively be seen as demasculinization—of the Church had begun earlier
than the French Revolution. This has allowed one historian to argue that
one of the most significant consequences of the Counter-Reformation
was the feminization of religious personnel.[10] Although we cannot be certain of precise figures, it has been estimated, on the basis of a list of religious pensioners in 1817, that there were approximately 80,000 members
of contemplative religious orders and congregations in 1790. Of these,
over 55,000 were women and 26,000 were men. Less than a century later,
in 1878, there were more than 125,000 women religious in France (excluding Alsace and Lorraine, which has been annexed by Germany following the Franco-Prussian War).[11] In 1878, 7 of every 1,000 women belonged to a religious community, in contrast to 4 of every 1,000 women
on the eve of the French Revolution. Regional studies of religious practice have revealed what religious historians have come to call an identifi-
able "sexual dimorphism" in religious practice as well as in religious vocations in the early eighteenth century. One historian has concluded, on
the basis of a study of requests for masses for the dead in Provence, that
the eighteenth century witnessed a veritable feminization of Catholicism.[12]

Of course, there were great regional disparities in religious practice
during the eighteenth century in France, just as there were discrepancies
between town and country. The religious surveys undertaken by the Catholic Church in the nineteenth century and by canon Boulard in 1947 do
not exist for prerevolutionary France, but there are reliable indications
that the religious map of modern France was already firmly in place by
the eighteenth century. Paul Bois observed, for example, that an invisible
boundary divided the department of the Sarthe, separating an irreligious
and nonpracticing east from a highly devout west.[13] Western France had
already acquired its reputation for religious devotion, even if there were
evident subregional contrasts. In the arrondissement of Rennes, for example, the number of men (90.6 percent) who performed their Easter

[10] Pierre Chaunu, *L'église, culture et société: Essais sur réforme et contre-réforme* (Paris, 1984),
p. 401.
[11] Hufton and Tallett, "Communities of Women," p. 77; and Gibson, *A Social History of French
Catholicism*, p. 105.
[12] Gibson, *A Social History of French Catholicism*, p. 10; and Michel Vovelle, *Piété baroque et déchris-
tianisation en Provence au XVIIIe siècle: Les attitudes devant la mort d'après les clauses des testaments*
(Paris, 1973).
[13] Paul Bois, *Paysans de l'Ouest: Des structures économiques et sociales aux options politiques depuis
l'époque révolutionnaire dans le Sarthe* (Le Mans, 1960).

duty was almost identical to the number of women (97.8 percent) in 1899.[14] In less practicing areas, such as Champagne, the number of those who went to mass and who did their Easter duty was very low among both sexes. In the arrondissement of Epernay only 1.1 percent of men and 16.6 percent of women made their Easter duty on a regular basis between 1886 and 1890, and a priest in the parish of Somme-Brionne noted in 1890 that in that year, "not a single man attended mass, even after a mission which, while well attended, has not had any results."[15] The south of France, moreover, was beginning to detach itself from the formal practice of Catholicism.[16]

Differences between town and country were also becoming readily apparent in the eighteenth century. Priests recruited from the great urban centers of France were fast becoming phenomena of the past. Marseilles, Paris, and Bordeaux were considered to be centers of unbelief on the eve of the French Revolution. These trends appeared to be all the more paradoxical in that the cities of France had been at the forefront of efforts to christianize the "pagan" countryside during the Counter-Reformation of the seventeenth century.

The work of religious sociologists and the studies of Boulard have confirmed that there was no linear progression from a christianized to a dechristianized country from the eighteenth to the twentieth century. There was a sharp decline in the formal practice of religion, as measured by attendance at mass and performance of Easter duty, from the French Revolution to the 1830s, but a process of rechristianization was observable between 1830 and 1880, particularly among the bourgeoisie. The great anticlerical crusade of the early Third Republic coincided with further declines in the formal practice of religion after 1880, however. In some regions there was more continuity than in others, but what all sociologists have observed is the marked difference in the religious behavior of men and women, which was particularly noticeable at the end of the nineteenth century.[17] If there were religious variations marked by class—the

---

[14] Pierre Barral et al., *Matériaux pour l'histoire religieuse du peuple français, XIX–XX siècles: Bretagne, Basse-Normandie, Nord, Pas-de-Calais, Picardie, Champagne, Lorraine, Alsace* (Paris, 1987), p. 220.

[15] Ibid., pp. 418, 421.

[16] Gibson, *A Social History of French Catholicism*, pp. 9–10; P.-F. Hacquet, *Mémoire des missions des Montforains dans l'ouest (1740–1779)* (Fontenay, 1964); Louis Pérouas, *Le diocèse de la Rochelle de 1648 à 1724* (Paris, 1964), pp. 453–71.

[17] Barral et al., *Matériaux pour l'histoire religieuse*, p. 9. Regional studies have confirmed the beginnings of a rechristianization of the bourgeoisie. See Yves-Marie Hilaire, *Une chrétienté au XIX siècle: La vie religieuse des populations du diocèse d'Arras (1849–1814)*, vol. 2 (Villeneuve-d'Ascq, 1977), pp. 600–622.

gradual alienation of the urban working class from the Church—and region, the "sexual dimorphism" observed by contemporaries by and large persisted.

The reasons for the decline in religious belief among men and women in eighteenth-century France are still largely obscure, but historians have often attributed it to Tridentine Catholicism. The reformed Catholicism that emerged from the councils at Trent exhibited features which evoked a hostile reaction in many quarters. Urban clerics began to attempt to impose a far more demanding religion on believers. This religion was often hostile to popular cultural practices and espoused a repressive sexual morality that expressed itself in the confessional. Much of the decline may also be attributed to the intellectual currents of the Enlightenment. Whatever the causes, some of the features of nineteenth- and twentieth-century Catholicism were already entrenched in the eighteenth century, one of the most prominent of which was the feminization, or to view it from another perspective, demasculinization of Catholicism.

Olwen Hufton and Suzanne Desan, among other historians, have argued that the French Revolution played a pivotal role in accelerating the process by which French Catholicism became further feminized.[18] They have sought to explain how the French Revolution created patterns of "sexual dimorphism" and why women stayed within the church and sought to express themselves in the ways that they did. The argument that women were closer to death because of the increased risk of death in childbirth has been advanced to explain women's attachment to religion. Hufton has argued that the Revolution alienated women by removing the social support network that the Church represented. The removal of this network and women's traditional role in the practice of religion meant that women were more sensitive to the disruption of religious ritual and to the attacks on religious institutions. Finally, Bonnie Smith attributes the religious fervor of bourgeois women in the North in the nineteenth century to the "reproductive life of women" and to the cult of domesticity that women came to embrace.[19]

In looking at the importance of the revolutionary decade in contributing to the "feminization" of Catholicism, I will focus less on the question of whether women were more naturally drawn to religion, more likely to embrace "superstition" or to remain within the Church during the Revolution, but rather on why contemporaries thought that this was so and on

[18] Hufton, "The Reconstruction of the Church"; and Desan, *Reclaiming the Sacred*, esp. pp. 197–216.
[19] Smith, *Ladies of the Leisure Class*, pp. 93–122.

how the association of women with religion shaped the status of women and political culture more generally in postrevolutionary France. Indeed, as Suzanne Desan has argued, women's leadership in religious riots in the French Revolution profoundly altered community dynamics and gender roles following the French Revolution. It contributed to the perception that "public religious expression" was a "woman's prerogative and women's duty in the family and community."[20]

Religiosity became tightly associated with the sphere of the feminine between 1791 and 1799. Revolutionaries came to transform a laudatory Counter-Reformation discourse concerning the "sexe dévot" into one of vilification. They did so at two crucial political moments: the oath crisis following the vote of the Civil Constitution of the Clergy in 1791, and the aftermath of the Jacobin dechristianization campaign of 1793, after which discredited and "counterrevolutionary" women were more often than not branded "fanatique." Ultimately, the implications of the revolutionary association of religion with the sphere of the feminine and the creation of the "femme fanatique" reached far beyond these specific revolutionary political moments and played an important role in shaping political debates and legislation governing the Church and female religious communities well into the nineteenth century.

THE CATHOLIC CHURCH AND REVOLUTION

Catholicism's renewed association with the sphere of the feminine coincided with its alienation from the Revolution. That alienation was by no means inevitable, however. In 1789, Catholicism was hardly incompatible with the French Revolution. Indeed, many of the most ardent revolutionaries were representatives of the First Estate. Throughout the early years of the Revolution a series of measures designed to dismantle the social, economic, and institutional basis of the Old Regime, including those associated with the Catholic Church, were implemented. Those that pertained to the Church were based on long-standing grievances among the clergy and laity alike, but its critics had no coherent or clear vision concerning what the relationship between the Church and a newly regenerated France should be. Between July 1789 and July 1790, when the National Assembly promulgated the Civil Constitution of the Clergy, which was designed to settle this question, the assembly began to reform the Church in a piecemeal fashion by, for example, nationalizing the property of the French Church on 2 November 1789 and prohibiting monastic

[20] Desan, *Reclaiming the Sacred*, p. 213.

vows. Early in 1790, the deputy Isaac-René-Guy Le Chapelier (1754–94), whose name is intimately associated with dismantling of the corporate world of Old Regime France, proposed discussing whether or not to suppress monastic orders and congregations entirely. By 13 February solemn lifelong monastic vows were no longer legally recognized, though active congregations devoted to education and charitable activities remained in existence, and nuns and monks were accorded state pensions. Ironically, this did not lead to the emptying of convents, and many nuns actively opposed the revolutionary legislation.[21] Many women returned to their families, who balked at the financial burden they imposed, and others continued to adhere to communal life in clandestine circumstances. Some married.

With the vote of the Civil Constitution of the Clergy on 12 July 1790, the relationship between the Catholic Church and the state became more clearly defined and turned into a highly contested terrain. Indeed, it divided the clergy and the laity into warring factions. In many respects the Civil Constitution of the Clergy responded to the grievances expressed by the First and Third Estates. It abolished the patchwork of Old Regime dioceses and created new dioceses that corresponded to the geographical boundaries of the departments. All clerical salaries were fixed and all ecclesiastical positions without cure of souls were abolished. Two features of the Civil Constitution of the clergy created dissent. First, all clergy were to be subject to election by an "active" citizen laity; and second, this clergy was required to swear an oath of allegiance to the nation.

Opposition to the Civil Constitution of the Clergy came from many sources. Much of it centered on issues of authority. Many members of the Church objected to being subject to lay authority, but the oath became the lightning rod of opposition, and those who refused to sign onto it, the *réfractaires*, were no longer recognized as legitimate priests. Most of these priests objected to the National Assembly's attempt to arrogate to itself the power to legislate in spiritual matters. Others objected to the fact of the Revolution itself, a position that the pope assumed when he condemned both the Civil Constitution and the French Revolution in a papal brief on 10 March 1791.

Opposition to the Civil Constitution of the Clergy and to the swearing of the oath was not confined to the clergy, however. Although many revolutionary officials attributed lay opposition to the machinations of the priests, there is considerable evidence to suggest that the laity opposed

---

[21] Alphonse Aulard, *La révolution française et les congrégations: Exposé historique et documents* (Paris, 1903), pp. 14–24.

the Civil Constitution for their own reasons. In some communities the imposition of the Civil Constitution was seen as the first step towards the closing of churches, and in others it fed into age-old confessional rivalries, particularly in areas where there was a significant Protestant presence. There were also regional variations in the opposition to the oath, but it was during the deepening crisis surrounding the Civil Constitution that revolutionary officials began to comment on the conspicuous and dominant role of women in public demonstrations and in the resistance to this revolutionary legislation. For example, in the spring of 1789 there were only rare mentions of women in rural crowds in southern Ile-de-France, but by 1791–92 they were mentioned more and more frequently.[22] To read the commentary of contemporaries, the conflict that the oath engendered could be interpreted as a battle between the sexes, which to a large extent cut across all social boundaries. Abbé Sevestre observed that in Normandy wherever riots occurred "the voices of women dominated," and abbé Gregoire came to lament that his Constitutional Church was "strangled by dissolute and seditious women."[23] In short, the oath crisis spawned an emerging discourse that associated religiosity, defense of refractory priests, and counterrevolution with women.[24]

What was the nature of this discourse and how was this association expressed? Male revolutionary Patriots would sometimes ironically adopt a religious or biblical language to demonize riotous women. Women in the Ardèche were accused of "tormenting their husbands, children, and servants like so many devils," while in the Brioude priests were accused of working "diabolically through women like the Serpent through Eve."[25] During the oath crisis the language used to denounce the alleged zealotry of women drew on a prerevolutionary religious vocabulary, and more often than not women who protested the oath to the constitution were branded "dévote," "fanatique," and "béguine," all terms of derogatory nature and intended as verbal insults. While "fanatique" and "fanaticism" came to have a common currency in the eighteenth century and were

---

[22] See, for example, Timothy Tackett, "Women and Men in Counterrevolution: The Sommières Riot of 1791," *Journal of Modern History* 59 (December 1987): 680–704, esp. 684; and Serge Bianchi, "Les femmes dans les troubles religieux et de subsistances dans le sud de l'Ile-de-France," in *Les femmes et la Révolution française*, ed. Marie-France Brive, vol. 1 (Toulouse, 1989), p. 95.

[23] Timothy Tackett, *Religion, Revolution and Regional Culture in Eighteenth-Century France: The Ecclesiastical Oath of 1791* (Princeton, N.J., 1986), p. 173; and abbé Gregoire, quoted in Mona Ozouf, "De-Christianization," in François Furet and Mona Ozouf, eds., *Critical Dictionary of the French Revolution* (Cambridge, Mass., 1989) p. 29.

[24] Tackett, *Religion, Revolution, and Regional Culture*, pp. 159–82, esp. pp. 172–77.

[25] Cited ibid., pp. 175–76.

used to denounce clerical abuses of all kinds, the pejorative connotations
of the term "dévote" could be traced to the seventeenth century, when it
was primarily applied to bluestocking, aristocratic women at court, who attempted to interfere in politics. By the French Revolution, the term
"dévote" had been democratized and generalized, so that it came to apply
to all women who appeared to be particularly religious, from the illiterate
peasant to the châtelaine. By 1791, the "dévote" was feminine and had become a code word to describe any person, masculine or feminine, who resisted the implementation of the Civil Constitution of the Clergy.

How did contemporary observers understand or explain the prominence of women in religious riots and movements of religious resistance?
They generally resorted to two explanations. They argued over and over
again that women's attachment to religion was "plus vif" and "plus ten-
dre," or they suggested that priests used them in households to act as "Tro-
jan horses."[26] As women were deemed to be more weak-willed and subject
to influence, they were easily duped by their spiritual guides. The two explanations dovetailed in the revitalization of the prerevolutionary anticlerical fear and charge that priests held undue power over women and
played the role of seducers, thereby undermining patriarchal authority in
the home.

With the Civil Constitution of the Clergy, the Revolution and the
Church "were set on a collision course."[27] Religion and revolution, in the
words of the historian Jules Michelet, became increasingly incompatible,
and matters religious became implicitly political. As a result of the debacle
over the oath, the Catholic Church came to be associated with counterrevolution, reaction, and France's prerevolutionary past, which the Revolution wished to eradicate. To this extent the conflict provided a basis for
the dechristianization campaign of the Years II and III of the Revolutionary era, and as that campaign proceeded, religion increasingly became associated with the empire of priests and women. A "fanatique," who was almost always female, could not be a good republican because she was by
definition an enemy of the republic.

DECHRISTIANIZATION

The government-sponsored dechristianization campaign of 1793 and
1794, the attempt to remove the influence of the Catholic Church from

---

[26] Ibid., p. 175.
[27] Gibson, *A Social History of Catholicism, 1789–1914*, p. 40.

France, was in part a popular grassroots movement and in part a policy that reflected governmental hostility to the Catholic Church as an institution. It took various forms.[28] After 10 August 1792 the government deported refractory priests in order to prevent them from influencing elections, and reassigned responsibility for recording vital statistics to secular authorities. The parish clergy lost one of its sources of power, and divorce and remarriage became permissible. By the fall of the Year II or 1793, dechristianization assumed violent and often sinister forms. In some communities churches were closed. Religious ceremonies were replaced with revolutionary ceremonies and festivals.[29] In others, icons and statues were smashed and destroyed. Detachments of the Revolutionary Army aided, abetted, and sometimes initiated these activities, as they defaced sacred objects. On 13 December 1793, a public official by the name of Dagorn, responsible for overseeing the accounts of the municipality of Quimper in Brittany, ordered the closing of churches in the city. In front of a crowd of peasants celebrating the feast of Saint Corentin, the patron saint of Quimper, two officials, guarded by troops from the Loir-et-Cher, systematically began to destroy statues and ornaments inside and outside the Cathedral. Dagorn concluded his exploit by urinating in a ciborium—a revered receptacle for holding the consecrated waters of the Eucharist.[30]

In an effort desacralize time and space, the leaders of the First Republic attempted to desacralize bells and to limit their use for religious purposes, thereby seeking to transform "the prevailing pattern of the culture of the senses" and village life more generally.[31] As Alain Corbin has persuasively argued, bells had enormous emotional power in France during the Old Regime and during the nineteenth century. Bells were used to punctuate the day. Villagers rang them on special celebratory occasions, for religious purposes, and to warn a community of imminent danger. Between the summer of 1793 and 1795 the revolutionary government began to requisition bells and melt them down for the national war effort, which resulted in considerable dislocation and consternation in village commu-

---

[28] Ozouf, "De-Christianization," pp. 20–32; *Annales historiques de la Révolution française*, no. 233, July–September 1978, special issue, "Dechristianization in the Year II."
[29] Mona Ozouf, *Festivals and the French Revolution*, trans. Alan Sheridan (Cambridge, Mass, 1988).
[30] Roger Dupuy, "La période révolutionnaire et la reconstruction concordataire," in *Histoire religieuse de la Bretagne*, ed. Guy Devailly (Chambray, 1980), p. 243.
[31] Alain Corbin, *Village Bells: Sound and Meaning in the Nineteenth-Century Countryside*, trans. Martin Thom (New York, 1998), chap. 1, pp. 3–44; and Desan, *Reclaiming the Sacred*, for revolutionary legislation and local responses.

nities. Communes were far more reluctant to give up their bells than silver sacred objects, and many viewed the confiscation of bells as a form of spoliation and an attack on their identity as communities.

As in the case of resistance to the oath, government officials attributed much of the negative reaction to the dechristianization campaign, whether orchestrated from above or initiated from below, to the machinations of women. In some cases women were caught ringing bells for the Angelus—devotional prayers to commemorate the Annunciation—leading religious celebrations, and insisting on the observance of religious festivals. In the winter of 1795, women in the department of the Yonne broke into a village church to ring the church bells and to sing offices.[32] The popular society of Charolles in Saône-et-Loire received a report in the month of Pluviôse (Rain), year III of the Republic (1795) that observed that "overturning altars of fanaticism in some country communes resulted in crowds gathering together, which consist entirely of women."[33] It was women who attacked administrators, reclaimed their bells, sat on the doorsteps of churches and jeered at public officials. In the month of Frimaire (Frost), year II of the Republic (1794), women in a small village by the name of Belmont protested the new revolutionary "religion of goats."[34] When local officials were instructed to read a paean to the Supreme Being in the village of Saint Vincent near Lavoûte Sur Loire in June 1794 the entire female audience turned to the back of the church—now the temple of reason—and raised their skirts to show their bare buttocks. This practice was a female sign of scorn and has a long history, of course, Mikhail Bakhtin noting that this is one of the most common "uncrowning gestures throughout the world."[35]

As the dechristianization campaign became increasingly violent, the language used to describe its opponents became more extreme, and the association of religion with the sphere of the feminine became more pronounced. A *commissaire civil* from Toulouse railed against fanaticism in Bec du Tarn, and decried the women in particular, who he argued were more easily seduced by it. Ignoring the October Days, during which 7,000

---

[32] Desan, *Reclaiming the Sacred*, p. 211.
[33] Cited in Michel Vovelle, *The Revolution against the Church: From Reason to the Supreme Being*, trans. Alan José (Cambridge, 1991), p. 158.
[34] Cited ibid., p. 156.
[35] Hufton, *Women and the Limits of Citizenship*, p. 118. Bakhtin, *Rabelais and His World*, trans. Hélène Iswolsky (Bloomington, Ind., 1984), p. 373. Also see Vivian Cameron, "Political Exposures: Sexuality and Caricature During the French Revolution," in *Eroticism and the Body Politic*, ed. Lynn Hunt (Baltimore, 1991), pp. 93–94. This practice is evoked once again in its nineteenth-century form in Emile Zola's novel *Germinal.*

women made a historic twelve-mile march to Versailles from Paris to demonstrate before the king in 1789, he asserted that the Revolution had been made by men and that women should not be allowed to impede its progress.[36] In Mailly-le-Vineux, a national agent reported in 1794 that "women's weakness has prevented them from losing sight of religious ideas which have nourished them since infancy," and the Jacobin publication *La Vedette*, which was published in Besançon, announced that "it is in the weakness of their [women's] minds that fanaticism grows."[37] The explanations advanced to understand this phenomenon in 1793 and 1794 resuscitated prerevolutionary fears about the seductive power of priests, the weakness of women, and their natural susceptibility to influence. When a Parisian soldier in the Revolutionary armies attempted to prevent a mass in a village he was passing in the month of Ventôse (Wind) of the year II (1794) and was thrown into jail, he pronounced: "You have destroyed many weeds, but others remain to imperil the fruits of our efforts. . . . it is those rascally priests who still lord it over towns and villages, who turn the heads of our wives and our children. . . . It is my opinion that all such people should be put under arrest . . . made to work from morning to night under a harsh commander, and that after they leave our wives alone and cease leading them astray in the confessional."[38]

The epithets used to describe the female religious fanatic became ever more colorful, and Jacobins began to embellish their language with references with a variety of derogatory epithets. Women resisting dechristianization were described as "uncivil bigots," "venomous *dévotes*," "fanatics in skirts," "hideous accomplices of papal authority," "mégères" (vixens), "druids," "énergumènes" (diabolically possessed), and "vermines malfaisantes." The women countered by calling officials "philosophes," disciples of the devil and his child the Republic.[39] Although references to religion and blasphemy were systematically evoked in complaints of verbal insults in early eighteenth-century Paris, they had virtually disappeared by the late eighteenth century, when one finds only an occasional religious insult, such as the woman accused of being a "bigote qui alloit tous les jours à confesser aux Carmes," to which the accuser added that she was a prostitute and a confidence trickster.[40] By 1793, religious insults were

---

[36] Richard Cobb, *The People's Armies: The armées révolutionnaires, Instrument of the Terror in the Departments*, trans. Marianne Elliott (New Haven, Conn., 1987), p. 450.
[37] Cited in Desan, "The Family as Cultural Battleground," pp. 181 and 183.
[38] Cited in Cobb, *The People's Armies*, p. 449–50.
[39] Hufton, *Women and the Limits of Citizenship*, pp. 121, 115.
[40] David Garrioch, "Verbal Insults in Eighteenth-Century Paris," in Burke and Porter, *The Social History of Language*, p. 109. Religious insult was also rare in the New World. See Peter

some of the commonest forms of offensive remark—almost exclusively directed toward women.

Insults are perhaps a natural means of venting frustrations that cannot be expressed in other ways. They signify disapproval, sometimes hatred, and they often implicitly evoke societal values and norms. Charges of infidelity and promiscuity were the most common forms of insult against women in the eighteenth century.[41] Insults are also, of course, a means of establishing dominance through a form of public declaration, and it is in this context that we can begin to understand the outpouring of religious insult directed against women between 1791 and 1794. When Jacobin officials stood before churches and heaped abuse on "les femmes crapuleuses et séditieuses," they were attempting to intimidate them. When officials reported on the resistance to dechristianization and identified it as female, they were denigrating religious belief, and they insulted male protesters by attributing a female identity and characteristics to them. During the Sommières riots of 1791, for example, a prominent male activist, Jean Durand, was given the ironic and defamatory feminine nickname of "La Dévote."[42] In attributing religious resistance to women, Jacobins wished to downplay its significance. While both men and women took part in religious riots and demonstrations between 1791 and 1794, male revolutionaries primarily chose to see the women.

MEN AND WOMEN IN THE REPUBLIC OF VIRTUE

Much of the reason that male revolutionaries came to associate religion with the sphere of the feminine is linked to the fact that as the Revolution radicalized it came increasingly to be defined in masculine terms. From their inception, the revolution and the Republic were contrasted with a corrupt and feminine Old Regime monarchy embodied in the person of Queen Marie Antoinette.[43] Much of the corruption and degeneracy of the

---

N. Moogk, "'Thieving Buggers' and Stupid Sluts': Insults and Popular Culture in New France," *William and Mary Quarterly* 36 (October 1979): 524–47.

[41] Garrioch, "Verbal Insults in Eighteenth-Century Paris," p. 109.

[42] Tackett, "Women and Men in Counterrevolution," p. 697.

[43] Sarah Maza, "The Diamond Necklace Affair Revisited (1785–86): The Case of the Missing Queen" in Hunt, *Eroticism and the Body Politic*, pp. 63–89; Chantal Thomas, *La reine scélérate: Marie-Antoinette dans les pamphlets* (Paris, 1989); and Jacques Revel, "Marie-Antoinette in Her Fictions: The Staging of Hatred" in *Fictions of the French Revolution*, ed. Bernadette Fort (Evanston, Ill., 1991), pp. 111–29. Also see Landes, *Women and the Public Sphere*.

monarchy was ascribed to the power and influence of women at court, and early revolutionary discourse was predicated on an antifeminine rhetoric.

Despite pressure exerted by Olympe de Gouges, Etta Palm d'Aelders, and a number of other prorevolutionary female activists, the institutions created to replace those of the Old Regime excluded women from the public sphere of politics. The First French Constitution of September 1791 divided the country into active and passive citizens on the basis of wealth and gender, excluding women and the majority of male citizens from political participation. This exclusion was justified in terms that revealed that the public space of politics and republican values were defined as a male sphere. Although republican "virtue" and the moral values on which the republic was founded were rooted in a long tradition of civic humanism, that "virtue" was increasingly articulated in gendered terms during the French Revolution. A section leader in Orleans remarked in 1792, for example, "Les mères approndront à leurs enfants à parler de bonne heure le langage mâle de la liberté."[44] When the First Republic was established, the constitution broadened the franchise to include all male citizens, but it continued to exclude women. Women's practical political participation nonetheless increased substantially in the first year of the new republic and reached a high point during the first six months of 1793 when the Society of Revolutionary Republican Women was founded. The society energetically supported the policies of the Terror, identifying hoarders, aristocrats, and all other enemies of the revolution. The society's members bore arms and soon began to criticize the Jacobin authorities for failing to implement the Constitution and the policies of the Terror assiduously. At a 16 September meeting of the Jacobin Club the society and its members were attacked as "counterrevolutionary sluts" who were the cause of all of the disorder and riots over bread and provisioning in the city of Paris.[45] In October 1793, the Committee of Public Security used the occasion of a popular protest against the society by the market women of Paris, who objected to their demands for a law requiring all women to wear Phrygian bonnets, to prohibit all popular societies of women. André Amar, speaking on behalf of the committee, argued that women did not have the requisite qualities needed to participate in politics.

[44] Cited in Outram, "*Le langage mâle de la vertu*," p. 127. Also see Lynn Hunt, "Male Virtue and Republican Motherhood," in Baker, *The French Revolution and the Creation of Modern Political Culture*, 4:195–208.
[45] Landes, *Women and the Public Sphere*, p. 142.

By the end of 1793, a growing number of women began to be viewed as suspect and to be branded "counterrevolutionary." The very same feminine qualities that were evoked to explain the behavior of women who defended the Church and religion were used to explain and condemn the actions of prorevolutionary, radical women belonging to political clubs. The term "fanatic" had been generalized to include prorevolutionary and counterrevolutionary women. The sole offense of all of the 327 women listed as "suspects" in the Toulouse region between October 1793 and the end of Ventôse year II was that they were "fanatics," to which their critics sometimes added that they were also aristocrats.[46] Amar asserted that "women are disposed by their organization to an over-excitation which would be deadly in public affairs" and that "interests of state would soon be sacrificed to everything which ardor in passions can generate in the way of error and disorder."[47] The historians Jules Michelet and Alphonse Aulard even made a causal link between the two groups of "counterrevolutonary" women, arguing that when the Committee of General Security closed their clubs, women turned from the "fanatisme de leurs clubs" to the "fanatisme des prêtres."[48]

In short, as the Revolution radicalized, women began to disappear from its ranks, through policies of exclusion and through choice, and this disappearance is even reflected in the representational symbols of the Republic itself. The deputies of the Convention chose the male figure of Hercules, rather than the female figure of Liberty, for the seal of the Republic.[49] Increasingly in revolutionary iconography the female figure came to represent discord, division, and fanaticism: political threat was very often represented as sexual and religious threat.[50] The feminization of the religious discourse of the Revolution must then in part be understood in terms of the masculinization of the language defining the Re-

---

[46] Jean-Claude Meyer, "Les femmes face aux problèmes religieux en pays Toulousain," in Brive, *Les femmes et la Révolution française*, 1:226.

[47] Cited in Landes, *Women and the Public Sphere*, p. 144.

[48] Jules Michelet, *Les femmes de la Révolution* (Paris, 1854); Alphonse Aulard, *Le culte de la raison et de l'Etre Suprême, 1793–94* (Paris, 1892).

[49] Lynn Hunt, *Politics, Culture and Class in the French Revolution* (Berkeley, 1984), pp. 103–119. Also see Eric Hobsbawm, "Man and Woman in Socialist Iconography," *History Workshop Journal* 6 (1978): 121–138 and the criticisms by Maurice Agulhon, Sally Alexander, Anna David, and Eve Hostettler in *History Workshop Journal* 9 (1979): 167–82.

[50] Madelyn Gutwirth, "The Rights and Wrongs of Woman: The Defeat of Feminist Rhetoric by Revolutionary Allegory," in *Representing the French Revolution: Literature, Historiography, and Art*, ed. James A. W. Heffernan (Hanover, N.H., 1992), pp. 150–68; and Neil Hertz, "Medusa's Head: Male Hysteria under Political Pressure," *Representations* 4(1983): 25–55.

public and in terms of the repudiation of a feminized monarchy in favor of a republic of masculine virtue.

POSTREVOLUTIONARY RECONSTRUCTION

While the revolutionary decade resulted in the disruption of everyday religious practices and called Catholic authority into question, it also witnessed the dismantling of female religious orders and congregations. While many monks and nuns left their orders to return to their families, to marry, or to begin a new life, many continued to practice their vocation clandestinely, and a significant number of those belonging to active teaching and hospital congregations persisted in their work.

During the Directory and Napoleonic periods, the Catholic Church began to be rebuilt. Gone were the abbeys, convents and monasteries of prerevolutionary France. Their land had been confiscated and sold off to the highest bidders. Female religious communities reconstituted themselves, and new communities began to spring up throughout France, however. The first real indication of a revival of female religious communities following the French Revolution can be found in a survey undertaken by Napoleon's Ministry of Religious Affairs in 1808. The report found that in spite of the revolutionary legislation designed to suppress female religious there were twelve thousand *religieuses* and *congréganistes* in France. The majority of these women religious belonged to active, secular congregations dedicated to teaching and charitable work (54 percent) or nursing (14 percent), while only 32 percent were contemplative. Most of these communities had prerevolutionary origins, and only a few were newly created. Among the largest were the Filles de la Charité, with 1,653 members. One of the smallest was the Breton order of Saint-Esprit de Plérin.[51] Former *religieuses* and *congréganistes* received a pension from the state, and close to sixty-seven hundred had been reintegrated into their former orders and congregations.[52]

Despite his wish to make peace with the Catholic Church and his promulgation of the Concordat, Napoleon was not particularly favorably disposed to the reemergence of religious orders and congregations. In 1804, he wrote that he had no objection to former nuns living together and finishing out their lives in a common community, but that he would not countenance the recruitment of novices or their appearance in public in

[51] Langlois, *Le Catholicisme au féminin*, p. 74.
[52] Ibid., p. 80.

FIGURE 1. Jean Henri Marlet (1771–1847), *The Foundling Nursery*. A number of charitable institutions staffed entirely by nuns were founded in the early years of the nineteenth century. Musée de l'Assistance Publique, Hopitaux de Paris, France. Courtesy of Bridgeman Art Library, U.K.

their religious habits.[53] Napoleon, however, while upholding revolutionary legislation governing religious orders, relented when he recognized the state's need for nuns to tend the sick during the Napoleonic Wars, and he began to authorize their existence in a series of decrees, which were issued in three stages, between 1800 and 1815. This began in 1800 when the minister of the interior, Jean-Antoine Chaptal, authorized Citizeness Dulau, mother superior of the Filles de la Charité, to accept and train novices for hospital work. Between 1800 and 1802 other congregations devoted to nursing made requests for authorization and official recognition. In 1802, these authorizations were extended to teaching congregations. The decree of 3 Messidor, year XII (22 June 1804) marked a new phase in the history of religious congregations in France, and it remained in place until the beginning of the twentieth century. The decree, which was intended to check the growth of Jesuits, banned any religious commu-

[53] Ibid., p. 70.

nity from forming without being granted an imperial decree, and the members of a community that did not seek or obtain authorization could be brought to court for prosecution. While this decree effectively checked the growth of male religious communities, the state demonstrated more leniency toward female communities, often turning a blind eye to those without authorization, or granting provisional authorizations in cases in which the Conseil d'Etat refused to approve an authorization. Indeed, there was a division of opinion about how religious communities should be treated in the ranks of the Napoleonic civil service. Joseph Fouché wished to follow the letter of the law by not tolerating the existence of any unauthorized community, while Joseph Marié Etienne Portalis favored the reconstitution of religious communities, even those that had been cloistered, provided that monastic rules were not restored and the establishment of a community could be justified in terms of its social utility. A new decree passed on 18 February 1809 marked a third and final phase in the history of authorizations. This decree pertained to hospital communities only and laid out a simple procedure by which they would be given official recognition.[54]

The status and position of religious communities were very different from what they had been during the Old Regime, and in many respects the growth of congregations as opposed to religious orders was encouraged. Napoleon tended to authorize communities that could indicate their public utility through their role in society. The legal basis on which they existed, moreover, was more in keeping with revolutionary legislation, which banned solemn vows. No longer could a nun or congréganiste "die a civil death," losing whatever rights she had over her property and person. Civil rights in the postrevolutionary order were inalienable. The vow, which could not be solemn, was a nonbinding act. The state only showed tolerance and leniency toward female communities consisting of women drawn together by their private religious convictions, but they were legally recognized as public bodies only if they made themselves "socially useful" through hospital work or primary school teaching.

The association of women with the religious sphere was thus a demonstrable reality by the end of the eighteenth century. The phenomenon was not, however, strictly speaking, the creation of the French Revolution. Women had played an active and well-recognized role in the success of the Counter-Reformation during the seventeenth century, when one can begin to speak of a feminization of Catholic religious culture, and the number of women entering religious congregations and orders continued to outstrip men throughout the entire eighteenth century. What is ironical is that while historians have recognized this, they have by and large come to reify revolutionary discourse and to see it as a reality, to view the revolutionary decade as a decisive turning point in the feminization of religion in modern France. They have chosen to see discontinuity rather than continuity. While the feminization of Catholicism was not a new phenomenon, the revolutionary experience transformed a laudatory discourse concerning *le sexe dévot* espoused by influential seventeenth-century clerics like François de Sales, the great Counter-Reformation evangelizer and bishop of Geneva, and Cotton, the confessor of Henri IV, beyond all recognition,[55] and that transformation was to have profound consequences for the civil and political status of French women in the nineteenth and twentieth centuries.

[55] Robert Mandrou, *Des humanistes aux hommes de science* (Paris, 1973), p. 139; Lucien Febvre, "Quelques aspects méconnus d'un renouveau religieux en France entre 1590 et 1620," *Annales, économies, sociétés, civilisations* 13, no. 1 (1958); Timmermans, *L'accès des femmes a la culture (1598–1715)*, p. 399.

CHAPTER 2

Private Lives and Public Order
in Restoration France

In December 1821, Douglas Charles Loveday, a Protestant Englishman who owned property in France, presented a petition to the French government that protested the conversion of his eldest daughter to Catholicism while she was in a French boarding establishment in Paris.[1] Loveday's private outrage over his daughter's repudiation of her Protestant faith was soon transformed into public melodrama with far-reaching implications when he alleged that his daughter's conversion and subsequent clandestine flight to a convent constituted a *rapt de séduction,* or kidnapping by seduction—until then a charge more associated with the circumstances of an amorous elopement. The Chambers of Peers and Deputies fiercely debated the issues of the case. By the spring of 1822 Paris and London publishers stoked the fire that these debates ignited by issuing pamphlet versions of Loveday's petition, responses by Emily and her teacher, family letters, and readers' commentaries on the affair.[2]

---

[1] *Pétition à la Chambre des Pairs par M. Douglas Loveday, anglais et protestant, se plaignant du rapt de séduction opéré sur ses deux filles et sur sa nièce dans une maison d'éducation où il les avait placée a Paris* (Paris, 1821; 2d ed., Paris, 1822). The original handwritten version of the petition is contained in the Archives Nationales {hereafter AN CC4323. Also see Achille de Vaulabelle, *Histoire des deux restaurations jusqu'à l'avènement de Louis Philippe* (de janvier 1813 à octobre 1830), 4th ed., vol. 6 (Paris, 1858), p. 174; J.-A. Dulaure, *Histoire de la Restauration,* vol. 3 (Paris, 1870), pp. 187–88; and Louis Grimaud, *Histoire de la liberté d'enseignement en France,* vol. 5: *La restauration* (Paris, 1956), pp. 533, 546–47.

[2] Loveday's petition led to the publication of no fewer than twenty pamphlets on the affair in France, several of which went through several editions, including translations into Alsatian. See, for example, *Réponse à la pétition de M. Loveday; par un des rédacteurs de "La Quotidienne"*

The Loveday affair provides a prism through which to regard the emerging conflicts surrounding female religious vocations and female religiosity more generally in France following the Napoleonic interlude, and it also became the center of public debate in Britain, where the Catholic Emancipation Act was soon to be passed. Indeed, it reveals the way in which religious differences shaped patterns of national stereotyping and expressions of collective identity in both countries. What made the Loveday affair a source of intense scrutiny among the French reading public were the ideological and cultural fissures in French society and politics in the immediate aftermath of the French Revolution.

The defenders and detractors of father and daughter drew battle lines that were in large part political. Clerical monarchists intent on restoring the authority of the Catholic Church following the French Revolution championed the rights of Emily Loveday, while a growing anticlerical liberal opposition rallied to her father's cause in order to stem the ominous counterrevolutionary tide that swept France in the early 1820s. Trouble in the Loveday family erupted soon after the demise of Napoleon's empire, in the midst of a popular religious revival, and on the eve of a political debacle over the passage of a general law authorizing the reestablishment of female religious orders and congregations in 1825. Like the tragic and far more celebrated Calas affair of 1762, the private drama of the Loveday family soon became a major political scandal and placed the power of the Catholic Church in French politics and society at center stage.[3]

At the heart of this family drama lay unresolved questions regarding the claims of religion, the role of the state in adjudicating family conflict, and the civil status and rights of women in postrevolutionary France. Ulti-

---

(Paris, 1822); *Réflexions sur la réponse d'un rédacteur de "La Quotidienne" à la pétition de M. Douglas Loveday* (Paris, 1822); *Lettre du majeur Loveday, gouverneur de Benarès, à son frère Douglas Loveday* (Paris, 1822); *Lettre de Sir Williams C. . . . à M. Loveday* (Paris, 1822); *Lettre d'un ministre protestant à un ministre de la même religion habitant en France, à l'occasion de la pétition de M. Loveday* (Paris, 1822); *Examen d'une pétition présentée aux Chambres par M. Loveday* (1st, 2d, and 3d eds., Paris, 1822); *Considérations à l'appui de la pétition présentée à la Chambre des Pairs par M. Douglas Loveday, par Michel (du Var)* (Paris, 1922); *Bittschrift an die Deputierten-Kammer, von Hrn D. Loveday* (Strasbourg, 1822); *Beweisstücke und Bermerkungen* (Paris, 1822).

[3] The *parlement* of Languedoc sentenced Jean Calas, a Protestant from Toulouse, to a gruesome death for allegedly murdering his son in order to prevent him from converting to Catholicism. Calas was ultimately rehabilitated in 1765 when Voltaire came to his defense. See Marc Chassaigne, *L'affaire Calas* (Paris, 1929); David Bien, *The Calas Affair: Persecution, Toleration and Heresy in Eighteenth-Century Toulouse* (Princeton, 1960); and Edna Dixon, *Voltaire and the Calas Case* (New York, 1961). Ten years later, in 1775, Voltaire came to the aid of the Protestant Sirven family, which was also condemned by the parlement of Languedoc for the murder of their apostate daughter. William Doyle, *The Oxford History of the French Revolution* (Oxford, 1989), p. 55.

mately, the affair showed how and why family relations remained a central political and social concern for a nation where the rights of both men and women continued to be sharply contested.[4]

The Loveday affair would normally have been a matter for the law courts because it centered on a legal dispute over child custody and the civil rights of a foreign subject residing in France. However, the case was never given formal legal consideration because the child in question, Emily Loveday, was over the age of twenty-one and had therefore reached the age of majority as defined by France's Civil Code of law. The legal issues that the case broached were nonetheless a conundrum for both the defenders and detractors of Emily Loveday because all shared a fundamental belief in the importance of the principle of paternal authority as a basis for political and social order. The ultraroyalist comte Louis de Bonald (1754–1840), who had defended the inviolability of the family as a vituperative opponent of revolutionary divorce laws in 1816, summarized the consensus on this matter well when he declared before the Chamber of Peers, "Divided on political questions, we are unanimous in our feelings of respect for our families and of tenderness for our children, and what kind of person is it who would have the sad initiative to come immolate the Loveday family at our tribune and entertain all of Europe with this scandalous debate."[5] While Catholic royalists claimed paternal authority, which provided the basis for public order in society, was established by God, liberals argued that that same authority was derived from nature.[6] Ultraroyalists upheld the sanctity of the patriarchal family as a means of reconstituting the prerevolutionary social order, whereas liberals saw it as "the protector of private property" and as "the guarantor of a barrier against the encroachments of the state."[7] Whether they saw paternal authority as founded in religion or in natural law, throughout the nineteenth century the bitterest of political enemies defended the principle in

[4] Lynn Hunt has recently argued that in eighteenth-century France, political societies were viewed as "families writ large" and that French political culture was "structured by narratives of family relations." Hunt, *The Family Romance of the French Revolution* (Berkeley, 1992), pp. xiii–xiv. This was no less true of the early nineteenth century, when family relations remained a keystone of political theory among figures as diverse as Bonald and Proudhon.
[5] M. de Bonald, *Réflexions préjudicielles sur la pétition du sieur Loveday* (Paris, 1822), p. 4.
[6] M. A. T. Desquiron wrote in 1821, for example, that paternal authority "was the most sacred of all magistracies; it is the only one which does not depend on conventions, the only one which preceded them." He went on to argue that this authority was derived from nature itself, and that nature, "stronger than law," would maintain this authority in spite of all efforts to get rid of it. Desquiron, *La puissance paternelle en France mise en rapport avec les intérêts de la société* (Paris, 1821), pp. 11, 15.
[7] Jacques Donzelot, *The Policing of Families* (London, 1980), p. 5.

both public and private life by arguing that the "good order of families" was "the first condition and the surest guarantee of good order in the state."[8]

While all the political antagonists thus agreed on the fundamental social and political importance of the principle of paternal authority, the Loveday affair raised uncomfortable questions regarding the limits of that authority, the civil rights of women, and the autonomy of daughters, wives, mothers, and sisters in postrevolutionary French law. That law was a product of new inventions and reinvented traditions. It fulfilled some of the fundamental demands raised by the French Revolution in establishing a single uniform legal code and the principle of juridical equality. However, when it came to women, particularly those who were married, France's civil and penal codes roundly dismissed that principle.[9] Paternal authority was strengthened immeasurably in postrevolutionary civil and criminal jurisprudence. Though women were accorded a civil status, it was subordinate, and they were denied any political rights in spite of the universalistic political language of the revolution. Indeed, that very language ironically supplied the basis for the exclusion of women from the public space of politics and bolstered the legal authority of husbands and fathers in the name of virtue and public order.[10] Although historians have explored the paradoxes of liberal theory in this regard to illuminate the history of women's demands for political rights, questions concerning women's civil and property rights in postrevolutionary French law have been viewed by historians as a shut case and have not received the same attention.[11] The Loveday affair brings into sharp relief one significant di-

---

[8] Philippe-Auguste Paget, *De la puissance paternelle dans le droit romain et le droit français* (Paris, 1869), p. 144.

[9] James F. Traer, *Marriage and the Family in Eighteenth-Century France* (Ithaca, N.Y., 1980), p. 191.

[10] "Women's personal virtue (virtue = chastity) is equated with political virtue (virtue = putting state above personal interests), like Brutus, who executed his sons when they attempted to betray the Roman republic. The continuum between the two senses carries a whole series of messages: that female chastity is the prerequisite for political innovation undertaken in the name of a universal will. . . . 'Virtue' was in fact a two-edged word, which bisected the apparently universalistic terminology of *le sovereign* [*souverain*] into two distinct political destinies, one male and the other female." Outram, "*Le langage mâle de la vertu*," p. 125. See Landes, *Women and the Public Sphere;* Joan Wallach Scott, "French Feminists and the Rights of 'Man': Olympe de Gouges's Declarations," *History Workshop* 28 (Autumn 1989): 1–21; Scott, "'A Woman Who Has only Paradoxes to Offer': Olympe de Gouges Claims Rights for Women," in *Rebel Daughters: Women and the French Revolution*, ed. Sara E. Melzer and Leslie Rabine (Oxford, l992), pp. 102–20; and Scott, *Only Paradoxes to Offer.*

[11] Géneviève Fraisse makes a similar observation in "Natural Law and the Origins of Nineteenth-Century Feminist Thought in France," in *Women in Culture and Politics*, ed. Judith Friedlander et al. (Bloomington, Ind., 1986), pp. 318–29. The subject of women's civil and property rights has attracted more attention among historians of Britain and America. See,

mension of women's civil status in postrevolutionary France: the rights of women in the domain of religious expression, vocation, and freedom of thought. Although the Civil Code sharply curtailed women's rights in French civil law, in successfully winning her case, Emily Loveday and her defenders forcefully and inadvertently subverted the juridical construction of paternal authority that the Civil Code enshrined. Indeed, one of the greatest ironies of the affair was the extent to which clerical monarchists, who were the most ardent proponents of that authority, found themselves championing Emily Loveday solely as a consequence of their unbridled defense of the institutional interests of the Catholic Church.

The legal and political issues raised by the affair remained contested and continued to resonate because the case of Emily Loveday was not the first or last of its kind. The archives of the courts as well as of the Ministries of Justice and Religious Affairs are replete with complaints and petitions concerning the spiritual seduction of women and their sequestration in convents between the 1820s and 1880s.[12] The long-term implications of the challenges to paternal authority that such cases represented must not be underestimated. As greater and greater numbers of French women entered religious life during the course of the nineteenth century, these challenges led the Right and the Left alike to demand legislation limiting the civil rights of French women, who had equal rights to inheritance under the Napoleonic Code, and in calls primarily among the Left for legislative checks on the prodigious growth of female religious communities.[13]

Historians have shown the private side of the peculiar virulence of French anticlericalism in the deep-seated opposition to clerical meddling

---

for example, Marylynn Salmon, *Women and the Law of Property in Early America* (Chapel Hill, N.C., 1986); Mary Poovey, "Covered but Not Bound: Caroline Norton and the 1857 Matrimonial Causes Act," in *Uneven Developments: The Ideological Work of Gender in Mid-Victorian England* (Chicago, 1988); and Susan Staves, *Married Women's Separate Property in England, 1660–1833* (Cambridge, Mass., 1990).

[12] One of the most dramatic of such legal cases occurred in 1843 and involved the spiritual and sexual seduction of a twenty-six-year-old nun by her confessor, sieur de Sainte-Colombe, in the convent of Notre Dame de Toulouse. Bernarde-Emilie Lecomte ultimately left her convent and became the clandestine mistress of Sainte-Colombe and the mother of three of his children. After this aristocratic priest and lover abandoned her, she took the matter to the royal court of Agen in 1843 and sued for damages as well as for a pension, which were denied. *Plaidoyer prononcé par M. Cazeneuve devant le cour royale d'Agen pour Dame Bernarde-Emilie Lecomte, ex religieuse, habitante de Toulouse, contre le sieur Sainte-Colombe, prêtre, son ancien confesseur, habitant de Montrède (Gers), pour rapt de séduction* (Toulouse, 1844).

[13] For accounts of the growth of female religious congregations and for the "feminization" of the Catholic Church in nineteenth-century France, see Langlois, *Le catholicisme au féminin*; Hufton, "The Reconstruction of the Church, 1796–1801," in *Beyond the Terror*; Gibson, *A Social History of French Catholicism*, pp. 105–7; 152–57.

in the intimate world of conjugal or family relations in the confessional.[14] The Loveday affair reveals another equally important private side to that anticlerical sentiment, namely, the fears created by female religious expression and the threat that a woman's potential religious vocation posed for property, paternal authority, and the integrity of the family. Between 1800 and 1880 the number of women who entered religious communities increased dramatically. In the context of a growing "feminization" of clerical vocations and a declining birthrate, these fears came to exercise a powerful hold on the popular and literary imagination in the postrevolutionary period and ultimately provided a particularly compelling justification for dismantling female religious communities toward the end of the nineteenth century.

As the Loveday affair represented opposing accounts of Emily Loveday's conversion by father, daughter, family members, the press, and public commentaries, it also raises a number of questions for historians concerning the "evidence of experience" and the relationship between history and narrative "fiction."[15] In order to understand the public scrutiny that the case provoked in France and the long-term implications of the Loveday affair for French politics and law, the narrative accounts of its participants and the ways in which the public read those accounts must be set within the field of competing discourses regarding the civil status and agency of women in postrevolutionary French society.

THE SEDUCTION OF EMILY LOVEDAY

"I am a foreigner," Douglas Loveday began his 1821 petition to the Chamber of Peers, "I came to France on the faith of treaties, and under the protection of the law of nations. I have faithfully observed the laws of the

[14] See Theodore Zeldin's pioneering article on the private side of French anticlericalism, "The Conflict of Moralities," which is largely based on Jules Michelet's *Du prêtre, de la femme, de la famille.*
[15] See Natalie Zemon Davis, *Fiction in the Archives: Pardon Tales and their Tellers in Sixteenth-Century France* (Stanford, Calif., 1987); Ross Chambers, *Story and Situation: Narrative Seduction and the Power of Fiction* (Minneapolis, 1984); Hayden White, "The Value of Narrativity in the Representation of Reality," and "The Question of Narrative in Contemporary Historical Theory," in *The Content of the Form: Narrative Discourse and Historical Representation* (Baltimore, 1987), pp. 1–57; Michel de Certeau, "History: Science and Fiction," in *Heterologies: Discourse on the Other*, trans. Brian Masumi (Minneapolis, 1986) pp. 199–221; Barbara Herrnstein Smith, "Narrative Versions, Narrative Theories," *Critical Inquiry* 7 (Autumn 1980): 213–36; Peter Brooks, *Reading for the Plot: Design and Intention in Narrative* (New York, 1984); Clifford Geertz, "'From the Native's Point of View': On the Nature of Anthropological Understanding," in *Local Knowledge: Further Essays in Interpretive Anthropology* (New York, 1983), pp. 55–70; and Joan W. Scott, "The Evidence of Experience," *Critical Inquiry* 17 (Summer 1991): 773–97.

country; and yet my most sacred rights have been violated: and amidst this misfortune that overwhelms me, I find no authority to which I can turn for protection. I am reduced to the necessity of appealing to the first body of the State—to the Deputies of the French nation—to obtain the satisfaction to which I am entitled."[16]

Douglas Loveday was an Englishman who came to France in the immediate aftermath of the French Revolution and bought property in Auteuil, a fashionable town on the outskirts of Paris. While he retained his British citizenship, Louis XVIII, king of the newly established Restoration Monarchy, granted him civil rights as a Frenchmen by royal decree on 3 December 1817. Loveday's troubles in France effectively began two years later, in the summer 1819, when he placed his two daughters, Emily and Mathilda, and his niece, Mary, in a Parisian boarding school run by Ernestine Reboul, a single lay schoolteacher, during the summer of 1819. His eldest daughter, Emily, was nineteen years of age, Mathilda eighteen, and Mary was twelve. Mr. Loveday alleged that one of the conditions of the boarding arrangement was that his daughters and niece, who were minors, would only be instructed in the arts of music, sewing, and etiquette and would not participate in the religious activities of the house, which consisted of religious instruction, confession, and attendance at mass. After the young charges were delivered to Reboul's care, Loveday and his wife made their way back to Britain. While we know that two years later all three girls converted to Catholicism, that they were returned to Loveday's care, that Emily fled her father's house, and that she took refuge in a convent, the circumstances of the girls' conversion and the motives and reasons for Emily's flight were bitterly contested by the affair's principal protagonists, the press, and by the reading public.

According to Loveday, he learned of the girls' conversion when he returned to France to remove his children from Reboul's school. The means used to effect this conversion, Loveday claimed, were tales of pretended miracles that had recently occurred in Amiens and other alleged acts of God.[17] One such tale was documented by Douglas Loveday for a British reading public and went through two editions.[18] Loveday attributed no

[16] *Pétition à la Chambre des pairs par M. Douglas Loveday*, p. 1. Loveday, who was born in Hammersmith, traveled between England and France frequently and became a prominent figure in French social circles in the Restoration and July Monarchies.

[17] The preserved body of a deceased nun in the city of Amiens was alleged to have been responsible for a number of miraculous healings.

[18] *The Miraculous Host Tortured by the Jew under the Reign of Philip the Fair in 1290, Being One of the Legends that Converted the Daughter and Niece of Douglas Loveday under the reign of Louis XVIII in 1820, with Mr. Loveday's Narrative*, 2d ed. (London, 1822).

formal blame or responsibility to his daughter, whose agency he denied, arguing that she had fallen prey to a seductive plot perpetrated by Reboul, the owner and director of the boarding establishment. Not only had she stolen his daughter, but she had corrupted her morals by teaching her the art of dissimulation through which Emily initially concealed her newfound religious beliefs. In short, to hear Loveday tell it, Reboul seduced his family, "usurped the rights that religion, nature and law gave me over her . . . shocking me at the idea of so cruel a violation of rights" that were "most respectable and sacred."[19] For Loveday, the seduction of his daughters was evidence of a larger problem of fanaticism in France, which penetrated "the bosom of families," causing domestic strife and discord.

Much of Loveday's account of Reboul's alleged *rapt de séduction* depended on his invocation of the schoolteacher's moral turpitude and her desire to keep the Loveday children for the monetary benefits that they afforded. These qualities and motives were portrayed largely through innuendo regarding the latter's willingness to allow Emily Loveday to enter into correspondence with an unknown gentleman, whose identity was later revealed as a sexagenarian priest, and by the suddenness of the children's conversion.

Douglas Loveday claimed that on bringing his daughters home after learning of their conversion, he had succeeded in winning back the souls of Mathilda, who was now twenty, and his niece. However, Emily remained steadfast in her newfound faith, and one week later she secretly left her father's house. Soon after, Loveday claimed to have received a letter postmarked from Amiens that indicated that Emily had taken refuge in La Maternité, a foundling institution run by a religious community. Emily Loveday confessed in her own response to Loveday's petition that she stayed in Amiens a month to wait for documentation from England that would prove her majority (in order to be free from parental control.)[20]

In the meantime, Douglas Loveday ostensibly appealed to the police and the English ambassador to intervene on his behalf and soon learned that his daughter had moved to the house of an English Catholic gentleman by the name of Jerningham and that she was still in contact with Reboul. Jerningham ultimately turned Emily over to her father, but in less than twenty-four hours she again fled Douglas Loveday's house. Although, her father claimed, he knew that she had taken refuge with the nuns of

[19] *Pétition à la Chambre des pairs par M. Douglas Loveday*, p. 4
[20] This explanation was provided by the duc de Saint-Aignan in his review of the case before the Chamber of Peers. *Archives parlementaires de 1787 à 1860, recueil complet des débats législatifs et politiques des chambres françaises*, 2d ser. (1800–60), vol. 34, 26 January 1822 (Paris, 1876), p. 209.

the Congregation of Notre Dame at no. 106, rue de Sèvres in Paris, according to Loveday's account the nuns belonging to this establishment
initially denied her existence. Loveday then made several unsuccessful attempts to regain custody of his daughter. On one highly publicized occasion he tried to force Emily into a hired carriage with the help of another
man while she was out for a walk near Montparnasse with two nuns belonging to the Congregation of Notre Dame.

After having entreated the public authorities and the English Ambassador in France to aid him in his unsuccessful efforts to regain his daughter from the Congregation of Notre Dame, Loveday took the unusual step
of petitioning the Chamber of Peers on 28 December 1821. According to
article 371 of the Civil Code, children remained under their parents' formal authority until the age of majority. While Mathilda and Mary had not
reached the age of majority, Emily had just turned twenty-one and was
therefore not legally bound to submit to all of her father's commands
under the Civil Code. Loveday, however, attempted to get around this fact
by arguing that Emily had converted to Catholicism *before* she had
reached the age of majority and that her conversion had been the result
of *rapt de séduction*, a criminal act perpetrated by Ernestine Reboul. At the
same time, twelve thousand of copies of the petition charging Ernestine
Reboul with *rapt de séduction* were printed to mobilize public opinion on
his behalf.

Although Loveday's petition resembled many of the diverse pleas (for
pensions, pardon, or property) that have found their way into remote corners of governmental archives, it bore a greater similarity to the *mémoire
judiciaire*, the published version of a lawyer's defense of his client, which
was originally intended for the eyes of judges alone.[21] During the eighteenth century, such *mémoires* were increasingly published in celebrated
cases, particularly after the Calas affair, and thus became the "main bridge
between the courtroom and the street."[22] Indeed, their often sensational
and titillating content soon made them into a popular form of pamphlet
literature by the beginning of the French Revolution. During the early
Restoration *mémoires judiciaires* reappeared, galvanizing public opinion on

[21] Sarah Maza, "Domestic Melodrama as Political Ideology: The Case of the Comte de
Saunois," *American Historical Review* 94 (December 1989): 1249–64. Maza has argued that
such cases played an important role in the construction of a "public" and "public opinion"
that transcended the corporate society of orders during the ancien régime. See Maza, "Le
Tribunal de la nation: Les mémoires judiciaires et l'opinion publique à la fin de l'ancien
régime," *Annales: économies, sociétés, civilisations* 42 (January 1987): 75–90. Also see her *Private
Lives and Public Affairs*.
[22] Maza, "Domestic Melodrama as Political Ideology," p. 1253.

behalf of either plaintiff or defendant, and were soon supplemented by the *Gazette des Tribunaux*, a newspaper which reported on the cases and court decisions throughout France for the legal community and the general public.

The author of Loveday's petition was none other than the renowned Restoration jurist, André Dupin (1783–1865), who worked to narrate "circumstances and feelings of Mr. Loveday in a manner calculated to produce the strongest sensation, especially as the Princes of the Blood and the Archbishop of Paris are charged with being parties to the abduction."[23] Born in a well-to-do legal family six years before the outbreak of the French Revolution, Dupin came of age as a jurist during the years in which Old Regime law was dismantled and replaced by new legal codes. The elder brother of the social statistician Charles Dupin, he was a respected member of the bar, and no stranger to political controversy. Dupin boasted of having pleaded cases for the humblest and the most renowned. His clients included political figures as diverse as Napoleon in 1821–22 and the duc d'Orléans in the affair of the Théâtre-Français in 1818.[24] As a supporter of constitutional monarchy who came to play a prominent role in the July Revolution of 1830, which toppled the Restoration regime, he often defended liberal causes. On a number of occasions Dupin acted as lawyer on behalf of the *Constitutionnel*, which took Douglas Loveday's side, against the attempts of the monarchy to shut down political opposition by muzzling the press.[25]

Loveday's petition and charge soon brought responses from Emily Loveday and the schoolteacher whom Loveday accused of *rapt de séduction*. Like Loveday's petition to the Chamber of Peers, these responses resem-

---

[23] The only record of Dupin's authorship is contained in the English translation of Loveday's pamphlet that was published in London in 1822 in *The Miraculous Host*. The anonymous introductory note to the translation claims that Loveday "caused M. Dupin, a celebrated French advocate, to draw up a petition, stating the case to the French Chamber of Deputies." *The Miraculous Host Tortured by the Jew*, p. 17.

[24] Dupin pleaded four thousand civil cases between his admission to the bar and his entry into political life as a deputy following the July Revolution of 1830. He argued that although civil suits often did not have the dramatic character of criminal affairs, they "implicated the state and honor of families, the self-respect of persons, and to a large degree their social status." André Dupin, *Mémoires*, vol. 1: *Souvenirs du barreau* (Paris, 1855), p. 248. For a less than flattering portrait of the jurist, see *Petit dictionnaire de nos grandes girouettes d'après elles-mêmes* (Paris, 1842), pp. 104–9. Also see Donald R. Kelley, *Historians and the Law in Postrevolutionary France* (Princeton, N.J., 1984), pp. 56–60.

[25] See, for example, André Dupin, *Mémoire pour les rédacteurs du Constitutionnel, en réponse de l'acte d'accusation en tendance sur la question de savoir si les ordres religieux peuvent s'introduire ou se maintenir sans loi qui les institue* (Paris, 1825); and Dupin, *Défense du Constitutionnel prononcé à l'audience de la cour royale, du 17 juillet 1827* (Paris, 1827).

bled *mémoires judiciaires.* Along with two lawyers, Jean-Baptiste-Louis-Joseph Billecocq and M. Hennequin, Reboul signed her response herself. As Emily's statement was written in the third person, she evidently received similar, albeit anonymous, help. Reboul and Emily Loveday refuted Douglas Loveday's representation of fact and intention in their telling of the story of Emily's conversion. These refutations centered on three principal areas: the nature of Emily's conversion; her motives in fleeing her father's house; and Reboul's role in Emily's conversion. Both Emily and Reboul contended that the former's conversion was one made of free will, that she had not been the object of any form of coercion, and that as she was over the age of twenty-one, she was responsible for her actions. Both portrayed her flight from her father's house as an act of fear (that Douglas Loveday would return her to England and forbid her from practicing her faith) rather than one of insubordination.

Voice and the appearance of authenticity were central to the narrative strategies of father, daughter, and teacher. For this reason, Loveday's December 1821 petition and his expanded version of February 1822 were written in the first person, as were Reboul's first and second responses. The first-person voice lent their stories an immediacy and personal pathos that a third-person account lacked because the participants allegedly spoke in their own voices, without any formal mediation that would temper the emotion that they evidently felt. Lawyers involved in the case were well aware of the power of the first person account. Indeed, the question of authorship of Loveday's petition and of Emily's and Reboul's responses was repeatedly raised in order to cast doubt on the veracity of the conflicting accounts of the conversion. For example, Douglas Loveday faulted Reboul for having had to resort to legal counsel to draft her response and suggested that she was in need of the artifice of lawyers, which he was not.[26] On the other hand, Emily and Ernestine Reboul claimed that her father's petition was "written for him" and suggested that it was more polemic than truth.[27]

In making their cases, Ernestine and Emily had to walk a narrow line. The voice that each assumed was inevitably shaped by their vulnerable legal status as women in postrevolutionary law. Unable to testify and afforded none of the rights that the head of a family could claim, each made

---

[26] "Par prudence, elle s'est associé aux deux jurisconsultes, elle eût trop de peine à répondre elle-même. Il fallait un certain art: elle a eu recours à ceux qui le possédaient." *Pétition ampliative à la Chambre des Députés par M. Douglas Loveday, anglais et protestant, avec les pièces justificatives de son contenu et des observations additionelles* (Paris, 1822), p. 48.
[27] *Réponse de Miss Emily Loveday à la pétition présentée au nom de son père à la Chambre des Pairs* (Paris, 1822), p. 5.

strategic use of her vulnerability by appealing to truth, virtue, and nature, rather than law in making her case. Ernestine admitted that the "contest" between herself and Loveday was "unequal": "I do not challenge the authority of the head of a family who holds his children to account of his children. I quite understand that in this sad debate, the contest is unequal" because "M. Loveday is a father, I am a schoolteacher. Trust has to give him preference . . . but there is something more imposing and even more worthy of respect: that is the truth!"[28] Like her teacher, Emily and her lawyers were careful not to repudiate the claims of paternal authority. She declared in the opening lines of her response that she was "torn between two sacred obligations," that of the "free exercise of religion" and "a father's will." "Ignorant of the law," she declined to discuss legal considerations, "which appalled her filial piety." Instead, she only sought to "reestablish factual truth distorted (dénaturé) in the petition of her father."[29] Representing herself as "submissive," she claimed not to respond to her father, but to speak in the name of her religion and, like Ernestine Reboul, "to avenge innocence and calumniated virtue."[30]

The different stories told by Douglas Loveday, Ernestine Reboul, and Emily Loveday all revealed a family gone awry. Loveday portrayed a daughter whose natural filial affection had been so corrupted that she willfully ignored the claims of paternal authority. When police officials expelled her father from the convent of Notre Dame after he tried to gain access to his daughter, Douglas Loveday claimed, she had smiled with malevolent satisfaction. In contrast, Emily Loveday painted a violent father, duped by "perfidious counselors," who used his expression of "paternal pain" to launch a political diatribe.[31] Reboul saw in Loveday and his wife absent or despotic parents and a family in which discord reigned. Indeed, she went so far as to assert that the disorder in the Loveday family was the root cause of their children's conversion. In so doing, she turned the tables and put Douglas Loveday under attack.

In order to give her conclusions weight in her "unequal battle" with Loveday, Reboul cast herself in the role of a dutiful daughter and sister, rather than as an unmarried schoolteacher. Her indictment of Mr. and Mrs. Loveday was preceded by a short autobiographical statement written, according to her lawyers, by her alone, to emphasize the veracity of her account. It began: "Raised by a father whose memory will always be vener-

[28] *Réponse de Mlle Reboul aux imputations dirigées contre elle dans une pétition présentée aux deux Chambres par M. Loveday* (Paris, 1822), p. 3.
[29] *Réponse de Miss Emily Loveday*, pp. 5, 7.
[30] Ibid, p. 6.
[31] Ibid., p. 5.

ated by his family [in contrast to Mr. Loveday], and whose solicitude was seconded by the most virtuous mother [in contrast to Mrs. Loveday], I have never left the family [paternal] home." She tended her sick father, who later died, and established a school to provide for her mother as well as for her widowed sister, who had two children and who had been suddenly left without means of support by an unforeseen accident. She asked the readers of her response to consider why she would "unnecessarily compromise the growing prosperity of our establishment" [and her livelihood] by effecting the conversion in the circumstances Loveday described.[32]

In contrast to her family's loyalty and affection, Reboul asserted, the relationships between parents and children in the Loveday family were strained and Douglas Loveday had concealed important facts in making his case. She claimed that it was Mrs. Loveday, who did not appear in the three editions of Loveday's petition, and not her husband who first placed Emily, Mathilda, and Mary in the boarding school. Mrs. Loveday allegedly lived in a pavilion attached to her school for some time afterwards and had ample opportunity to observe the establishment.

When Emily and her sisters first arrived at her establishment, Reboul claimed, she had been struck by Emily's sad and sickly demeanor as well as by her distinguished manner. Emily was in a state of suffering, requiring a great deal of attention. Reboul worried anxiously about her health and came to observe an unhappy relationship between mother and daughters that ultimately resulted in Mrs. Loveday moving out of the pavilion, with the full knowledge and approbation of Mr. Loveday.

According to Ernestine Reboul, the Lovedays were, moreover, indifferent to the religious education of their daughters. She claimed that she hesitated to admit the Loveday sisters into her establishment because of their religion, but Douglas Loveday had insisted on his belief that one religion was as good as another. On one occasion, Reboul noted, he gave her a painting entitled "Christ on the Cross," for her chapel, a painting whose existence he now denied. When Mr. Loveday did see his daughters on Sunday outings, Reboul claimed, he preferred to take them to the Tuileries rather than to a Protestant service held at the residence of the British ambassador.

Reboul asserted that the Lovedays were largely absent from their daughters' lives for three years, and she soon suspected deeper familial problems on learning of "the pain and worries that the two unhappy daughters of Mrs. Loveday experienced." For example, when Douglas

[32] *Nouvelle réponse de Mlle. Reboul, provoquée par la pétition ampliative de M. Loveday* (Paris, 1822), pp. 18, 21.

Loveday took his daughters to see the festivities in honor of the birth of the duc de Bordeaux (in 1820), they returned in a "state of affliction," confiding their "secret" as to the cause and repeated "a thousand times that they had no one but us [the Reboul sisters] in the world."[33] Reboul did not reveal the young girls' "secret," but suggested that it was sufficiently troubling to cause her concern. Ultimately, Ernestine Reboul attested, she and her sister, who lived at the school, came to be the "veritable mothers" of the children who shied away from the conflict and disorder of their real family. After Emily was returned to her father following her conversion, Reboul allegedly received letters from Emily's seventeen-year-old brother which disclosed that Emily had been repeatedly pilloried with verbal abuse. Reboul thus concluded her response to Loveday's allegation by asserting that the conversion of the Loveday sisters was the direct result of parental neglect and domestic strife: "Undoubtedly, before comparing the catechisms of her beliefs, Emily compared the calm that she enjoyed in my house with the storms of the paternal home! Yes . . . Mr. and Mrs. Loveday are the true authors of their daughters' conversion. . . . If the two sisters had found in their parents examples and consolations that they had the right to expect, they would never perhaps have thought of this change in religion."[34]

THE PUBLIC'S JUDGMENT

While the protagonists in the Loveday affair gave different accounts and interpretations of the circumstances of Emily's conversion, the French public asked, more specifically, whether Emily Loveday had the right to renounce her Protestant faith, convert to Catholicism, and leave her father's house. For the historian, the Loveday affair raises questions about the nature and limits of paternal authority in postrevolutionary French society. The questions that the affair posed for the French reading public resonated because of the large number of petitions and cases involving the conversion and abduction of children from Protestant and Jewish communities surfaced between the Old Regime and the Restoration. The most highly publicized case of the early nineteenth century was that of Emily Loveday.

The debate over the rights of Douglas and Emily Loveday in the Chamber of Peers was preceded by a discussion of two lesser-known cases, one of which concerned Claudine Salles, an artisan's daughter from Nîmes,

---

[33] Ibid., pp. 12–13. *Quelques mots clairs et distincts adressés à Mlle Reboul par M. Loveday fils, protestant éclairé à l'âge de dix sept ans* (Paris, 1822).
[34] *Nouvelle réponse de Mlle Reboul,* p. 13.

and the other involved the daughter of a thief from La Rochelle. The case of Claudine Salles was brought to the Chamber of Peers by her father after he had appealed to legal authorities. Although she had been returned to her father by magistrates, she had repeatedly run away from home. Claudine's father thus petitioned to the Chamber of Peers to protest the conversion of his eighteen-year-old daughter to Catholicism following a stay in a Catholic hospice, and demanded that she be returned to her father's house. Like Emily Loveday, Claudine Salles fled her father's house several times, first taking refuge with the *soeurs grises* and then with a seamstress in Aix-en-Provence. Claudine pleaded for the state's protection, claiming that her parents had vowed to kill her and that they had physically abused her in the past. As a result of these circumstances, the Chamber did not act on her father's behalf.

In the case of Salles, a father's paternal authority was matched against a daughter's freedom of conscience and right to protection from alleged physical abuse. However, other issues entered into the case of Daucourt, who also petitioned the state for the return of his six-year-old daughter, who he alleged had been carried off by a Sister of Charity. He claimed that the nun then refused to allow him to see his daughter, and he petitioned the peers for her release. While the thief's daughter had not formally converted to Catholicism, this case centered on the conditions under which a father might be deprived of his civil and paternal rights over his children. The peers were quick to point to the many dangers of restricting the authority of fathers in the domestic sphere. When the Chamber refused to act on the case because of Daucourt's "paternité redoutable," one deputy, General Maximilien Foy, strenuously protested that a "father can have faults; these faults must be punished when they assume the form of crimes." However, "as much as the law can occupy itself with these faults" it was impossible to claim on this basis that a father be deprived of his paternal rights over his child. He concluded by asking, "who is going to protect paternal power if it is not the legislator who instituted it?"[35] Foy went on to warn that one could go too far in arguing that a father's delinquency removed his right to paternal authority. He asked, "And who is to say that there will not come a day when paternal authority would be removed from the hands of the political prisoner?"[36]

After voting against the thief's petition, the peers considered Douglas Loveday's petition. The duc d'Aignan first presented a report of a committee's investigation into the affair. He concluded the report with the

[35] *Archives parlementaires, chambre des deputés*, 11 April 1822, vol. 36, pp. 219–20. Also see AN, BB³⁰194 for an investigation of the Salles case.
[36] Ibid.

recommendation that the petition be rejected. The duc d'Aignan reasoned that Loveday had willingly placed his daughters in a Catholic establishment and cited his unruly behavior to illustrate his bad faith. He recalled Loveday's actions in the convent and on the rue de Montparnasse, where he tried to force his daughter into a carriage. Despite the protests of the liberal deputy Jean Dénis Lanjuinais, the ultraroyalist Chamber of Peers voted eighty to fifty-seven to reject Loveday's claims.

Douglas Loveday did not stop there, however. He submitted a revised petition to the Chamber of Deputies, and the debate that took place in the Chamber several months later became a public sensation. Its sessions, unlike those of the peers, were open to the public, and reporters of all political stripes were on hand to observe the proceedings. On 12 April 1822, the *Journal des débats* reported that at dawn spectators were camped out on the steps leading to the public entrance to the gallery of the Chamber of Deputies and that the crowds of people were no smaller outside the reserved seating section. From nine in the morning swarms of people filled the streets surrounding the Chamber of Deputies, and when the doors of the gallery were opened at one thirty in the afternoon, the room was immediately packed with spectators, among whom were foreign visitors, "some of the most distinguished ladies," and a larger number of deputies than was the norm, especially on the right of the chamber.[37] As the available seats and standing area of the Chamber of Deputies filled, the previous day's proceedings were read but barely heard by a "public eager with emotion and [sensing] scandal."[38]

When peers and deputies were asked to weigh a father's authority against a daughter's right to freedom of conscience and her liberty to chose her domicile, their consideration of the problem was largely determined by party politics. Ultraroyalist conservatives defended the religious rights of Emily Loveday, and liberals, ironically perhaps, championed the paternal claims of her father. However, political divisions did not prevent opposing sides from stressing the importance of the principle of paternal authority for the maintenance of public order. In making their cases for and against Emily Loveday and her father, liberals and ultraroyalists frequently found themselves contradicting their most revered principles.[39]

[37] *Journal des débats*, 12 April 1822, p. 1; and *Gazette de France*, 12 April 1822, p. 1. The debate was also reported in the clerical *Tablettes du clergé et des amis de la religion* (Paris, 1822), p. 310.
[38] *Journal des débats*, 12 April 1822, p. 1.
[39] Crane Brinton has made a similar argument in his analysis of illegitimacy in Revolutionary and Napoleonic law. Debates on illegitimacy soon revealed "the clash between competing ideas and emotions *in the same set of men.*" *French Revolutionary Legislation on Illegitimacy, 1789–1804* (Cambridge, Mass., 1936), p. 4.

For Douglas Loveday and many of his supporters in the Chambers of Peers and Deputies what was at issue in the affair was the preeminence of paternal authority in face of the claims of religion. "If one could tolerate, in France, a violation as unworthy of all that men hold to be the dearest and most sacred, those of other nations will all flee. . . . vainly would she [France] display before their eyes artistic marvels and all her titles for the admiration of nations; a man, understanding his dignity, would never stop in a land where the rights of paternal authority would be trampled under foot, where fanaticism would penetrate the bosom of families to disturb the peace, where conscience would have stopped being an inviolable sanctuary!"[40] Paradoxically, Loveday and even his opponents argued that this authority was founded in religion. Loveday asserted that "the respect for paternal authority is linked to the respect for Divinity; filial piety is a cult. . . . in the eyes of the world, the paternal curse is the most terrible of scourges: this language is that of all times, of all places, of all beliefs."[41] Reboul had thus usurped the rights that religion, nature, and the law gave Loveday over his family, and for many of his defenders these rights were also founded on property and public order. Indeed, since the abolition of the revolutionary family tribunal and the introduction of the Napoleonic civil and criminal legal codes, the reassertion of the principle of paternal authority was a central concern in political, academic, and legal circles. In 1801, an essay competition sponsored by the Institut de France focused on "the extent and limits of paternal authority in a well-constituted republic," and one of the successful aspirants argued that "paternal authority must be propagated" for reasons of state.[42] Like Montesquieu, a number of jurists argued that paternal authority was "of great use towards the preservation of morals" and it was particularly important in life decisions taken by daughters and sons alike.[43] The Napoleonic Code stipulated that

---

[40] *Pétition à la Chambre des Députés par M. Douglas Loveday*, pp. 19–20.

[41] *Pétition ampliative à la Chambre des Députés par M. Douglas Loveday*, p. 19.

[42] Quoted in Alain Cabantous, "La fin des patriarches," in *Histoire des pères et la paternité*, ed. Jean Delumeau and Daniel Roche (Paris, 1990), p. 335. For a discussion of the importance of the principle of paternal authority in French society and in the immediate aftermath of the French Revolution, see R. Deniel, *Une image de la famille et de la société sous la Restauration* (Paris, 1965); Jacques Mulliez, "La volonté d'un homme," in *Histoire des pères*, pp. 279–312; Jacques Mulliez, *"Pater is est . . .* la source juridique de la puissance paternelle du droit révolutionnaire au code civil," in *La famille, la loi, l'état de la Révolution au Code Civil*, ed. Irène Théry and Christian Biet(Paris, 1989), pp. 412–31. For a discussion of the eighteenth century and the use of *lettres de cachet*, by which the king could imprison or liberate his subjects without recourse to the law courts, see Arlette Farge and Michel Foucault, *Les désordres des familles* (Paris, 1982).

[43] Charles de Secondat, baron de Montesquieu, *The Spirit of the Laws*, trans. T. Nugent (New York, 1949), book 5, chap. 7, and book 23, chaps. 7 and 8, p. 48. Montesquieu argued that pa-

daughters required paternal consent to be married until the age of twenty-one, paternal counsel being required thereafter, and sons were bound to seek paternal consent until the age of twenty-five, the age of majority notwithstanding. As all male and female religious orders had been abolished in 1791 and had no legal status, the code was silent on the question of consent required for religious vows.

The comte Daru claimed before the Chamber of Peers that Emily's actions thus posed a threat to public order, which provided the basis of French civil law. Could a twenty-one-year-old girl, who required parental consent to be married, have the right to leave her paternal house to live where she wanted and how she wanted? The fact that it was religion that had "seduced" Emily Loveday did not make her actions less serious an offense for Loveday's supporters. It appeared to make them worse. If condoned, they suggested, women could behave independently in a variety of different contexts: "Take note that if she has the right to shut herself up in a religious house, she has the right to go anywhere."[44] The social consequences of Emily's alleged insubordination were all too clear and were summarized in an anonymous pamphlet: "If one tried to justify the behavior of Miss Loveday . . . tomorrow all [kinds of] romantic young women, urged by their desires, will listen to the voice of a seducer more than ready to give a false appearance to an escapade with fair words inspired by the heavens, the voice of God whom none should resist."[45] Fathers and families were warned to take heed. Emily Loveday may have been seduced by God, but a daughter could easily be seduced by a more tangible lover, which would inevitably destroy the honor of fathers and the fabric of society.

While it was not unexpected for an ultraroyalist political body to defend religion and the interests of the Church, it was surprising to see peers like Bonald appear to sacrifice the principle of paternal authority which he had so successfully used to attack the Civil Code's divorce law in 1816. Indeed, Bonald had argued in his *Du Divorce considéré au XIX siècle, relativement à l'état domestique et à l'état public de la société*, that "husband, wife, and children are indissolubly *united* . . . because natural law makes it a duty, and because universal reason, from which it [the family] emanates has

ternal consent was more important in French law than in British law probably because children in Catholic France, particularly women, could choose between marriage and a religious vocation.

[44] *Archives Parlementaires de 1787 à 1860*, 2d ser., vol. 34. p. 212.

[45] *Réfutation du mémoire justificatif de Mlle. Ernestine Reboul, suivie de considérations sur l'abus du prosélytisme* . . . par M. S . . . L . . . (Paris, 1822), p. 4.

founded society on a basis less fragile than the affections of man."[46] In short, he suggested that "the child is minor or subject in the family even when he has reached majority" within the state because "public society" does not destroy or alter familial relationships.[47]

What made it possible for men like Bonald to defend Emily's right to independence and stress the importance of paternal authority at one and the same time was the invocation of paternal responsibility. In this regard, Emily Loveday's defenders answered Douglas Loveday's claim to paternal authority with the charge that Loveday had been delinquent in his paternal duty. They thus shifted the focus of the debate from Emily and her schoolteacher to the alleged delinquency of her father. Bonald asked the Chamber of Peers, "If the father of a family complained to the Chamber of Deputies that having placed his daughter in the Opera conservatory for lessons, that they had acquired a taste for the theater, and that their teachers or companions seduced them and urged them to embrace the theatrical profession against their parents' will, with what contempt, or rather with what a sentiment of pity would the Chamber of Deputies rebuff such a foolish complaint?"[48] Bonald emphasized the fact that Loveday had willingly and knowingly placed his daughters in Reboul's care. Although fathers had the right and duty of guardianship, surveillance, and education under the Civil Code, that duty had in practice been handed to Reboul. A Francophobic English reader following the affair in magazines and newspapers in London, who invoked the much-maligned figure of the governess, concurred in this argument but drew different conclusions: "As a mother who values the immortal interests of her children above all other things, I declare that worlds should not tempt me to entrust the education of my daughters to a French governess." She went on to attribute the Loveday scandal not to Loveday's actions, but to those of his wife, to the "present race of thoughtless and fashionable mothers, who in their imprudent zeal for insubstantial accomplishments sacrifice the best interests of their children."[49]

[46] De Bonald, in *Oeuvres de M. de Bonald*, 3d ed., vol. 5 (Paris, 1818), p. 69.
[47] Ibid., p. 96.
[48] Bonald, *Réflexions préjudicielles sur la petition du sieur Loveday*, p. 1.
[49] *Gentleman's Magazine*, February 1822, p. 135. For a discussion of the unease that the governess aroused in British society during the nineteenth century, see Mary Poovey, "The Governess and Jane Eyre," in *Uneven Developments: The Ideological Work of Gender in Mid-Victorian Britain* (Chicago, l988). The figure of the morally compromised governess reemerged in the scandal surrounding the murder of the duchess Choiseul-Praslin by her husband, who had developed a passion for the family governess, in 1847.

CIVIL RIGHTS AND PATERNAL AUTHORITY

Although a central issue that the Chambers of Peers and Deputies considered in the Loveday affair concerned paternal rights and responsibilities as weighed against the political power of the Catholic Church, Emily Loveday's conversion also posed questions concerning the nature of her civil rights and her agency. Emily Loveday resolutely declared that her conversion was free and voluntary and boldly argued that religion always took precedence over paternal authority: "Religion is a natural right that no law, that no power can touch, that all nations that are the least bit enlightened respect, and before which paternal authority, as powerful as it is through the natural sanction that God gave it, must bend."[50] She based her arguments against the omnipotence of paternal authority in both religion and natural law.

The question of agency and right, to which Emily Loveday laid claim, were subjects of intense discussion in the press and legislative chambers during the spring of 1822 because of the unusual nature of the charge of *rapt de séduction* brought against Ernestine Reboul. In his 1782 dictionary of judicial terms, the jurist Guyot traced *rapt* to the Justinian Code, and he defined it broadly as a crime committed by a man who abducts a woman to corrupt, rape, or marry her, or a combination of the three.[51] He also applied the term to the abduction of a minor (son or daughter)[52] for the purpose of marriage without the consent of his or her family. He went on to make a distinction between two forms of *rapt*, one committed through violence and the other through seduction. While the former in effect constituted rape, the latter, *rapt de séduction*, implied a degree of consent on the part of the victim and the removal of the victim from his or her family. According to another jurist the latter was more dangerous because it was more difficult to resist, particularly when it was perpetrated by the "weaker sex."[53] Whereas Guyot drew a distinction between rape and seduction, Fournel in his *Traité de la séduction* defined *rapt de séduction* more narrowly as a "crime against the authority of parents, who have as an ob-

---

[50] *Réponse de Miss Emily Loveday*, pp. 6–7.
[51] Guyot, *Répertoire universel et raisonné de jurisprudence civile, criminelle, canonique et bénéficiale* (Paris, 1782), p. 548.
[52] Ibid. Jean François Fournel cites a 1602 case in which a woman was charged with *rapt de séduction* for marrying a minor without his family's consent. M. Fournel, *Traité de seduction, considerée dans l'ordre judiciaire* (Paris, 1781), p. 336. On *rapt*, also see Claude-Joseph de Ferrière, *Dictionnaire de droit et de politique*, vol. 2 (Toulouse, 1787), pp. 537–40.
[53] De Ferrière, *Dictionnaire de droit et de politique*, 2:540.

ject the [socially] advantageous marriage of a child, against the wishes of the family."[54] He also made a distinction between simple seduction and a *rapt de séduction*: "seduction is an injury done to the person seduced, rather than to the family, but *rapt de séduction* is an injury that directly harms the family whose authority it wounds."[55] By implication, a child without a family is by definition not subject to the crime of *rapt de séduction*, for the only object of the law on this matter is the "honor of families, and the parent's choice of marriage partners."[56]

During the Old Regime *rapt de séduction* was a capital crime, though in practice the severity of punishments was determined by the social and corporate status of the perpetrator. The lower the station of the *ravisseur* and the higher the station of the victim of the crime, the harsher the punishment as the intent of the law was to prevent "marriages rendered unworthy by the corruption of morals and even more so by the inequality of [social] condition."[57] In short, while a rape or "simple seduction" was a crime committed against the individual, *rapt de séduction* was a crime against the family, state, and society as a whole, and its punishment was designed to protect the property and lineage of aristocratic families and to ensure the stability of the corporate order of society predicated on privilege.

For this reason, it is not perhaps surprising that the offense of *rapt de séduction* should have disappeared from France's criminal code during the French Revolution, which eradicated titles of nobility and the corporate society of the Old Regime. The offense was not resurrected in postrevolutionary law. It was replaced by laws governing the abduction and sexual abuse of minors. Article XXXI, title II of the revolutionary criminal code made the abduction of girls under the age of fourteen a crime punishable with twelve years in irons, and article 354 of the Napoleonic criminal code punished the abduction of any minor regardless of sex with imprisonment. The Napoleonic penal code, moreover, drew a distinction between abduction through the use of violence and through the use of fraud.

---

[54] Fournel, *Traité de séduction*, p. 305.

[55] Ibid., p. 306.

[56] Ibid., pp. 335–36.

[57] De Ferrière, *Dictionnaire de droit et de politique*, 2:540. For a discussion of the evolution of marriage law in early modern France, see Sarah Hanley, "Family and State in Early Modern France: The Marriage Pact," in *Connecting Spheres: Women in the Western World, 1500 to the Present*, ed. Marilyn Boxer and Jean Quataert (New York, 1987), pp. 53–63; and Sarah Hanley, "Sites of Political Practice: Lawsuits, Civil Rights, and the Separation of Powers in Domestic and State Government, 1500–1800," *American Historical Review* 102 (Feb. 1997): 27–52.

Under revolutionary and postrevolutionary law the severity of punishment was no longer determined by the social status of the victim and the
accused but rather by the age and sex of the former.[58]

Although *rapt de séduction* was not a part of the postrevolutionary civil
and penal codes in France, the term nonetheless continued to be used in
legal treatises and commentaries. It gradually disappeared from legal
commentary only toward the end of the nineteenth century. Whereas the
1845 edition of Victor Alexis Désiré Dalloz's *Jurisprudence générale, table an-
alytique des vingt-deux années du recueil périodique (1845–1867)* contains references to *rapt*, which appear under entries devoted to the kidnapping of
minors, such references cannot be found in the subsequent edition.[59]
Writing in 1869, one jurist wrote that the law did not "punish the act of
what our older authors called *rapt de séduction*" if the victim of this offense
was not a young girl under the age of sixteen.[60] By 1870 it was clear that the
language of gender and age had replaced corporate privilege and social
status in the definition of such crimes.

What was so extraordinary about the Loveday affair was not that Douglas Loveday used the language of prerevolutionary law, but that the abduction charge did not involve a clandestine elopement or abduction for
sexual purposes and the perpetrator of the alleged crime was not a man,
but rather an unmarried female schoolteacher. As Barbara Diefendorf has
argued, parents did use the fevered language of the charge of *rapt de séduction* to oppose their children's religious vocations during the Counter-
Reformation, and one might suspect that they used the language for
rhetorical and sensational effect. She cites a 1590 case in which a father
deplored a Jesuit's abduction of his son, characterizing it as a *rapt de séduction*.[61] The charge, however, was more frequently used in cases of sexual
abduction and marriage without parental consent. The use of the charge
in the Loveday affair demonstrated a transference of the concept of seduction from the body to the soul, from the domain of sexual and marital

---

[58] *Code criminel et correctionnel ou recueil chronologique des lois . . .*, vol. 1 (Paris, 1805), p. 66; and
M. Carnot, *Commentaire sur le code pénal*, 2d ed., vol. 2 (Paris, 1836), pp. 162–63. According to
article 356 of the penal code, in circumstances in which a girl under the age of sixteen had
consented to her abduction and the accused had not reached the age of majority, the latter
would be imprisoned for three to five years. If the accused were over the age of twenty-one
he would be subject to hard labor for life.

[59] Dalloz, *Jurisprudence générale* (Paris, 1877).

[60] Paget, *De la puissance paternelle dans le droit romain et le droit français*, p. 144.

[61] Barbara Diefendorf, "Give Us Back Our Children: Patriarchal Authority and Parental Consent to Religious Vocations in Early Counter-Reformation France," *Journal of Modern History*
68, no. 2 (June 1996): 290.

relations to that of religious behavior, and it is this transfer that in part contributed to the public sensation surrounding the affair.[62]

By January 1822 Loveday's petition and the responses of Emily Loveday and Ernestine Reboul generated a lively public commentary in the Restoration's two principal opposition newspapers, *La Quotidienne* and *Le Constitutionnel*. This journalistic commentary was in turn followed by a spate of pamphlets by anonymous authors on the subject, newly expanded and documented accounts of the events that led up to Emily's conversion by Loveday and Reboul, and reprinted family letters. These letters, some of which were obviously fake, were published in pamphlet form and purchased for as little as forty centimes.[63] They included a letter to Emily Loveday from her mother; letters to her father from her uncle and her self-professed husband-to-be, and a letter to Mademoiselle Reboul from Emily's seventeen-year-old brother.

The competing interpretations of Emily Loveday's conversion and the self-representations of the affair's protagonists were thus transformed into a powerful melodrama, whose mode could be characterized by an "indulgence in strong emotionalism; moral polarization and schematization . . . inflated and extravagant expression" as well as by "dark plottings" and "breathtaking peripety."[64] This "melodramatic mode," which has been used to describe the emergence of new literary and dramatic forms in France during the late eighteenth century, had increasingly come to permeate the court system as well as cases of family dispute toward the end of the Old Regime. This mode played no small part in contributing to the construction of a public sphere that transcended the corporate and political order of Old Regime society. Indeed, melodrama was in part a creation of the desacralizing political culture of the French Revolution and was "radically democratic" in its self-conscious appeals to public opinion within a larger moral universe.[65]

---

[62] Carnot, for example, remarked on the unusual nature of this case in his 1836 commentary on crimes against children in the penal code. Carnot, *Commentaire sur le code pénal*, 2:150–51.

[63] For example, the letter allegedly written to Douglas Loveday by his brother (father of the young Mary) was obviously a fake. It consisted of a barely veiled attack on Loveday for exposing his family to publicity. See *Lettre du majeur Loveday, gouverneur de Benarès, à son frère Douglas Loveday* (Paris, 1822).

[64] Peter Brooks, *The Melodramatic Imagination: Balzac, Henry James, Melodrama, and the Mode of Excess* (1976; reprint ed., New York, 1985), pp. 11–12.

[65] For a discussion of the "melodramatic mode" in postrevolutionary European culture, see ibid., esp. pp. ix–55, 198–206. Sarah Maza makes a similar point in "Domestic Melodrama as Political Ideology." According to Brooks it was Diderot who first articulated a new genre of melodrama, which mixed tragedy with comedy and took as its subject the drama of everyday

Readers who commented on the Loveday affair supplied several competing explanations of Emily Loveday's conversion to Catholicism and ultimate flight to the congregation of the sisters of Notre Dame. I would
argue that these narratives and those of the affair's protagonists themselves were already inscribed in a rich claustral literature, which played
such an important role in the emergence of melodrama as a literary form
in France in the latter half of the eighteenth century and flourished between the 1830s and 1860s.[66] Indeed, this literature supplied those who
took part in the affair with the plot lines and motives of conflicting narrative accounts.

Melodramatic narrative and tropes were reflected in the accounts of
Emily Loveday's conversion. Her flight to a convent was turned into a
story of abduction and incarceration. She was not only being held against
her father's will, but also against her own. To this extent, it was portrayed
by some observers less as seduction than as mental rape, which had profound consequences for Emily's role as a woman. Many responses to the
affair suggested that this form of seduction or rape was all the more re-
pugnant because it was religious and threatened to destroy Emily's natural
vocation as a future wife and mother. Indeed, much was made, in many
accounts of the affair, of the fact that Emily was extraordinarily beautiful,
which some commentators believed made her situation all the more
tragic.[67] One commentator explicitly equated Emily's departure from the
family home to throwing herself into the arms of a lover, even if that lover
happened to be God.[68] For a Protestant minister who had known her since
childhood, Emily's actions represented a renunciation of all possibility of
enjoying the fruits of earthly life, particularly that of wife and mother:
"Condemned by a deathly vow to an eternal celibacy, you will never be a
wife or mother. . . . you will grow old before your time."[69] Another com-

---

life. Brooks, *The Melodramatic Imagination*, p. 13. See Diderot, "Entretiens sur le Fils naturel,"
in *Oeuvres esthétiques*, ed. Paul Vernière (Paris, 1959); and Michael Fried, *Absorption and The-
atricality: Painting and the Beholder in the Age of Diderot* (Chicago, 1980), esp. pp. 76–105. Also
see Hunt, *The Family Romance of the French Revolution*, pp. 181–91.

[66] For a discussion of the relationship between this claustral literature and the emergence of
melodrama, see Brooks's pathbreaking book on the functions of melodrama, *The Melodramatic Imagination*, and Robert Shackelton, "The Cloister Theme in French Preromanticism,"
in *The French Mind: Studies in Honor of Gustave Rudler*, ed. Will Moore, Rhoda Sutherland, and
Enid Starkie (Oxford, 1952).

[67] Dulaure noted in his account of the affair that the eldest of the Loveday's sisters was "strik-
ingly beautiful." Dulaure, *Histoire de la Restauration*, 3:187.

[68] *Réfutation du mémoire justificatif de Mlle. Ernestine Reboul*, p. 3.

[69] *Instruction paternelle du docteur D., ministre de la religion anglicane, à Miss Emily Loveday* (Paris,
1822), p. 18. In trying to convince her to go back on her decision, he asked "What rank
would you hold in society where you would always be a stranger? You could not go back into

mentator, who remarked on her beauty, suggested, in contrast, that it was perhaps impending motherhood that drove her to the foundling hospital in Amiens. It was Loveday's claim that she took refuge in La Maternité in Amiens that gave rise to this speculation, and Loveday's allegation allowed Ernestine Reboul and her defenders to fault Loveday and his lawyer for encouraging such innuendo, exposing Emily to public scandal and destroying her reputation. While Douglas Loveday himself resolutely backed away from the suggestion that Emily was pregnant, his defenders used a highly sexualized language to explain her conversion: "it is not a question of marriage in the affair of Mademoiselle Loveday; but love often does not go with marriage. . . . here it is a question of love of God, it is true."[70]

Other narratives suggested more sinister reasons for Emily's conversion and flight in alluding vaguely to trysts, secret entanglements, and romantic attachments. The publication of a letter from "Sir William C. . . . ," in particular, raised the question of whether Loveday's anger at Emily's conversion and her hasty departures from her father's home could be explained by her explicit repudiation of a marriage and a future which her father appears to have planned for her.[71] Alternatively, Reboul's response to Loveday's petition, in which she claimed that the Loveday daughters were unhappy and returned from an outing with their father in a "state of affliction," suggested more troubling motives—possibly emotional, sexual, or physical abuse—for Emily's attempt to escape her father.

Charges concerning the spiritual seduction of daughters, their entry into religious communities without parental consent, or their forced sequestration were not confined to the Loveday affair or to the early years of the Restoration. They grew in number during the course of the nineteenth century, judging by the files extant in the Archives Nationales,[72] and many of them provide windows onto the situations of poverty, parental discord, and physical and sexual violence from which young women fled. These petitions came from rich and poor alike, and although many of these cases found their way into the law courts, a large number of complaints were submitted to the state by plaintiffs who were unwilling or

---

the world [from the convent] despite the *éclat* of your name" (p. 17). Emily Loveday never indicated a desire to assume the veil.

[70] *Réfutation du mémoire justificatif de Mlle. Ernestine Reboul,* pp. 3–4.

[71] *Lettre de Sir William C. . . . à M. Loveday* (Paris, 1822).

[72] The relevant files containing the petitions and documentation for such cases for a period beginning in the 1820s and ending in the 1880s can be found in BB[30]194 and BB[30]436 (Justice Files on religious affairs) and Ministry of Religious Affairs files in the F19 series concerning female religious associations. These include notably F[19]6313–15 and F[19]6427.

Miss Emily Loveday.

FIGURE 2. "Portrait of Miss Emily Loveday," frontispiece to *Le bon sens ou entretien d'un fermier avec ses enfans sur Miss Emily Loveday,* par Ferdinand S.-L. (Paris, 1822), one of the many pamphlets published at the time of the affair. She is shown reading "Oeuvres de Bossuet." Courtesy of the Service Reproduction, Bibliothèque Nationale, Paris.

unable to seek formal legal action. The state was soon forced to develop a standard procedure for handling them. As petitions arrived at the ministries of Justice, Religious Affairs, or Foreign Affairs, they were forwarded to the bishop of the diocese in question, and in many cases, to the *procureur du roi* of the arrondissement in which the alleged seduction or sequestration had occurred. He in turn investigated the merits of the complaint, and reported back to the ministry in question, before a final determination was made. While the circumstances and scripts of these cases were unique, and the petitioners dealt with vastly different political bodies in a century that witnessed five different political regimes, each case raised anew questions concerning agency, filial and paternal responsibility, the civil rights of daughters, and the relationship between private lives and public order. They revealed telling contradictions in the ideology and practices of the Right and the Left alike.

While the Church was a bulwark of public order, the story of Emily's seduction revealed to many a commentator the danger that the Church posed for good order in the family and for women's "natural" role as wives and mothers. Many petitions that followed the Loveday affair caused the government and the public to express concern that convents and the education they provided young women were in many cases undermining social and class relationships in French society. The 1866 case of Nathalie Salers, who had been educated in a convent in Toulouse and who decided to leave her father's house to become a nun, revealed the extent to which the state and the public worried that too much of an education provided by nuns would permanently alienate young women from their social origins. Nathalie's father was a self-made wine merchant in Miossac (Tarn-et-Garonne) who possessed a considerable fortune, but his lack of education and refinement allegedly became a source of difficulty in his relationship with his daughter. After Nathalie spent six years in a convent school where her father had proudly placed her, she returned home, in the words of one official, a "déclassée."[73] He went on to suggest that the religious education and the refined manners that she learned from the nuns of Sacré Coeur in Toulouse had alienated her from her parents despite the tender affection that they evidently felt for her. He argued that she therefore found refuge from the coarseness of her surroundings in a convent, and suggested that similar incidents threatened to upset good order in society. Although age was the single most important criterion in determining issues of conscience and religious vocation in conflicts between fathers and daughters and between parents and children, the value attached to family

[73] AN F¹96321, report, 7 March 1866. The *procureur impérial* remarked that Nathalie, like Emily Loveday, was extraordinarily beautiful.

relationships and political considerations increasingly came to determine administrative decisions concerning the claims of paternal authority.[74]

Many of the cases that came before the public authorities raised questions as difficult to adjudicate as those posed by Emily Loveday. While Douglas Loveday had been formally granted full civil rights as a Frenchmen and owned property in France, foreign subjects or citizens, who had not formally been granted those rights, found themselves in a more ambiguous position. Did French laws governing paternal authority apply to foreign parents, "who had not been admitted to establish their residence in France in conformity with article 13 of the Napoleonic Code?"[75] The answer of the jurist who posed the question in these terms appears to have been affirmative. He argued that paternal authority was established not only in the interests of children, but "also in the interests of society as a whole," and "if the authority of the father and mother over their children has its base in public order, as it is hardly possible to doubt, it necessarily comes under the rubric of laws governing police and safety."[76] Nonetheless, at different political moments the state was also asked to take into account the age, will, and interests of the child. The cases of Emily Loveday and a number of other young girls from England and Germany who entered convents in France in the nineteenth century showed how, in varying contexts, these considerations worked. The 1865 situation of Emily Kelson is a case in point.

Like Emily Loveday, Emily Kelson was a young English girl who abjured her Protestant faith and converted to Catholicism. She then decided to leave Britain, join the community of the Soeurs du Saint-Sacrement in Romans, and to take her vows at the age of eighteen. Her brother requested an interview with his sister the day before she was to take her vows to ensure that they were freely pronounced. The request, forwarded by the English ambassador to the minister of justice and religious affairs, was acted on swiftly and the minister expedited the "confidential and urgent" plea to the bishop of Valence. Emily Kelson's brother was granted his interview and was satisfied with her choice of a vocation.[77]

---

[74] An 1853 case indicated that consideration of the claims of paternal authority was also predicated on the legitimacy of the child. In that year the government determined that Emilie Digeon, who was illegitimate, was free from the parental claims of her parents because of her illegitimate status. AN F¹⁹6315, letter from Ministry of Justice to Madame Agalure, 16 December 1853.

[75] Paget, *De la puissance paternelle dans le droit romain et le droit français*, p. 144.

[76] Ibid.

[77] AN F¹⁹6324, letter from the bishop of Valence to the minister of justice and religious affairs, 13 April 1865. A similar case occurred in 1867 when the brother of Alice Wigney, who was thirty-one, alleged that his sister, who had converted to Catholicism and entered a convent in the Haute-Vienne, had written to her former pastor and indicated that she was being held

The 1860 case of Pauline Gerstlé, a young Protestant girl from Württemberg who had abjured her Protestant faith to become a novice in the convent of St. Joseph at Rançon, presented more difficult problems for the Ministries of Justice, Religious, and Foreign Affairs. Pauline Gerstlé was twenty-two, but she had fled her father's house three years earlier, while he was living in Paris. Having learned of her whereabouts, her father demanded her return through the diplomatic offices of the government of Württemberg. According to Württemberg law, she was still a minor, and the question involved "a very delicate appreciation of the character and extent of paternal authority" in relation to civil status (*statut personnel*). The minister of foreign affairs wrote: "I am inclined to think that the courts are the only ones competent to rule on the request. . . . Nonetheless, I feel some scruples in thinking that there is perhaps in this debate a question concerning liberty of conscience."[78] The Ministry of Justice nonetheless concluded that if her father could prove that Pauline Gerstlé was his daughter and that she was a minor, she could probably be returned to his custody.[79]

These cases, some of which occurred, as in the case of Pauline Gerstlé, almost forty years after the Loveday affair, attested to the complexity of the issues that the state had to confront. Their outcome was also shaped by the political climate (and regime) that existed when a petition was submitted to the state. In the political context of the staunchly pro-Catholic Restoration Monarchy (1815–30), the resolution of the Loveday affair was largely determined by political considerations, but the invocation of age, family relations, and the fact that Emily Loveday had taken refuge in a convent also influenced the final determination. The Chamber of Deputies voted to dismiss Douglas Loveday's claims. His request for the custody of his daughter was denied, and Emily Loveday was allowed to remain in the convent of the Sisters of Notre Dame in Paris.[80]

---

against her will. When her brother was granted an interview, he was satisfied about her free choice of a religious vocation. AN F¹⁹6327.

[78] AN F¹⁹6323, Memorandum from the minister of foreign affairs, 21 April 1860.

[79] Ibid., and memorandum from the ministry of justice, 3 May 1860. A similar case occurred in September 1878 when a twenty-year-old German woman from Hanover wished to join the Benedictines of Bayeux without her father's consent. Although laws governing paternal authority were stricter in Hanover, the Ministry of Religious Affairs concluded that it would be difficult for her father to lodge a protest, as she was twenty-one. The deciding issue in both cases was the age of the daughter. AN F¹⁹3615.

[80] While Emily Loveday disappeared from the public record after 1821, her father became the center of considerable attention seventeen years later when the celebrated musician Niccolò Paganini threatened to sue Douglas Loveday for his failure to pay for piano lessons that Paganini allegedly gave to another of Loveday's daughters, Clara. *Gazette des Salons, Journal des Dames et des Modes*, 25 July 1838, pp. 641–44. The *Gazette des Salons* commented on the extraordinary talent of the eighteen-year-old girl, whom it compared to Chopin and

RELIGION AND POLITICS IN RESTORATION FRANCE

The political outcome of the Loveday affair could, in many ways, be antic-
ipated, but the larger issues raised remained unresolved. They continued
to pose troubling questions for politicians and lawyers alike throughout
the nineteenth century. It is hardly surprising that the Chamber of
Deputies, elected in 1819 and deemed to be one of the most conservative
and pro-Catholic bodies imaginable, should dismiss Loveday's claims. The
ultraroyalist majority in the Chamber stood staunchly behind the political
prerogatives of the monarch and defended the temporal interests of the
Catholic Church at any cost. The Chamber's reactionary political stance
hardened even further in 1820, when the duc de Berry, heir to French
throne, was assassinated upon leaving the Opera in Paris and as threats of
a Carbonari conspiracy assumed tangible form. As unrest in the University
and in provincial cities emerged in these years, ultraroyalists became even
more convinced of the necessity of standing behind the Catholic Church
as a bulwark of social and political order.[81] Both liberals and ultraroyalists
saw the conversion of Emily Loveday as a victory for the Catholic Church
and by implication for the counterrevolutonary Right.

It is no accident that Loveday's petition became a major political scandal during a period marked by clerical resurgence that culminated in the
notorious 1825 law of sacrilege, which introduced the death penalty for
blasphemy.[82] The law coincided with a popular religious revival, but it also
spawned fears that the monarchy intended to return to the Old Regime.
The growing power of the Catholic Church could be seen everywhere.
The amount of state money filling church coffers and feeding clerical vocations, immortalized in Stendhal's Restoration novel *Le Rouge et le Noir*,
increased significantly. The Restoration Monarchy had also put its political muscle behind a series of missions that targeted provincial cities soon
after the reestablishment of the monarchy, which generated strident opposition in liberal circles.[83] France had for many in the Catholic Church

---

Liszt. *Gazette des Salons*, 10 March 1838, pp. 216–17. Also see *Lettres authentiques sur les dif-
férends entre Paganini et M. Loveday* (Paris, 1838).

[81] The left-wing Carbonari were an international secret society, which had about forty thou-
sand members in France. The French movement was galvanized by revolutions that occurred
in Spain and Naples during this period. See Alan Spitzer, *Old Hatreds and Young Hopes: The
French Carbonari against the Bourbon Restoration* (Cambridge, Mass., 1971); Spitzer, *The French
Generation of 1820* (Princeton, N.J., 1987), pp. 35–70; and Sheryl Kroen, *Politics and Theater:
The Crisis of Legitimacy in Restoration France, 1815–1830* (Berkeley, Calif., 2000).

[82] For a discussion of the law, see Mary Hartman, "The Sacrilege Law of 1825 in France: A
Study in Anticlericalism and Mythmaking," *Journal of Modern History* 44 (1972): 21–37.

[83] Ernest Sévrin, *Les missions religieuses en France sous la Restauration,* 2 vols. (Saint-Mandé,
1948–59).

become a country requiring missionary activity. Various regional and diocesan societies sprung up to encourage a renewed commitment to religion. These included the Jesuits, the Missionaires de Provence, the Missionaires de Toulouse, the Chartreux de Lyon, and the Missionaires de Saint-Martin de Tours, among others. Between the advent of the Restoration and its fall in 1830, it has been estimated that twelve to fifteen hundred missions were undertaken.[84] These missions assumed a variety of forms in the countryside and in different cities of France that centered on preaching, ceremonies of baptism, consecrations to the Virgin Mary, and processions to cemeteries. The arrival of missions often spelled the disruption of ordinary daily rhythms.

The purported influence that religion had in the lives of women was central to the fear of religious extremism that began to emerge among French liberals in the last years of the Restoration. A few years before the Loveday affair came before the French public, an anticlerical tract written to oppose the work of the religious missions cited the case of a fourteen-year-old girl who was "seduced" into choosing the religious life after being placed in a school run by nuns. Her family, informed of this resolve, were incensed enough not to approve it. Her mother and her sisters tried to remove her from the convent, but the young novice refused even to listen to them. The father demanded her return from the nuns, and they refused him. He therefore sought the help of the prefect, who gave him the authority to recover his daughter. The nuns relented, but the young woman, transported by an alleged saintly anger, declared that she would never follow him. The author of the anonymous tract, in an obvious attempt to gain sympathy for the father, reported that she hurled insults at him and tore at his face and hands, and returned to the convent, where she allegedly continued to "serve God with a fervor with which to make the faithful admire her."[85] At the end of many missions, the missionaries' female flock were inconsolable, only finding distractions for their sorrows and boredom by imposing penance on their husbands, children, and fathers. The most zealous allegedly left home, running after the priests who had seduced them, or "went to bury themselves in some convent."[86]

The private face of this public fear was the growing unease concerning the sway that the Catholic Church had over the minds of French women. This fear was given tangible form in the image of men deserting church pews in greater and greater numbers as women by and large remained

---

[84] Ibid., 1:96.
[85] *Histoire des missionaires dans le Midi de la France: Lettres d'un marin à un hussard* (Paris, 1819), p. viii.
[86] Ibid.

loyal to the Catholic Church. By 1820 France also began to witness the very dramatic explosion in the number of women entering religious congregations. This phenomenon had consequences for the principle of paternal authority and the unity of the family.

The emotions that the Loveday affair stirred in the French public reflected deep concerns that were revealed in many of the narrative accounts of Emily's conversion and flight. The sexual language of seduction, which was an inherent part of the Loveday affair, resurfaced in Michelet's prose where seduction did not assume the gentlest of forms: he argued that the priest "always has the stick of authority in his dealings with the woman, he beats her, submissive and docile, with spiritual rods. There is no seduction comparable to this."[87] Michelet went on to argue that religion merely served to undermine the natural harmony of the family and to construct an invisible wall between husbands and wives, fathers and daughters. The Loveday affair also revealed the extent to which religion could be a source of familial strife and conflict which challenged a father's as well as a husband's authority. Although Michelet and many other anticlerical writers lambasted the priest, particularly if he were a Jesuit in the confessional, he was far more wary of the mother superior in a religious community consisting of women. In a contest between the Jesuit confessor and the mother superior, Michelet declared himself to be on the side of the confessor: "Priest, monk, Jesuit, I am here, on his side," when faced with the "Jesuitess, a great converted lady, who believes herself born for government with a sword of Bonaparte among a troop of trembling women."[88]

What was the significance of the charge of *rapt de séduction*, which had disappeared from France's criminal code, and its transfer from the domain of marriage and the body to that of the spirit during the postrevolutionary period? The charge of *rapt de séduction* leveled against Ernestine Reboul by Douglas Loveday represented more than a sensational rhetorical device intended to attract the attention of the French public. The growing importance of religious vocations in the lives of French women during the Restoration was just as direct a danger to the principle of paternal authority as elopement and clandestine marriage among ruling elites—in whose interests the legal charge of "rapt de séduction" was written—during the Old Regime. Female religious communities potentially

---

[87] Quoted in Zeldin, "The Conflict of Moralities," p. 15. Jules Michelet's *Du prêtre, de la femme, de la famille* was reprinted at least eight times by 1875. Michelet's equation of violence with seduction in this context is telling and warrants further consideration.

[88] Michelet, *Du prêtre, de la femme, de la famille*, 7th ed. (Paris, 1861), pp. 242–43.

threatened family, state, and society. In contrast to Protestant Britain, women in Catholic France increasingly chose religious celibacy as a way of life, creating the possibility of a "separate identity and organization for women in religious life."[89] That separate identity and organization certainly did not call existing gender roles into question, but the ambiguous legal status that women occupied in the realm of religious expression and vocation implicitly destabilized the juridical construction of paternal authority that the Napoleonic Code enshrined.

CONSEQUENCES

These concerns were soon translated into the political arena two years after the Loveday affair, in 1824, in proposed legislation governing the reestablishment of female religious congregations. Debates on the issue revealed significant opposition to the potential economic power that such communities might represent and the devastation that they could bring to family wealth. The Napoleonic Code of 1804, which replaced the prerevolutionary criminal and civil codes that had been abolished during the French Revolution, had made no mention of the associational rights of religious communities, the civil status of their members, or property dispositions governing their existence. Religious communities had been authorized on an ad hoc basis. The code did carefully define the civil status and property rights of secular single and married women. Under the terms of the Napoleonic Civil Code, the property rights of women were very limited. Although the code abolished primogeniture and established the principle that inheritances should be divided equally among offspring regardless of sex, a single woman's right to dispose of her property was subject to the approval of male relatives until she reached the age of twenty-one, while a married woman's property became subject to her husband's will. The right to give or bequeath property to religious institutions was unclear, as female religious congregations had no formal legal existence. This legal lacuna was soon addressed as complaints poured into the government about the potential threats that religious communities posed to the integrity of family patrimonies. Although male religious congregations were never authorized, the legislative chambers of the highly clerical Restoration Monarchy passed a law on 24 May 1825 that granted formal legal recognition to female religious communities that requested authorization and that performed important public services.

[89] Natalie Zemon Davis, "City Women and Religious Change," in *Society and Culture in Early Modern France*, p. 95.

A reading of the debate over the law reveals that a large part of it focused on the threat that such congregations posed to paternal authority, family relations, property, and by implication, public order. Members of the Catholic Right, who had so ardently defended Emily Loveday's rights, countered these arguments on utilitarian grounds and, ironically, in terms of public order. Bonald pleaded, "what is more useful in the political order than this devotion of young persons, who give up the family from which they came . . . in order to consecrate themselves to the service of the larger family, to become daughters of society, and mothers to all its children . . ."[90] He went on to suggest that women religious, in providing services to the state, helped to spare the treasury: "Don't fear a luxury that costs nothing to the state, and which, in giving the lower ranks of the people education and virtue, can save the government the cost of policing and repression."[91] One of Bonald's most striking arguments was that the religious vocation provided an alternative to suicide. He contended that "the Revolution only left one door [open] for leaving the world voluntarily," and that was suicide, which he claimed was a route that many had taken since the Revolution. He suggested that it was "more enlightened and more humane to open the doors" to those who wished to leave the world in order to serve it.[92]

Property dispositions were a central issue shaping the text of the 1825 law, which abolished perpetual vows. Nuns could not take vows for more than five years, though these could be renewed, and they were obliged to declare these vows before both civil and ecclesiastical authorities. Moreover, such vows could only be taken without parental consent if the woman in question was over the age of twenty-one. Most importantly, women religious did not lose their civil status or capacity or their right to property: they did not become "morte civilement." In the spirit of a legal code that abolished the corporate bodies of the Old Regime, the law stipulated that nuns retained their civil rights and individual claims on their property. However, nuns who took formal vows could neither bring nor bequeath more than one-quarter of their property to a female religious community when they entered it if that property exceeded ten thousand francs in value. The *rapporteur* of the 1825 law defended this clause by arguing that as nuns no longer lost their civil status or individual rights to their property in joining an order, it provided them some protection in

---

[90] *Chambre de pairs de France: Session de 1824. Séance du mardi 13 juillet 1824: Opinion de M. le Vicomte de Bonald sur le projet de loi relatif aux communautés religieuses de femmes* (Paris, 1824), p. 5.
[91] Ibid., p. 25.
[92] Ibid., p. 24.

the event that they left or were expelled from a community. More importantly, however, the law was designed to "protect families . . . against . . . spoliation."[93] The law specifically curtailed the property rights of women religious in order to shield families from ruination, to maintain public order, and to protect women from themselves. The legislation was one of the first in a series of postrevolutionary decrees and laws that were passed in order to restrict the influence of religion in civil society. It thus represented one important stone in the edifice that was to become the *état laïque* in France.

[93] Quoted in L.-L. Charrier, *Commentaire de la loi des congrégations religieuses de femmes* (Paris, 1825), p. 93.

CHAPTER 3

Storytelling and the Social Imagery of Religious Conflict

In 1830, the Bourbon Restoration was swept away in a three-day revolution that ushered in a new constitutional monarchy. The July Monarchy (1830–48) and its king, Louis Philippe, repudiated many of the pro-Catholic initiatives and measures that had been put in place during the Restoration, but this did not eradicate anticlerical sentiment. Nor did it calm fears generated by the increasing number of women religious in civil society. Indeed, in the period between 1830 and the Revolution of 1848, concerns about religious seduction and abduction only seemed to grow. They were reflected in novelistic literature and in legal cases involving the alleged forced incarceration of women in convents. This became clear in 1845 when Jeanne-Françoise Le Monnier, who had been a nun in the Norman monastery of the Saint Sacrament in Bayeux, brought a case to court charging the superior of the order and four other women religious for incarcerating her first in a convent and then in the insane asylum of Bon Sauveur in the nearby city of Caen. Her lawyer, Léon Tillard, presented her case to the court in the form of a *mémoire judiciaire*, which narrated the facts of the affair from his client's point of view, and he concluded with a legal justification for her allegations.[1] Like the Loveday affair, the case of

---

[1] *Affaire de Dame Jeanne-Françoise Le Monnier contre dame Marie Le Caplain, Dame Caroline de St.-Séverin, Dame Reine Jourdain, et Dame Renée-Charlotte Le Chasseur* (Caen, 1845). The *mémoire*, as the case became more widely publicized, went through two editions. Publishers in Bayeux refused to print it. *Soeur Sainte-Marie Bénédictine. Récits par elle-même. Mémoire, débat*

Jeanne-Françoise Le Monnier captured the attention and the imagination of the French public and the French state. Le Monnier's lawyer, Léon Tillard, wrote that "the name Soeur Marie [Le Monnier's religious name] is popular in our city."[2]

In March 1845 the Minister of Religious Affairs wrote to the prefect to ask for information about the case, having read accounts of it in the newspaper *National*. On 28 March, the prefect wrote to the minister that while he could not know the outcome of the case, he could be positive that it would "produce a great impression" in Normandy and would deeply stir the public in Bayeux in particular.[3] This chapter explores how Le Monnier's story was told to the court by her lawyer, in order to examine the elements comprising the social imagery that was employed in public debates surrounding conflicts between the Church and the state in nineteenth-century France. In particular, I wish to assess how Tillard appealed to a set of moral categories and images that reveal some of the underlying bases of the anticlerical initiatives that were proposed in these years, and in particular that of secularizing the asylum system.

I will examine Le Monnier's *mémoire* from three perspectives in this regard. First, in terms of how changes in the law and legal procedure following the French Revolution contributed to the way in which Le Monnier's story was told to the court, and second, in terms of how courtroom narratives intersected with contemporary social commentary and novelistic literature during the first half of the nineteenth century. Finally, I wish to explore how such cases helped to define a new relationship between secular and canon law.

Storytelling is, of course, a part of any legal system and frequently reveals in a clear and compelling way prevalent social stereotypes that can range widely and reveal much about how individuals in specific historical settings fashion themselves and their motives in the eyes of others. Natalie Davis has studied, for example, how ostensibly contrite wives or husbands tried to exonerate themselves in the wake of violent acts through strategies of self-presentation in order to justify their actions. Ruth Harris has shown how women accused of crimes of passion in late nineteenth-

---

judiciaire. Comptes rendus et jugement (Caen, 1845), p. 10. A final version, with Tillard's commentary on the case and proceedings, was also published in 1846 under the title *Soeur Sainte-Marie, Bénédictine. Récits par elle-même. La procédure—les enquêtes—la preuve. Orgueil et placement au B.-S.* (Caen, 1846).

[2] "Le nom de Soeur Marie est populaire dans notre ville." *Soeur Sainte-Marie, Bénédictine. Récits par elle-même. La procédure. Les enquêtes. La prevue. Orgeuil et placement au B.-S.*, p. 9.

[3] F¹⁹6314, 28 March 1845.

century France spoke directly on their own behalf in court and drew on the tropes of melodramatic literature and on moral assumptions about female honor to defend their behavior. The extent to which they successfully avoided conviction often depended more on how effectively they told their stories and appealed to these categories than on rules of procedure and law.[4] The study of narrative in legal courts thus provides a window onto the social and moral categories of a given society as well as onto hidden and sometimes unspoken cultural codes and societal fears that might otherwise go undetected by the historian.[5] Indeed, these narratives reveal how these cultural codes were often created out of collective anxieties, and they allow one to reflect on why certain anxieties become particularly charged at given historical moments.

I have chosen the Le Monnier case to explore these issues for three reasons. First, other cases or charges of the same kind were brought during a long period extending from the 1820s to the 1880s whereas these kinds of cases are entirely absent from the eighteenth- and twentieth-century public record. This was a nineteenth-century case par excellence. Courts and the Ministry of Religious Affairs were asked to intervene to investigate, and the cases therefore became a matter of state concern. Second, I wish to explore why charges of sequestration and confinement were so prevalent during this period and to place them within the context of the fascination with Gothic narratives and novels in this period. Third, I will examine how such narratives structured broader discussions about the relationship between Church and state as well as between religious and secular authority.

The Le Monnier case must first be placed within the context of the transformation of the French legal system following the French Revolution, a transformation that changed the relationship between secular and canon law. This is important because, in the words of Peter Brooks, "the law at least implicitly recognizes the power of story-telling" and for this reason, in different social contexts, "it has been intent . . . to formalize the conditions of telling—to assure that narratives reach those charged with judging them in certain rule-governed forms."[6] I will then explore the nar-

---

[4] Davis, *Fiction in the Archives*; and Ruth Harris, *Murders and Madness: Medicine, Law, and Society in the Fin-de-Siècle* (Oxford, 1991), pp. 208–42.

[5] For discussions of storytelling in forensic trials, see Lance Bennett, "Story-Telling in Criminal Trials: A Model of Social Judgement," *Quarterly Journal of Speech* 64 (1978): 1–22, and Lance Bennett and Martha Feldman, *Reconstructing Reality in the Courtroom: Justice and Judgment in American Culture* (New Brunswick, N.J., 1981), pp. 3–10.

[6] Peter Brooks, "The Law as Narrative and Rhetoric," in *Law's Stories: Narrative and Rhetoric in the Law*, ed. Peter Brooks and Paul Gewirtz (New Haven, Conn., 1996), p. 19.

rative strategies of Le Monnier's lawyer, before concluding with a discussion of the theme of claustration and legal storytelling during this period.

CHANGES IN THE LAW

Secular law in France during the eighteenth and nineteenth centuries was based on an inquisitorial as opposed to an accusatorial model.[7] Most criminal trials during the eighteenth century were conducted entirely in private, and the first stage of criminal investigation was carried out by judges. This amounted to questioning the principal witnesses as well as the plaintiff and defendant, out of which a dossier would be created that would complete the *instruction préparatoire*. In the second stage of the investigation, the *instruction définitive*, witnesses were required to repeat testimony, and plaintiffs and defendants sometimes confronted each other for the first time. All evidence and paperwork collected during these two stages of investigation became part of a general file which the judge consulted in deciding a case. Two distinct features characterized this system. First, the proceedings were conducted almost entirely in private and although plaintiffs and defendants had recourse to lawyers, they often faced judges without their counsel present. So the role of the lawyer was, in essence, to advise and draw up legal documents setting out the facts of the case and then to argue legal points to the court.[8]

These legal briefs, or *mémoires judiciaires*, were initially handwritten documents intended for the eyes of the judges alone, and they were the principal means through which the facts of a case were presented to judges in written form. *Mémoires judiciaires* were constructed in the form of stories. They could range from a few pages to several hundred pages in length. With time they were printed and circulated among family members and other parties interested in a case. The *mémoire judiciaire* and later the newspaper became the principal conduit between the courtroom and society at large.[9] It soon became a form of popular pamphlet literature, especially when the *mémoire* centered on a cause célèbre or a particularly titillating legal case.

While the *mémoire judiciaire* presented the facts of a case and made legal arguments to the court, it increasingly spoke in the name of and appealed

---

[7] Katherine Fischer Taylor, *In the Theater of Criminal Justice: The Palais de Justice in the Second Empire* (Princeton, N.J., 1993), pp. 5–9.
[8] For a discussion of these procedures see Maza, *Private Lives and Public Affairs*, pp. 34–35. Also see David Bell, *Lawyers and Citizens: The Making of a Political Elite in Old Regime France* (Oxford, 1994), p. 31.
[9] Maza, *Private Lives and Public Affairs*, p. 36.

to a new social entity known as the "public" from the late eighteenth century onward. It is for this reason that historians of eighteenth-century France have in recent years devoted considerable attention to these legal documents. They have argued that they played an important role in the creation of the very concept of "public opinion," which increasingly came to represent a distinct secular authority in opposition to a morally and politically flawed monarchy. In doing so, the *mémoire judiciaire* contributed to the democratization and secularization of the political and corporate culture of the Old Regime. In some cases, *mémoires judiciaires* in the Old Regime became a form of opposition journalism which criticized political and social elites for their exclusivity and high-handedness and argued for more democratic legal norms. Ultimately, they played an important role in challenging the authority of the French monarchy, thus laying some of the ideological groundwork for the French Revolution.[10]

The legal system of the Old Regime and all the privileges attached to it were, of course, abolished during the French Revolution and replaced by institutions based on principles of ostensible equality before the law. However, with the Revolution and the writing of the Napoleonic Code, certain rules and procedures were retained, including the use of the *mémoire judiciaire* in presenting the facts of a case. While the accusatorial model also survived the Revolution and judges continued to play an important role in the direct investigation of cases, important aspects of the system changed. The courts of the Old Regime were abolished as well as the privileges attached to them. The legal profession was opened, in principle, to all. One of the greatest changes in the nature of French criminal law was to render public what had been essentially private during the Old Regime: court proceedings and cases. The new legal system also gave more advantage to the accused through trial by jury. *Mémoires judiciaires* remained a significant part of postrevolutionary legal culture, and historians have argued that they continued to foster a new secular and democratic morality in the nineteenth century.

But, how did changes in the law affect the status of ecclesiastical cases during this period? It must be stated clearly that Le Monnier's case would never have been brought before a secular court during the Old Regime. All matters governing cloistered religious orders and their members fell under the jurisdiction of canon law. This was because an aspirant who wished to enter a religious order was required to take a solemn, lifelong

---

[10] Sarah Maza, "Le tribunal de la nation: Les mémoires judiciaires et l'opinion publique à la fin de l'ancien régime," *Annales, économies, sociétés, civilisations* 42 (1987): 73–90, and *Private Lives and Public Affairs.*

vow as a result of which he or she died to the secular world or became "mort civilement." Indeed, a nun's civic death was expressed through ritual. In taking her vows, the nun would lie prostrate before the grille, covered by a funeral pall, while the office of the dead was recited.[11] All disputes governing her property or person came under the jurisdiction of her order and canon law. She had no rights or protection under civil law as technically she did not exist as a legal being. Indeed, the Church had more power to adjudicate its own affairs in the eighteenth century, independent of secular legal authority, and religious authorities also had an extraordinary influence over the secular justice system.

Napoleonic law, which established the legal system for postrevolutionary France, rationalized what were a confusing set of procedural practices based on customary law and royal *ordonnances*. However, the Napoleonic civil and criminal codes were silent about the rights and status of the clergy in secular society, and the boundary between secular and canon law was exceedingly unclear. It is true that the Concordat of 1801 established the formal relationship between Church and state until their separation and the abrogation of the Concordat in 1905, providing general guidelines for governance, but it did not define how conflicts between members of the clergy could be resolved in case of deadlock, even after the law governing female religious congregations was passed in 1825.[12] No legislation was ever passed for male religious orders, many of which remained unauthorized, existing at the margins of the law for most of the nineteenth century.

Until the 1860s, governments tried to keep cases involving priests or nuns out of secular courts because in the increasingly public world of the courtroom they feared that religious scandals and conflicts might undermine morals and public order.[13] So prefects, subprefects, *procureurs* and the Ministry of Religious Affairs often stepped in to seek administrative solutions. But in cases of serious crime, like murder or rape, or when a conflict became intractable, the clergy found itself in court. Le Monnier's case fit this pattern in that the subprefect of the arrondisse-

---

[11] Elizabeth Rapley, *The Dévotes: Women and the Church in Seventeenth-Century France*, p. 175.

[12] For revolutionary legislation governing religious congregations, see Alphonse Aulard, *La révolution française et les congrégations: Exposé historique et documents* (Paris, 1903). For the legal status of religious congregations following the Revolution, see Paul Nourrisson, *Histoire légale des congrégations religieuses en France depuis 1789* (Paris, 1928); A. Vuillefroy, *Traité de l'administration du culte catholique: Principes et règles d'administration* (Paris, 1842); Armand Ravelet, *Traité des congrégations religieuses: Commentaire des lois et de la jurisprudence* (Paris, 1869).

[13] Jean Maurain, *La politique ecclésiastique du Second Empire de 1852 à 1869* (Paris, 1930), pp. 77–79. This was one of the "privileges" that the clergy enjoyed until the 1860s.

ment of Bayeux first intervened in order to try to adjudicate the conflict, but to no avail. So cases like hers increasingly found their way into
secular court.

The cultural and social context in which cases were tried in the nineteenth century was quite different from that of the eighteenth. *Mémoires
judiciaires* addressed the general public more directly and could assume a
much broader readership. Cases would be reported in other ways, notably
through the newspapers—and principally, in legal cases, in the *Gazette des
Tribunaux*. Legal cases also provided plots for the theatre and the novel.
One need only think of the famous murder trial of Antoine Berthet, accused of shooting his former mistress, which was recast by Stendhal in
1830 as *Le Rouge et le Noir*. And all these printed materials reached a vastly
expanded readership, which now included large numbers of people who
had not had access to them before. This new readership was reflected in
the success of the *cabinets de lecture*, which were in their heyday during the
1820s, 1830s, and 1840s, and in the popularity of serial novels, of which
Eugène Sue's *Mystères de Paris* and *Le juif errant* were two of the most important examples.[14] Nineteenth-century *mémoires judiciaires* were now frequently filled with literary references.

The effect of these legal and cultural changes are immediately apparent in Léon Tillard's statement of Jeanne Le Monnier's case. The *mémoire
judiciaire* was, for example, printed for public consumption and soon went
into a second edition. From the start, Tillard addressed himself to the
general public, although he dedicated the *mémoire* to the subprefect of
Bayeux, and he invested the case with a larger political significance. He
placed Le Monnier's complaint squarely in the context of then current
press debates concerning the need for new legislation to govern religious
orders, and he suggested the case represented a kind of unresolved prerevolutionary atavism: "No doubt," he told his readers, "we no longer
have the lettre de cachet, those Bastilles . . . but every day reveals miser-
able feminine antipathies in the shadow of cloisters, supported by the in-
flexibility of hierarchical will. . . . The victim perishes, not hierarchical ab-
solutism. . . . Is this the liberty and the equality of our national
charters? . . . How these unhappy women murmur in the silence of mon-

---

[14] Ernestine Dumont wrote to Eugène Sue in November of 1843, "your work is everywhere—
on the worker's bench, on the merchant's counter, on the little lady's divan, on the shop-
girl's table, on the officeworker's and magistrate's desk. I am sure that of the entire popula-
tion in Paris, only those who cannot read do not know your work." Quoted in James Smith
Allen, *In the Public Eye: A History of Reading in Modern France, 1800–1940* (Princeton, N.J.,
1991), p. 55; and Françoise Parent-Lardeur, *Lire à Paris au temps de Balzac: Les cabinets de lecture à Paris, 1815–1830* (Paris, 1981).

asteries without their voices being heard by public authority . . ."[15] By implication he suggested that until the voices of these women were heard the specter of the Revolution would continue to haunt French society. The issues of the case thus became immediately inscribed in broader arguments regarding the necessity of asserting secular authority over religious authority—a concern that dominated French politics for much of the nineteenth century and was expressed in the conflict between Gallicanism and Ultramontanism.[16]

TELLING THE STORY

Tillard's *mémoire*, like the *mémoires* of the late eighteenth century, created a Manichean world and used the devices of theatrical melodrama. Tillard himself acknowledged at one point in his narrative that he knew that he might be accused of employing cheap theatrics in presenting the facts of the case.[17] The characteristics of this melodrama included "extreme moral polarities, hyperbolic expressions and gestures, sketchy characterization, complicated plotting, and emphatic moral didacticism."[18] The narrative strategies used by Léon Tillard consisted of a first-person account by the nun in question, which lent immediacy and pathos to her story—a practice that was increasingly common in the eighteenth century—direct literary references to two of the best-selling texts of the day, notably Eugène Sue's *Le juif errant* and Jules Michelet's hugely popular 1845 attack on the power that priests had in the confessional, *Du prêtre, de la femme, de la famille*, and the use of plot lines and imagery drawn from claustral literature of the eighteenth and nineteenth centuries.

The relationship between the copious claustral literature produced between 1760 and the 1840s and courtroom storytelling during the early nineteenth century is a fascinating one, and has not received the consideration it deserves.[19] The literary critic Peter Brooks has argued that the theme of claustration was crucial to the development of melodrama in its

---

[15] *Affaire de Dame Jeanne-Françoise Le Monnier*, p. 5.

[16] For a discussion of the Ultramontane-Gallican divide, see the introduction.

[17] "Ici, nous ne craignons point que l'on nous taxe d'une sensibilité théâtrale, factice, montée pour le besoin de la cause." *Affaire de Dame Jeanne-Françoise Le Monnier*, p. 64.

[18] Maza, *Private Lives and Public Affairs*, p. 66.

[19] Denis Diderot's tale of the victimization of Suzanne in *La religieuse* (1760) is perhaps the best-known example of a genre of literature that explored the forced confinement and/or libertinage of women within religious institutions. Diderot's novel was followed by a plethora of literature on the subject. Jeanne Ponton, *La religieuse dans la littérature française* (Laval, 1969), pp. 382–86. Also see Mita Choudhury, "Despotic Habits: The Critique of Power and its Abuses in an Eighteenth-Century Convent" *French Historical Studies* 23, no. 1 (Winter 2000):

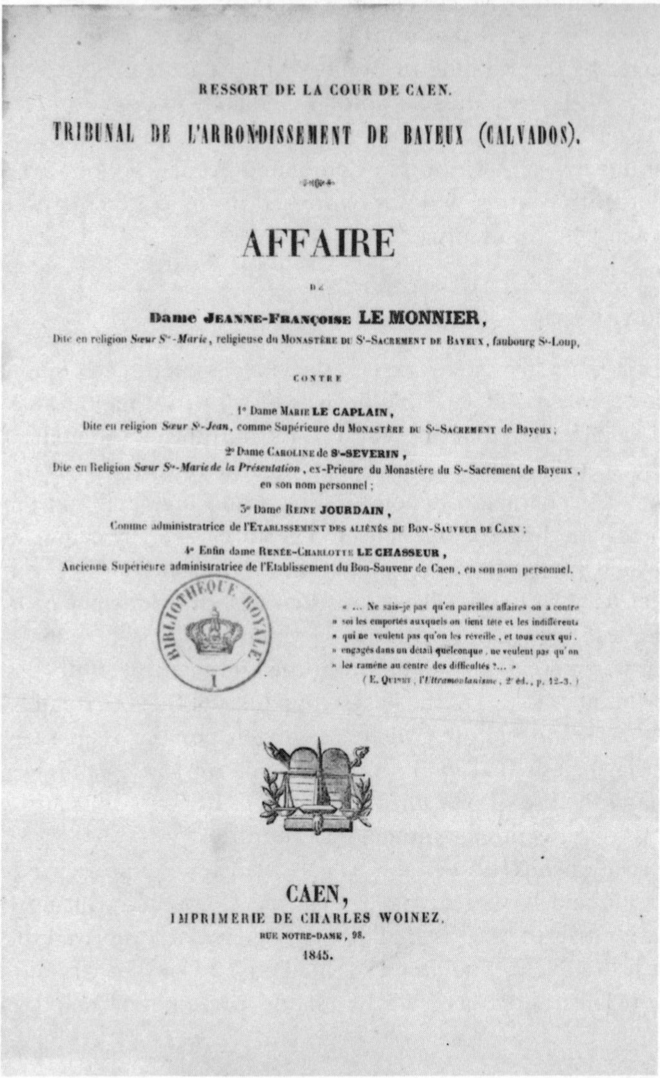

RESSORT DE LA COUR DE CAEN.

TRIBUNAL DE L'ARRONDISSEMENT DE BAYEUX (CALVADOS).

AFFAIRE

DE

Dame Jeanne-Françoise LE MONNIER,

Dite en religion *Sœur Ste-Marie*, religieuse du Monastère du St-Sacrement de Bayeux, faubourg St-Loup,

CONTRE

1° Dame Marie **LE CAPLAIN**,
Dite en religion *Sœur St-Jean*, comme Supérieure du Monastère du St-Sacrement de Bayeux;

2° Dame Caroline de **St-SEVERIN**,
Dite en Religion *Sœur Ste-Marie de la Présentation*, ex-Prieure du Monastère du St-Sacrement de Bayeux, en son nom personnel;

3° Dame Reine **JOURDAIN**,
Comme administratrice de l'Etablissement des aliénés du Bon-Sauveur de Caen;

4° Enfin dame Renée-Charlotte **LE CHASSEUR**,
Ancienne Supérieure administratrice de l'Etablissement du Bon-Sauveur de Caen, en son nom personnel.

« … Ne sais-je pas qu'en pareilles affaires on a contre
» soi les emportés auxquels on tient tête et les indifférents
» qui ne veulent pas qu'on les réveille, et tous ceux qui,
» engagés dans un détail quelconque, ne veulent pas qu'on
» les ramène au centre des difficultés ?… »
(E. Quinet, *l'Ultramontanisme*, 2e éd., p. 12-3.)

CAEN,
IMPRIMERIE DE CHARLES WOINEZ,
RUE NOTRE-DAME, 98.
1845.

FIGURE 3. Frontispiece of *Affaire de Dame Jeanne-Françoise Le Monnier* (Caen, 1845). Courtesy of the Service Reproduction, Bibliothèque Nationale, Paris.

earliest forms. It represented the "ultimate (Gothic) nightmare of burial alive, loss of mobility and of identity."[20] Between 1789 and 1799 twenty-six claustral plays, including one authored by Olympe de Gouges, the author of the *Declaration of the Rights of Woman* (1791), were performed in Paris alone.[21] One of the most popular, Boutet de Monvel's *Les victimes cloîtrées* (1791), was performed eighty times between 1791 and the Restoration and was a great success. Indeed, the play has been considered the first example of a new type of melodrama in France. It concerns the incarceration of the novel's hero and heroine in separate religious houses by monks and nuns working for a nefarious aristocrat. Ultimately, both are liberated from their subterranean cells in a final scene by a republican mayor wearing the tricolor. In Brooks's words, "the play suggests the connection of the claustral space of the Gothic on the one hand, to the Revolution on the other: the Revolution as the opening up of and liberation from the claustral, the victory of democracy as virtue and innocence."[22]

Olympe de Gouges, *Le couvent, ou les voeux forcés*, which was performed eighty-nine times between 1790 and 1792, follows a similar plot line. She tells the tale of a mother and infant daughter confined to a convent by their wicked brother and uncle, the marquis of Leuville. The latter, a violent man who disapproved of his sister's marriage, has murdered her husband. When the daughter, Julie, reaches the age of sixteen, her uncle and the mother superior in effect force the unwilling young girl to take her vows by threatening to withdraw her pension. The marquis does so to hide his infamy, while the mother superior looks forward to a fat dowry. However, the marquis's young son, who has fallen in love with Julie during visits to the convent with his father, is intent on liberating the heroine. The young chevalier gains access to the religious house by dis-

---

33–65. The subjects of the nun and the convent were not confined to literature or to France during this period. See Susan p. Casteras, "Virgin Vows: The Early Victorian Artists' Portrayal of Nuns and Novices," in *Religion in the Lives of English Women, 1760–1930*, ed. Gail Malmgreen (London, 1986), pp. 129–60.

[20] Brooks, *The Melodramatic Imagination*, p. 50.

[21] See Louis-Caroogis Carmontelle, "Le couvent des religieuses, comédie en un acte" (1789), Ms. B.N. f.f. 9326; Maurin de Pompigny, *La bonne soeur ou elle en avait besoin* (Ambigu-Comique, 17 December 1789); Anon., *Le couvent, drame* (Théâtre de la Nation, April 1790); Joseph Fiévée, *Les rigeurs du cloître* (Les Comédiens italiens ordinaires du Roi, 23 août 1790); Olympe de Gouges, *Le couvent, ou les voeux forcés* (Théâtre français, October 1790); Pierre Laujon, *Le couvent, ou les fruits du caractère et de l'éducation* (Théâtre de la Nation, 16 April 1790); Anon., *La religieuse danoise, ou la communauté de Copenhague* (Théâtre de Montansier, 1791); Boutet de Monvel, *Les victimes cloîtrées* (Théâtre de la Nation, 29 March 1791); Carbon de Flins, *Le mari directeur, ou le déménagement du couvent* (Théâtre de la Nation, 25 February 1791); Pujoulx, *Amélie, ou le couvent* (Théâtre Feydeau, 28 February 1791); Jacques-Benoît Demautort, *Le petit sacristain* (Théâtre de la Vaudeville, 13 March 1792); Desprez et Rouget de Lisle, *Les deux couvents* (Opéra-Comique, 16 January 1792).

[22] Brooks, *The Melodramatic Imagination*, p. 50.

guising himself as a Capuchin monk and declares, "I will only leave here to bring Julie to the marriage altar."[23] Ultimately, the young chevalier frees Julie, with the help of an honest priest and commissaire, and the marquis de Leuville begs his family's forgiveness. The convent's servant, who acts as a kind of chorus, concludes: "Undoubtedly God does not forbid living honestly and quietly in a convent; but I am of the opinion that he much prefers marriage."[24]

The political metaphors of bondage and liberation set within these moralistic tales were immensely popular during the revolutionary decade, and demand for such literature does not appear to have abated during the immediate postrevolutionary period.[25] In 1836, Madame Adèle Daminois published a novel whose central character was a half-English, half-French girl, not wholly unlike Emily Loveday. She comes to France from the West Indies with her French mother, who dies during the ocean passage, and must then live with her mother's sister and uncle. Alone and subject to the salacious advances of the aunt's husband, she flees to a convent. After being forced to suffer inhuman treatment at the hands of the nuns to whom she has freely entrusted herself, she ultimately regains her freedom.[26]

In evoking a prerevolutionary social imagery regarding bondage and liberation drawn from claustral literature, Tillard conjures up a fascinating mixture of conflicting social types and is provided with a wealth of plot lines and motives. He makes Le Monnier into a romantic heroine whose purity was assaulted by the evil machinations of a cabal of women. Tillard makes an emotional appeal to the court and the public by presenting her as a feminine victim in need of protection, a damsel in distress, who is denied her natural vocation as wife and mother through incarceration in a convent. On another level, he must subvert this plot line and reassert her rights as an individual because Le Monnier actually wants a pension or to return to her order. Her case was one that involved a breach or "rupture" of a *contrat d'association* brought before the Tribunal de Bayeux in the Norman department of Calvados.

---

[23] Olympe de Gouges, *Le couvent ou les voeux forcés* (Paris, 1792), p. 48.

[24] Ibid., p. 83.

[25] Among the many works published on the subject between 1800 and 1821, see Charles Nodier, *Les méditations du cloître* (1801); baronne de Méré, *L'abbaye de Saint-Rémy, ou la fille de l'abbesse*, 4 vols. (Paris, 1807); Eusèbe Salverte, *Nelia, ou les sermens*, 2 vols. (1812); Mme. Perin de Grandenstein, *La dame grise, ou histoire de la maison de Beauchamp* (1816); Abel Dufresne, *Le monde et la retraite, ou correspondence de deux jeunes amies*, 2 vols. (1817); Mme. de M. . . . , *L'abbaye de Saint-Aure, ou encore victime de l'amour* (1818); baronne de Méré, *La soeur grise, ou mémoires de Mme de Canès*, 3 vols. (1819); Jeanne-Edme Paccard, *L'abbaye de la Trappe, ou les révélations nocturnes*, 3 vols. (1821).

[26] Madame Adèle Daminois, *Le cloître au XIXe siècle* (Paris, 1836).

NARRATIVES OF CAPTIVITY

The bulk of the *mémoire* and the story of Le Monnier's ordeal is taken up with the story of her incarceration. To this extent, the social image of the incarcerated nun, which is central to the construction of Le Monnier's story, becomes a larger metaphor, in Tillard's telling of it, for the intolerance and hierarchical oppression of the Ultramontane Church in postrevolutionary France. It allows him to attempt to gloss over the conflicting images of the nun as vain, disobedient, and self-regarding—characteristics which emerge in the text. How is this achieved?

Tillard's narrative covers a nineteen-year period, from Le Monnier's entry into the Benedictine convent in 1825, at the age of twenty-seven, to her transfer to the asylum of Bon Saveur in Caen in 1841, at the age of forty-three; from then until 1842, when she left the asylum and was forced to enter the secular world; and finally, to the beginning of the case in 1844.

Le Monnier was born near Coutances in the Norman department of Manche in 1798. Her parents were shopkeepers. Her father was also a municipal official, who provided his daughter with an education. At seventeen she became a schoolteacher. She had long been drawn to the religious vocation, particularly to a cloistered order, despite the fact that she was offered a more than satisfactory position in secular life, according to her lawyer. This point is made for the purpose of indicating that she did not simply enter a religious order because she had no other options.

After taking her vows, Le Monnier's intellectual gifts were immediately recognized. She became the de facto bursar for the convent and ran its school for girls. Le Monnier's difficulties began in 1827, barely two years after she entered the convent. In her own telling of it, she was resented for her accomplishments and was the object of jealousy because of her intelligence. She suffered many small humiliations as a result. She was ordered, for example, to be the last nun to receive confession and was frequently banned from the confessional and denied communion.

It was at this point that Tillard introduced Le Monnier's first-person account of her persecution. Le Monnier's story consisted of a detailed description of various punishments and her growing alienation from the other members of the convent. By 1840 she had ceased associating with the other nuns in the order, she was banned from recreation and the confessional, and the mother superior installed a lock and iron bar on her cell where she frequently found herself an unwilling prisoner. She was allegedly then placed in a kind of boarded-up prison which contained only a straw mattress and which received no light and little air. She was given a ration of bread, apples, and a small measure of cider.

If Tillard drew on the most important literary texts of the day, he also used religious narratives in constructing his tale. Le Monnier, for example, allegedly stayed in her "prison" for a biblical seven days, and during each of those seven days a nun came to ask her if she would consent to go to another religious house. She refused. She was taken to the Bon–Sauveur de Caen, an insane asylum for women, along with a letter written by her superior, a priest, and a doctor, attesting to her deranged mental state.[27] Tillard added in a note to Le Monnier's account that the space where she was incarcerated in the convent was no larger than the mattress, that her hands had been tied behind her back, and that when she was taken to Bon Sauveur, one of the servants was required to carry her because of her weakness.

Part 2 of the *mémoire* is an account of Le Monnier's incarceration in the asylum of Bon Sauveur and begins with a commentary introducing her resumed narrative: "Here we have Sister Marie taken from her monastery and transported to a house of crazy women for alleged madness—does it not seem that the family of this nun should have been alerted to this event immediately?"[28] At this point we return to Le Monnier's personal narrative and her attempts to free herself from her frightful surroundings.

She wrote to the bishop and to her community. The bishop allegedly replied that even if she were not mad, she was still guilty and should remain where she was. The drama continued: "Here I am detained pitilessly, in the midst of noisy din, cries, frenzy, agitation, swearing, blasphemy, and the imprecations of the mad among whom are found fallen women [as well]."[29] She demanded to see the *procureur du roi*, a secular authority, and was refused.

Finally, one day the doctor came to inform her, at the instruction of the superior, that she had lived a long time as a nun and that she should now reenter secular life, and that she was to set her rosary aside to work each day at sewing. She refused. As a result, she was allegedly cast out of the asylum to earn her living in the world. She therefore found herself, in her words, "on the pavement, without any human aid, without money, without clothing or linen. It was thus that after having tasted the sweetness of celestial life in the cloister and not being able to force the doors

---

[27] The asylum of Bon–Sauveur in Caen was one of the most important asylums serving in a public capacity in the 1840s. The nuns also ran asylums in Saint-Lô in the Manche and in Albi in the Tarn. See Jan Goldstein, *Console and Classify: The French Psychiatric Profession in the Nineteenth Century* (Cambridge, 1987), pp. 311–12.

[28] *Affaire de Dame Jeanne-Françoise Le Monnier*, pp. 19–20.

[29] Ibid., p. 21.

to return to it, I was forced into the world."[30] Tillard wrote: "one can now see: it is not at all scandal that we are after. We are asking for bread; we are asking for certain guarantees for the future. . . . we understood that the time has come for social justice that has been refused us. . . . We count on all that is generous . . . in all classes of society."[31]

The persuasiveness of the story told by Tillard and Le Monnier was predicated on how Le Monnier's actions and motivations were perceived within the general context of social stereotypes regarding cloistered nuns and what one might call collective fantasies of claustration. We have seen the way in which Tillard used the claustral narrative to gain sympathy for his client and how he focused on her industry and zealous dedication to the rule of the order. The mother superior undoubtedly saw Le Monnier as a pretentious troublemaker who refused to adhere to the order's rule of obedience, and it was this that accounted for her troubles and for the punishment that she received. Her doctors, while seeing her as entirely sane, nonetheless supported the views of her religious superiors regarding her personal qualities. M. Faucon, the doctor assigned to Bon Sauveur, wrote that she was "perfectly orderly" in her behavior. "She has continued in her pious exercises and although ardently desiring to return to her community, she was never impatient. She appeared to us to have in her character a very pronounced tendency toward stubbornness, which explains her recalcitrance in not recognizing the wrongs she did to her community." Other than that, he concluded, she could certainly leave Bon–Sauveur.[32] Tillard was not able to suppress entirely the "troublesome" aspects of Le Monnier's personality, but at the same time he emphasized her religiosity and industry. Indeed, this was crucial to his case because the public would not necessarily view the plight of the nun sympathetically.

Tillard faced two problems in this regard. First, the cloistered nun was a distinctly unpopular figure in eighteenth- and nineteenth-century France. The social stereotype of the avaricious, lazy, and debauched monk and nun who lived off the honest toil of others was an inherent part of much of the revolutionary caricatures and broadsides against the Catholic Church. This view of men and women religious pervaded debates over banning religious orders and dispersing their members in 1791. Although most of the anticlerical revolutionary caricature centered on the figure of the corrupt priest or monk, where women religious appeared in such car-

---

[30] Ibid., p. 26.
[31] Ibid., p. 49.
[32] Ibid., p. 26.

icature, it was in the figure of the cloistered nun.[33] Stereotypes regarding the cloistered nun persisted after the Revolution and were perpetuated in novelistic literature. Women who assumed the religious vocation and who lived behind the iron gate of the cloister were frequently regarded as the saddest women of all because they lacked a purpose and had renounced their natural calling as women.[34] The cloistered nun, who lived isolated from the world and who had no identifiably useful role in society, in contrast to the *congréganistes* who taught school or cared for the sick, was frequently an object of suspicion or scorn.[35]

Tillard countered the image of the debauched or idle nun with a counterimage—that of the woman as victim of sequestration. In so doing, he consciously tapped into both the tradition of claustral literature, but also into one of the most popular literary works of the day, Eugène Sue's immensely successful anticlerical novel, *Le juif errant.* The novel, an explicit attack on the Jesuits, tells the story of Adrienne de Cardoville, who is incarcerated in an asylum by relatives intent on stealing her inheritance. Tillard sprinkled his text with quotations from Sue.

Tillard began his account of Le Monnier's incarceration with a passage from Sue describing Adrienne de Cardoville's imprisonment and, having concluded his narrative, he prefaced his critical examination of the facts with another quote from Sue regarding the doctor's diagnosis of Adrienne.[36] Like Adrienne, Le Monnier is diagnosed as suffering from "exalted ideas."[37] Like Adrienne, she is unsuspecting when she is carried away by two sinister female attendants with evil intent, and like Adrienne, she suffers greatly. And let us not forget that Sue ends *Le juif errant* with a plea for greater regulation of religious personnel, particularly the Jesuits.[38] The melodrama of this event and the nefarious figure of the Jesuit are well captured in the prints of Gavarni and J.-A. Beaucé, which illustrated Eugène Sue's text.[39]

Tillard not only faced the problem of having to counteract a pervasive social stereotype in the figure of the cloistered nun by capitalizing on the

---

[33] Antoine de Baecque, *La caricature révolutionnaire* (Paris, 1988), pp. 89–143.
[34] See above, chapter 2.
[35] While the figure of the *congréganiste*, the active nun who taught or cured the sick, was generally positive in the nineteenth century, the image of the contemplative nun continued to be very negative. See Ponton, *La religieuse dans la littérature française.*
[36] Adrienne de Cardoville exclaims during the visit, "si folle que je suis, je sais . . . qu'il y a des lois. . . ." Quoted in *Affaire de Dame Jeanne-Françoise Le Monnier,* p. 81.
[37] Ibid., p. 51.
[38] Eugène Sue, *Le juif errant,* vol. 3 (Paris, n.d.), p. 531.
[39] *Oeuvres illustrées d'Eugène Sue. 200 dessins par MM. Gavarni, J.-A. Beaucé, etc., etc. graves par A. Lavieille,* vol. 18 (Paris, n.p., 1850).

La visite du docteur Baleinier à Mlle de Cardoville. — PAGE 89.

FIGURE 4. Adrienne de Cardoville is visited by her doctor while being held by her two female jailers. *Oeuvres illustrées d'Eugène Sue: 200 dessins par MM. Gavarni, J.-A. Beaucé, etc., etc. gravés par A. Lavieille,* vol. 18 (Paris, 1850). Courtesy of the Service Reproduction, Bibliothèque Nationale, Paris.

themes of claustral literature. He faced another problem. Unlike most of the female victims of claustral literature, Le Monnier wanted to return to the world of the cloister and to the order that had expelled her. If, up to this point in the narrative, Le Monnier is presented as a victim of the cloister, as the woman in bondage, Tillard uses a language of right and contract to make his final arguments. It is this language that links the three separate parts of her complaint: the charge that she has been a victim of incarceration against her will, the demand for monetary damages, and the demand that she be allowed to return to cloistered life. Her rights and individual liberties had been violated by being imprisoned against her will, and her order had unlawfully violated its contract with her without just cause.

But how did Tillard make the case for Le Monnier's return to her order and for a promise that it would continue to support her financially? Tillard likened religious vows to marriage vows, the marriage contract to a kind of religious contract. He asserted that just as a husband is legally obligated to support and honor his wife, so a religious order must do the same for its nuns. Marriage and entering an order are forms of contract. Le Monnier's expulsion was nothing more than an illegal breaking of an associational contract between herself and the community of Benedictines of Bayeux. (He glosses over the fact that under postrevolutionary law lifelong religious vows, unlike marriage vows, were illegal. They had to be renewed every five years, and even then, they were not binding on the nun, who could leave whenever she wished.) While Le Monnier's order might claim that she was subject to expulsion because she was intractable and disobedient, and therefore violated the order's rule, Tillard argued that whether or not she was "reasonable or mystical, obedient or rebellious, humble or vain," this could not justify—"canonically, judicially and constitutionally, philosophically"—her incarceration in an insane asylum.[40] The act of incarceration constituted an attack on the civil liberties of the citizen. In short, the core of Tillard's argument was that Le Monnier was a nun, but she was a citizen in civil society first.

Set within an almost novelistic narrative of bondage and liberation, right, contract, and finally the last piece of the argument, social justice, were the basis of Tillard's arguments to the court. This was not simply a case of a recalcitrant nun, who for her sins found herself incarcerated among the insane against her will, but it was a case of woman left without resources or a means of a living. It is here that the narrative of the incarceration of Eugène Sue's heroine, Adrienne de Cardoville, and the narrative of Le Monnier's ordeal intersect. Sue ends his novel with a plea for social justice: "we have said and we repeat that there are terrible and innumerable miseries; that the masses, more and more conscious of their rights, but still calm, patient, resigned, ask that those who govern finally concern themselves with the amelioration of their deplorable position. . . . Permit us to summarize in a few lines the questions raised in this work. We have tried to prove the insufficiency of women's wages and the horrible consequence of this insufficiency. We have asked for new guar-

---

[40] *Affaire de Dame Jeanne-Françoise Le Monnier*, p. 77.

La promenade des jésuites. — PAGE 253.

FIGURE 5. Three ominous-looking Jesuits. *Oeuvres illustrées d'Eugène Sue: 200 dessins par MM. Gavarni, J.-A. Beaucé, etc., etc. gravés par A. Lavieille,* vol. 18 (Paris, 1850). Courtesy of the Service Reproduction, Bibliothèque Nationale, Paris.

antees against the facility with which someone can be put in an insane asylum."[41]

Tillard concludes his *mémoire* with the following remarks: "A poor nun, victim of an abuse of revolting power and who has been pitilessly refused daily bread and a few faithful guarantees for the future . . . but above all these are larger interests, more philosophical, social. . . . that is the struggle of individualism against monastic despotism, the Gallican spirit against the Ultramontane spirit, of civil liberties against the oppressive character of certain establishments forgetful of their philanthropic mission."[42] And so ends the *mémoire* of Léon Tillard.

The case that he constructed, drawing on what I would call fantasies of claustration, revealed a myriad of cultural assumptions and social archetypes regarding women, the religious life, and the veiled nun. But how do we explain these fears and anxieties centering on the theme of claustration, which is a staple part of Gothic literature in this period? Why were there so many cases of this type and why did they abruptly disappear in the late nineteenth century? A simple answer might be that the law had changed. These cases were brought as the state began to involve itself in the regulation of religious institutions, but they then disappeared as the state's involvement grew deeper and the courts successfully asserted the primacy of secular law over canon law. Their disappearance might then be seen as a reflection of the victory of secular republicanism during the early Third Republic, which was manifested in the widespread laicization of educational and medical institutions.

The fact that the Le Monnier case became a cause célèbre in 1845 is no accident. It followed close on the heels of the 1838 law governing asylums, and during a period of intense anticlerical ardor directed at the Jesuit order.[43] Both of the principal texts on which Léon Tillard depends, notably Eugène Sue's *Le juif errant* and Jules Michelet's *Du prêtre, de la femme, de la famille,* center on the figure of the nefarious priest. Indeed, anti-Jesuit agitation was rife in 1844–45. The serialized publication of *Le juif errant*

[41] Sue, *Le juif errant,* p. 581.
[42] *Affaire de Dame Jeanne-Françoise Le Monnier,* p. 98. Léon Tillard was responsible for reprinting a text by the well-known seventeenth-century priest, Mabillon, a member of the order of the Benedictines of St. Maur, who protested against the incarceration of nuns and priests and their ill-treatment in religious houses. Tillard wrote the introduction and publicized contemporary cases as well. Mabillon, *Réflexions sur les prisons des ordres religieux* (Caen, 1845).
[43] See Geoffrey Cubitt, *The Jesuit Myth: Conspiracy Theory and Politics in Nineteenth-Century France* (Oxford, 1993).

(from June 1844 to June 1845) told a story of Jesuit conspiracy, for which the newspaper *Le Constitutionnel* was paid handsomely. Its owner, Dr. Véron, saw his subscriptions increase from thirty-six hundred at the beginning of 1844 to twenty thousand the following year.[44]

Social stereotypes of the kind that informed the Le Monnier case create the stuff out of which a culture's *imaginaires sociaux* are created.[45] The constituent elements of this imagery were many and varied, revealing anxiety about the porous boundaries between Church and state as well as between secular and canon law. As trials no longer took place in a climate of secrecy, they increasingly galvanized the public and spawned debates over the need to regulate religious institutions. Much of this public discussion came to a head during the Second Empire, in the early 1860s, a period which laid the groundwork for the anticlerical legislation governing religious congregations in the early 1880s. Pamphlets such as *Crimes, délits, scandales au sein du clergé pendant les derniers jours,* published in 1861, and Charles Sauvestre's *Les congrégations religieuses devoilées,* published in 1870, documented numerous cases of abduction, incarceration, and coercion exercised by religious communities. Debate focused on some of the most lurid cases of sequestration, the most prominent of which was the Bluth case of 1861 involving the conversion of several young Jewish sisters and their imprisonment in different convents over a number of years. In sum, cases involving the alleged incarceration of religious women became a larger metaphor for the tyranny of the hierarchical Catholic Church and dramatized the symbolic stakes inherent in the conflict between Gallicanism and Ultramontanism. Women religious were at the center of this conflict, just as the adolescent girl wearing the Muslim veil in French classrooms has come to symbolize the backwardness of Islam and to justify the need to reassert the primacy of secular republican values in French society.

[44] Dr. Louis Désiré Véron, *Mémoires d'un bourgeois de Paris,* 6 vols. (Paris, 1853–55), 4:272–74.
[45] I borrow this term from Bronislaw Baczko, who defines the concept in terms of "representations of social reality and not simple reflections of it. Invented and elaborated by material taken from a symbolic store, they have a specific reality which resides in their very existence, in their variable impact on mentalities and collective behaviors, in the multiple functions they exercise in social life." Baczko, *Les imaginaires sociaux: Mémoires et espoirs collectifs* (Paris, 1984), p. 8.

ANTICLERICALISM AND THE NINETEENTH-CENTURY
SOCIAL IMAGINATION

Léon Tillard's storytelling played an important part in settling the case in
Le Monnier's favor. After calling over sixty-four witnesses over a period of
twenty-seven days, Le Monnier was successful in making her claim, with
the court ruling in her favor on 9 May 1845. But what does his legal story-
telling reveal about the *imaginaire social* of nineteenth-century France? Although this was a case based on the real distress experienced by a woman
expelled from a religious order, it was a story constructed and presented
by a republican anticlerical man. While we know little of Tillard, we do
know he ultimately became a *quarante-huitard* who supported the new republic in 1848.[46] His *mémoire* must be read on several levels. He devoted
two years of his life to the trial and his zeal came from political conviction,
rather than expectation of financial gain. His tale of bondage and liberation was one that allowed him to make his case in powerful and unequivo-
cal terms. This kind of tale was the principal metaphor through which critiques of royal despotism and ecclesiastical intolerance were made during
the eighteenth century. It became a central republican trope for expressing political emancipation. It had a particular resonance in the 1840s. Following the law of 1838, which established France's first system of public
asylums, there was huge concern about possible abuses of this system—as
in Eugène Sue's remarks on the subject—a fundamental ambivalence,
even among the bourgeoisie, about what Michel Foucault has called the
great confinement. In short, the case was a way of talking about and expressing a variety of social and political anxieties.

It may also have tapped into a new sensibility and deeper societal concerns. Karen Haltunnen has recently argued that narratives of captivity as
expressed in the Gothic novel and other forms of popular literature in
this period abounded. In Anglo-American culture it expressed a kind of
"pornography of pain."[47] The fear and titillation they inspired dovetailed,
in her view, with profound changes in views about pain and the human
body at the end of the eighteenth century and with the emergence of a
new humanitarian sensibility. To this extent the appearance of the same

---

[46] Léon Tillard was born in Bayeux on 14 June 1813. He was the author of *Février révolutionnaire et la situation actuelle, mai 1849* (Bayeux, 1849). Tillard was responsible for reprinting a
short work entitled *Réflexions sur les prisons des ordres religieux* (Caen, 1845) and an overview of
the case, Soeur Sainte-Marie, *Bénédictine. Récits par elle-même, la procedure, les enquêtes, la preuve,
orgueil et placement au B.S.*
[47] Haltunnen, "Humanitarianism and the Pornography of Pain in Anglo-American Culture,"
American Historical Review 100, no. 2 (April 1995): 303–34.

themes in the Le Monnier case reflected the appearance of new attitudes toward violence and bodily suffering, which has been documented in France by Alain Corbin.[48] Thus the issues raised by the case of the recalcitrant nun may well reflect broader cultural transformations that occurred in France during the eighteenth and nineteenth centuries.

Social anxieties and fears regarding the stunning rise in the number of women entering religious life contributed to the indignation that the case provoked. The phenomenon of the "feminization of religion," with all the implications that this might have for a growing cultural divide between men and women, shaped the way in which Tillard presented his evidence. The existence of these fears, which expressed collective fantasies of various kinds, is worthy of consideration. Jacqueline Lalouette, for example, has recently discussed the pervasive late nineteenth-century French fantasy of nuns who habitually and sadistically forced their young charges to sit on red-hot stoves—satirically called *rôtisseries congréganistes*.[49] The extent to which these events happened is one question; how and why they became constituent elements of an *imaginaire social* at a particular moment in time is another. In short, the case of Jeanne-Françoise Le Monnier raises larger questions for the historian about why cases are brought at some historical moments and not at others; how legal storytelling is constrained by the social and political context in which it takes place; about the ways in which it appeals to unwritten moral categories; and about how the types of legal cases that are brought before courts are themselves markers of social, political, or moral preoccupations that in turn shape the ways in which stories are told to the court.

---

[48] Corbin, *A Village of Cannibals: Rage and Murder in France, 1870*, trans. Arthur Goldhammer (Cambridge, Mass., 1992).

[49] Lalouette, *La libre pensée en France*, p. 241.

CHAPTER 4

The Politics of Sainthood and
the Cult of Sainte Philomène

The increasingly vocal anticlericalism evidenced in the Le Monnier affair was in part fueled by anxieties surrounding both female religious devotions as well as a variety of new popular cults that emerged during the course of the nineteenth century. These included the cults of the Sacred Heart, of the Miraculous Medal, and of the Virgin Mary at La Salette and Lourdes. These cults spawned new forms of devotion associated with Ultramontane piety and they were expressed in what came to be derisively referred to as Saint-Sulpice art. At the same time, they frequently assumed strong political or ideological overtones.

The phenomenon of Lourdes and the cult of the Sacred Heart have been the subject of two important recent books on the subject, but the history and meaning of other nineteenth-century saintly cults is less well known.[1] One the most popular new nineteenth-century cults was that of Sainte Philomène, an adolescent Christian martyr, who was allegedly tortured and killed for resisting the sexual advances of the emperor Diocletian in the third century AD. Baptismal records reflected her growing renown, and itinerant colporteurs contributed to her fame by hawking countless copies of the *Neuvaine en l'honneur de sainte Philomène, vierge et martyre, Thaumaturge au XIX siècle*. By 1886, a confraternity devoted to Philomène established at the Church of Saint-Gervais in Paris boasted

---

[1] See Harris, *Lourdes*; and Raymond Jonas, *France and the Cult of the Sacred Heart: An Epic Tale for Modern Times* (Berkeley, Calif., 2000).

seven thousand members.[2] Philomène ultimately became the subject of literary work as well.[3] When the Goncourt brothers wrote a novel about a young nun in 1861, it was not surprising that they entitled it *Soeur Philomène.*[4]

Philomène became the subject of painting as well. In 1837, for example, a group of women from the Norman city of Bayeux were granted permission by their bishop to dedicate a cathedral chapel to Sainte Philomène. The women assumed the entire cost of furnishing the chapel and wrote to the Parisian painter François-Louis de Juinne (whose fees they could not afford) to ask him to recommend an artist to paint the chapel's devotional centerpiece.[5] De Juinne proposed Théodelinde Dubouché, a young woman working in his studio. She gladly accepted the commission for the sum of four hundred francs and devoted much of the winter of 1837–38 to painting the martyred young saint. When the work was first unveiled in the Parisian church of Saint-Sulpice, de Juinne was greatly impressed by the skillful quality of its execution, and other painters remarked on its mix of classical and romantic styles which "so often conflicted with one another."[6]

Théodelinde Dubouché's painting of Philomène became one of many images of the saint that adorned chapels, churches and cathedrals in France from the 1830s onward.[7] Her popularity is, in retrospect, astonishing, however, because she was by and large a figment of imagination.[8]

---

[2] Its mission was to honor the saint, encourage the imitation of her Christian virtues, and obtain divine mercy for France. Abbé Gauthier, *Manuel de la dévotion à Sainte Philomène*, 2d ed. (Paris, 1911), p. 99.

[3] Charles Nisard, *Histoire des livres populaires ou de la littérature de colportage*, 2 vols. (Paris, 1864), 2:51; and Catherine Rosenbaum-Dondaine, *L'image de piété en France, 1814–1914* (Paris, 1984), pp. 52–53.

[4] Edmond and Jules Goncourt's *Soeur Philomène* (Paris, 1861) was turned into the play by Jules Vidal and Arthur Byl. Ponton, *La religieuse dans la littérature française*, p. 400. Also see Fouilland, *Sainte-Philomène ou le triomphe de la virginité: tragédie en cinq actes* (Lyon, 1852). Characters bearing the name Philomène began to appear in a number of nineteenth-century novels. See, for example, Emile Zola's *Germinal* (1885).

[5] Some of France's most illustrious aristocratic names, including Polignac and d'Aubigny, were associated with the enterprise. Marie-Thérèse du Coeur de Jésus, *Souvenirs d'une amie sur la vie de Théodelinde Dubouché, par une religieuse ursuline*, 2 vols. (Paris, 1882), 2:7–8.

[6] Ibid., p. 10.

[7] The Parisian church of Saint-Gervais alone contained eight paintings of the martyred virgin. One of them was executed by the female artist Clémence Fernal in 1839. *Inventaire général des richesses d'art de la France.* vol. 3: *Paris, monuments religieux* (Paris, l901), pp. 153–54. Also see Mrs. Anna Brownell Jameson, *Sacred and Legendary Art*, 2 vols. (Boston, 1865), 2:287–89.

[8] For the cult of Sainte Philomène, see Mgr. Povèda, *Memorie storiche riguardanti il martiro e culto della vergine Santa Filomena & l'inventione del suo corpo nel cimiterio di Priscilla* (Foligno, 1834); Jean Darche, *Vie très complète de Ste Philomène* (Paris, l876); Mgr. Francis Trochu, *La pe-*

Even though all saints are, in the words of Pierre Delooz, "more or less constructed," Sainte Philomène, unlike Anthony of Padua or Saint Perpetua, left no historical record of her life in the form of a name, a place of birth, a life story, or a date of death.[9] Her cult sprang up after the discovery of a young girl's bodily remains during excavations of the Roman catacombs in the early nineteenth century. Her name, vital statistics, and the story of her martyrdom were only later supplied by the visions of an Italian nun.

This chapter explores the emergence of the cult of Sainte Philomène and the political meanings with which it was invested by the Catholic Church in response to allegedly impious anticlerical assaults on Catholicism. The cult centered on a model of female martyrdom and femininity, which the Church wished to foster. Ironically, however, the narratives of Philomène's martyrdom resembled those surrounding secular female republican martyrs during the French Revolution. Her martyrdom and theirs were expressed entirely in terms of the virtues of bodily containment and purity. Although sexual renunciation and virginity are old themes in Western Christianity, they were given distinctive forms in the narratives of sexual danger and violence surrounding Philomène and the martyred female revolutionary saints of the late 1790s.[10]

---

tite sainte du curé d'Ars, sainte Philomène, vierge et martyre (Paris, 1929). Théodelinde Dubouché's biographer remarked on the considerable attention that "this young Greek princess, martyred for having refused the hand of the emperor Diocletian," received in the late 1830s. Marie-Thérèse, *Souvenirs d'une amie*, 2:8. For a regional perspective, see Yves-Marie Hilaire, *Une chrétienté au XIX siècle? La vie religieuse des populations du diocèse d'Arras (1840–1914)*, 2 vols. (Villeneuve d'Ascq, 1977), 2:406–47.

[9] Delooz, "Toward a Sociological Study of Sainthood," in *Saints and Their Cults: Studies in Religious Sociology, Folklore, and History*, ed. Stephen Wilson (Cambridge, 1984), p. 207.

[10] Modern historians have devoted a great deal of attention to representations of the female body and the meanings with which it has been invested through time. See, for example, Michel Foucault, *The History of Sexuality*, trans. Robert Hurley, 3 vols. (New York, 1978); Catherine Gallagher and Thomas Lacqueur, eds., *The Making of the Modern Body: Sexuality and Society in the Nineteenth Century* (Berkeley, Calif., 1987); Lynn Hunt, ed., *Eroticism and the Body Politic* (Berkeley, Calif., 1991); Susan Suleiman, ed., *The Female Body in Western Culture* (Cambridge, Mass., 1986); Marina Warner, *Monuments and Maidens: The Allegory of the Female Form* (London, 1985); and Dorinda Outram, *The Body and the French Revolution: Sex, Class, and Political Culture* (New Haven, Conn., 1989). Religious representations of the martyred female body have failed to evoke the same interest, but these representations have provided historians of antiquity and early modern Europe with an excellent lens through which to view changing conceptions of self and community. See, for example, Giulia Sissa, *Greek Virginity*, trans. Arthur Goldhammer (Cambridge, Mass., 1990); Peter Brown, *The Body and Society: Men, Women, and Sexual Renunciation in Early Christianity* (New York, 1988); Brent D. Shaw, "The Passion of Perpetua," *Past and Present*, no. 139 (May 1993): 3–45; Averil Cameron, "Virginity as Metaphor: Women in the Rhetoric of Early Christianity," in *History as Text: The Writing of Ancient History*, ed. Averil Cameron (London, 1989), pp. 181–205; Caroline Walker Bynum, *Holy Feast and Holy Fast: The Religious Significance of Food to Medieval Women* (Berkeley, Calif., 1987); Clarissa Atkinson, "'Precious Balsam in a Fragile Glass': The Ideology of Vir-

Cults of saints have long been important cornerstones of Catholic Christianity, but models of martyrdom and the fortunes of individual saints have changed significantly through time. Although historians of late antiquity and early modern Europe have devoted considerable attention to saintly cults, they have been less a subject of inquiry among historians of modern Europe, and there have been few sustained attempts to reveal the contexts that give rise to martyrs and inspire their followers.

What were the polysemic meanings with which Philomène was invested? What were the representations of Philomène's martyred body and the narratives of sexual danger surrounding her and the revolutionary martyrs of the 1790s in the context of France's revolutionary past and the growing importance of the female religious vocation in the nineteenth century, and a widespread preoccupation with sexual violence in nineteenth-century French society?[11] While I will argue that the propagation of Philomène's cult was an evident part of the Catholic Church's search for new sources of legitimacy in the aftermath of the French Revolution, her popular appeal, particularly among women, had much to do with the nature of her martyrdom and her alleged miraculous healings.[12] The eventual decline of the cult of Sainte Philomène—for unlike Sainte Geneviève, the patron saint of the city of Paris, Philomène's popularity was very short-lived—had much to do with the triumph of secularism, which was heralded by the Third Republic and its strict separation of Church and state in 1905. Also, by the turn of the century a new generation of Catholics preferred to honor Joan of Arc and Sainte Thérèse de Lisieux, both of whom had supplanted the young virgin martyr by the First World War, as men came back to the Catholic fold.

---

ginity in the later Middle Ages," *Journal of Family History* 8 (1983): 131–43; and Bynum's essays in *Fragmentation and Redemption*. For an illuminating study of the significance of the nude female body in Christian art, see Margaret M. Miles, *Carnal Knowing: Female Nakedness and Religious Meaning in the Christian West* (Boston, 1989).

[11] For a discussion of the "polysemic" nature of religious symbols, see Caroline Walker Bynum, "Introduction: The Complexity of Symbols," in *Gender and Religion: On the Complexity of Symbols*, ed. Caroline Walker Bynum, Steven Harrell, and Paula Richman (Boston, 1986) pp. 1–20. The multivalent or changing meanings with which "real" or imagined saints have been invested is reflected, for example, in the cult of Mary Magdalene, the repentant prostitute, who was first venerated by women, but gradually became the patron saint of male and female penitents. Victor Saxer, *Le culte de Marie Magdaleine en Occident des origines à la fin du Moyen Age* (Paris, 1959).

[12] This argument has been convincingly made by Philippe Boutry in his pathbreaking article, "Les saints des catacombes: Itinéraires français d'une piété ultramontaine," *Mélanges de l'Ecole française de Rome* 91, no. 2 (1971): 875–930.

A SAINT'S MARTYRED BODY

The bodily remains of Sainte Philomène were discovered on 25 May 1802 when a group of workmen digging in the cemetery of Priscilla on the outskirts of Rome came upon a tomb inscribed with the words "Lumena Paxte Cum Fi"[13] and with symbols that included three arrows, two anchors, and an object that resembled a lily or a virgin's lamp. The presence of what appeared to be a vial of dried blood near a decapitated skeleton of the young girl aged between thirteen and fifteen quickly led to the belief that the remains were those of an early Christian martyr. When her bones were unearthed, according to one account, they were transformed into "luminous bodies," which further confirmed their sacred character.[14] Her remains were transferred to the Sacred Reliquary in Rome until a priest from Mugnano, near Naples, convinced the Vatican to allow him to transfer the relics to his church in 1805. It was only after their transfer to Mugnano that miracles were reported. These included miraculous cures and a sudden rain that occurred in drought-stricken Mugnano when the saint was brought to the town.

Little was known about Philomène's life or her martyrdom until the 1830s when her personal history was unveiled in a series of visions that came to three people: a young artisan, a priest, and most importantly, a Dominican tertiary nun in Naples, Mother Luisa. These visions revealed that Philomène, a young adolescent girl, whom the nun claimed was a princess from a small state in Greece, refused the emperor Diocletian's sexual advances and offer of marriage. The rebuffed and enraged emperor had her stripped, flagellated, and thrown into the Tiber with an anchor around her neck. According to the visionary, two angels saved her and brought her to shore. She was therefore shot at with arrows, which reversed their course to kill the soldiers charged with the duty of killing her. Finally, Diocletian was said to have resorted to lancing her to death and decapitating her body.

The cult of Philomène was given official sanction in 1837—the same year the women of Bayeux created a chapel in her honor—when Pope Gregory XVI accorded her a mass. In 1855, Pius IX assigned 10 August to her in the calendar of saints. After the miraculous cure of a Frenchwoman, Pauline Jaricot, in Mugnano in 1835, Philomène's cult found a

---

[13] Arranged in another order the inscription could read "Pax Tecum Filumena," or "Peace be with you Philomena."

[14] *Sainte-Philomène: Sa vie, son martyre, ses premiers miracles. Pratiques de dévotion* (Montreal, 1910).

home in France, where it rapidly gained a significant following.[15] The archbishop of Paris gave a small relic of the saint to Sempigny, a small town near the city of Noyon, and a large number of chapels, including that of Bayeux, were dedicated to her.

To the extent that historians have commented on Sainte Philomène in France, they have examined her cult from two interconnected perspectives. One regards the cult in psychological terms, using a psychoanalytic language of repression or masochism.[16] Ralph Gibson has argued, for example, that the vision of the Italian nun who supplied the narrative of Philomène's life "contained strong elements of repressed sadomasochism."[17] Philomène's popularity has also been given a sociological interpretation, as evidence of the "feminization" of Catholicism in postrevolutionary France.

The narrative of Philomène's martyrdom might well warrant a psychological interpretation as far as the vision of the individual nun is concerned, but this interpretation cannot explain what her martyrdom meant to her followers and why her cult became popular when it did. Any analysis of the cult of Sainte Philomène must elucidate the reasons that lead certain saints and devotions to become popular or unpopular, without reducing religious expression to social history or psychology.[18] To point to the feminization of devotion to explain both the causes and the consequences of new forms of popular devotion, which the cult of Sainte Philomène represented, only reifies the category of the feminine without explaining what devotions meant to those concerned and how changes in devotional patterns related to other kinds of historical change or continuity. In short, while the psychological interpretation does not account for the historical specificity of the cult, the sociological interpretation is inherently tautological because devotion to the cult of Sainte-Philomène is cited as both a consequence and a cause of the feminization of religion in nineteenth-century France.[19]

The cult of Sainte Philomène cannot simply be reduced to psychological problems among its adherents or to the Church's changed social constituency in nineteenth-century France. The cult would not have spread

---

[15] Pauline Jaricot was an important figure for French Catholicism in her own right. She was the foundress of the Society for the Propagation of the Faith, one of the largest voluntary organizations in France.

[16] Kselman, *Miracles and Prophecies in Nineteenth-Century France*, p. 104.

[17] Gibson, *A Social History of French Catholicism*, p. 152.

[18] Delooz, "Towards a Sociological Study of Sainthood," p. 207.

[19] For a discussion of this tautology see Caroline Ford, "Religion and Popular Culture in Modern Europe," *Journal of Modern History* 65 (March 1993): 169.

without the sponsorship of the French clergy, and it would not have flourished unless it provided lay men and women with a means of making
sense of their world. The cult must therefore be placed within the social,
ecclesiastical, and political context of postrevolutionary France, but the
narrative of Philomène's martyrdom must also be viewed as a manifestation of a "lived religion" experienced by men and—more significantly—
women in nineteenth-century France.

OLD AND NEW SAINTS

The Roman catacombs have undergone successive periods of excavation
since late antiquity, and they have provided an almost inexhaustible store-
house of relics to the Christian world. When the unregulated traffic in
relics became a source of increasing embarrassment and scandal for the
Vatican in the late seventeenth century, the catacombs were closed to the
public and papal authorities established criteria to determine whether or
not bodily remains found in them could be designated as those of Christian martyrs. These criteria included the inscription of a palm in the tomb
and the presence of a vase containing the martyr's blood. The test of these
identifying characteristics persisted into the nineteenth century when interest in the Roman catacombs and the bodily remains allegedly belonging to early Christian martyrs became the object of renewed interest.

Between 1800 and 1850, 1,347 new bodies judged to be those of martyrs, including that of Philomène, were discovered and removed from the
catacombs—the majority after 1815—and they were distributed throughout the Christian world.[20] Two characteristics distinguished the nineteenth-
century "saints of the catacombs" from earlier periods. First, the majority
of saints were young adolescents and many of them were female, like the
great visionaries of the postrevolutionary period. Second, a very large
number of these relics found a permanent home in France. France im-
ported 23.2 percent of the martyrs' remains between 1800 and 1850 and,
after Italy, was the second most important recipient of saintly relics.[21] The
1830s, 1840s, and 1850s marked the "gallicization" of the traffic in alleged
saintly bodies, and Sainte-Philomène, in the words of Boutry, played a "pioneering role" in the development of this phenomenon.[22]

---

[20] For an analysis of the discovery of a large number of new catacomb saints during the first
half of the nineteenth century see Boutry, "Les saints des catacombes." Lacunae in Vatican
records between the years 1824–37 make the exact number uncertain, but it could be as
high as sixteen or eighteen hundred. Ibid., p. 885.
[21] The largest number of relics—642 or 47.66 percent—remained in Italy. Ibid., p. 887.
[22] Ibid., p. 895.

The diffusion of cults attached to the saints of the Roman catacombs was the deliberate work of a largely Ultramontane clergy in France and Sainte Philomène had the particular good fortune to have an influential proselytizer in the person of Jean-Marie-Baptiste Vianney, the Curé d'Ars. The priest had almost single-handedly rechristianized the parish of Ars, which had been largely indifferent to religion at the beginning of the nineteenth century, thus becoming the marvel of clericals and anticlericals alike. The curé's reputation for saintliness and extraordinary spiritual power was known far and wide by the middle of the nineteenth century, and the parish ultimately became a pilgrimage site. The Curé d'Ars was one of the chief propagators of the cult of Sainte Philomène in nineteenth-century France and made a concerted effort to direct his attention to a female audience. He entered into correspondence with a number of women who wrote to him of their concerns, and he gradually became the object of saintly veneration himself.[23]

The Curé d'Ars first learned of the virgin saint from Pauline Jaricot, after she had been allegedly cured of a serious illness while in Mugnano in 1835.[24] Vianney immediately obtained a relic of Philomène for his church. The first baby carrying the name of Philomène was baptized in Ars in 1835, and between 1836 and 1845, Philomènes represented 43 percent of all girls born in the parish.[25]

As soon as Philomène's relics were transported to Ars, the parish became a site of holy healings. Indeed, Philomène ultimately came to be known as the "thaumaturge of the nineteenth century."[26] While the Curé d'Ars placed the healing hand, he attributed the miraculous cure to Sainte Philomène. In the process, Philomène was very important in the Curé d'Ars's own progress toward sainthood.

If the cult of Sainte Philomène legitimized the work of the Curé d'Ars, who was in part responsible for popularizing the cult, Philomène and other saints of the catacombs became a source of legitimation for the Catholic Church itself. The French Church had suffered severe blows during the French Revolution. Many religious sites had been vandalized and desecrated. Holy objects and relics had been destroyed,

---

[23] For the Curé d'Ars, the patron saint of parish priests, who was canonized in 1925, see Philippe Boutry, "Un sanctuaire et son saint Jean-Marie Baptiste Vianney, curé d'Ars" *Annales, économies, sociétés, civilisations* 36 (1980): 353–79; Mgr. Francis Trochu, *Le curé d'Ars: St. Jean-Marie-Baptiste Vianney* (Montsuris, 1903); and Gibson, *A Social History of French Catholicism*, pp. 100–102.

[24] Boutry, "Un sanctuaire et son saint," p. 371.

[25] Ibid.

[26] Ibid.

and hundreds of parishes had been without priests or any form of religious direction for years. The early years of the nineteenth century witnessed a full-scale effort on the part of the Catholic Church, aided in part by governments of the Restoration, to revitalize the Catholic religion through missions, conversions, proselytizing, and the encouragement of religious vocations.[27] These efforts met with uneven success. While female religious congregations witnessed extraordinary growth during the course of the nineteenth century, few men entered male orders. The Restoration did, however, bring an upsurge in clerical vocations and the emergence of a largely Ultramontane clergy. The social face of this clergy was very different from that of the clergy of the ancien régime in that the majority of young men came from the popular classes to whom they ministered.[28] This clergy faced the difficult task of bringing entire villages back into the fold, as the Curé d'Ars was reputed to have done with miraculous speed. Methods of conversion or reconversion varied, but by the 1840s, it became clear that forms of officially sanctioned devotion had changed significantly from those of the eighteenth century. The nineteenth-century clergy, unlike their largely urban and bourgeois counterparts of the eighteenth century, were far more tolerant of popular religious practices and "superstitions." Instead of attempting to repress them, they sought to control and encourage them.[29]

Clerical recuperation of popular religion reflected new forms of institutionalized popular piety that were simultaneously fostered by the intellectual currents of Romanticism and by the fascination with tombs, ruins, and the dead.[30] Ultramontane sentiment among the clergy manifested itself in a shift to Latin liturgical forms in the 1840s, and the "romanization" of popular piety was reflected in the revival of cults of saints and the veneration of relics, a practice that had been frowned upon by many members of the French clergy in the eighteenth century.

Interest in the early Christian martyrs was also thoroughly in keeping with a new Ultramontane aesthetic reflected in French religious art and articulated by Alexis François Rio's influential *De la poésie chrétienne dans sa*

---

[27] See Sévrin, *Les missions religieuses en France sous la Restauration.*
[28] See Timothy Tackett, *Priest and Parish in Eighteenth-Century France: A Social and Political Study of the Curés in a Diocese of Dauphiné, 1750–1791* (Princeton, N.J., 1977), pp. 305–6.
[29] See Kselman, *Miracles and Prophecies in Nineteenth-Century France*, pp. 141–88; and Gibson, *A Social History of French Catholicism*, pp. 134–57.
[30] These themes are an integral part of René Chateaubriand's *Génie du Christianisme* (Paris, 1802), published in the same year that Philomène was discovered, and of his novel *Atala* (*1801*).

matière et dans ses formes, published in 1836, a study of Italian painting from the recent to the early Renaissance, which led to a revival of interest in the art of Fra Angelico.[31] The disparagement of the Renaissance as well as of the art of the eighteenth century was echoed by the renowned Charles de Montalembert in a combative essay, "De l'état actuel de l'art religieux en France," published in the *Revue des Deux Mondes* in 1837 and reprinted several times. Montalembert launched an attack on the art of the eighteenth century, arguing that it was a final chapter in the degeneration of Christian art, a process which began during the pagan Renaissance. This French form of Pre-Raphaelitism, embodied in Ultramontane aesthetics and religious art, in turn stimulated a renewed interest in the styles and art of the early Christian Church and in the early Christian martyrs, both old-established and newly discovered.

Nineteenth-century priests, bishops, and laymen became avid collectors and traders of relics belonging to the saints. The Curé d'Ars, for example, collected more than five hundred relics. Between 1860 and 1873 the house of the eighteenth-century saint Benoît Labre was periodically ransacked by those in search of relics, after which an iron grille was installed to protect it. The correspondence of one priest from Périgeux contained bills for nearly six hundred saintly remains, reflecting payment of an average of forty to fifty francs for a half-skull, tibia, or femur.[32]

A disproportionately large number of these relics came from across the Alps and were the bodily remains of the saints of the catacombs. About four hundred or more were brought into France and placed in countless holy edifices before Pope Leo XIII closed the catacombs and forbade further exhumations in 1881. The relics were distributed unevenly throughout France. By far the largest proportion found their way to the diocese of Paris—the remains of nineteen alleged martyrs—and to the diocese of Lyon, where more than twenty catacomb saints were housed.[33]

Relics and the veneration of saintly remains have long been a part of Catholicism, but they have served different functions over time. They have provided communities and individuals with a sense of protection and identity. They have played a thaumaturgic role, and they have been a source of wealth to communities that became pilgrimage sites.[34] The pres-

---

[31] For a discussion of the aesthetics of Ultramontanism, see Michael Paul Driskel, *Representing Belief: Religion, Art, and Society in Nineteenth-Century France* (University Park, Pa., 1992) esp. pp. 59–67.

[32] Gibson, *A Social History of French Catholicism*, pp. 151–52.

[33] Boutry, "Les saints des catacombes," p. 893.

[34] See F. Pfister, *Der Reliquienkult im Altertum* (Giessen, 1909–12); Hippolyte Delehaye, *Les origines des cultes des martyrs* (Brussels, 1933); Delehaye, *Sanctus: Essai sur les cultes des saints*

ence of relics and cults devoted to the young saints of the catacombs in
France in the aftermath of the French Revolution gave holy sites new and
tangible sources of sacrality following the destruction and desecration of
the Revolutionary decade. In the words of one nineteenth-century episco-
pal biographer, "France, physically and morally ruined by the impious
Revolution, had seen the majority of its venerable relics dispersed and destroyed. One began to sense the necessity of recuperating the numerous
[Christian] treasures, and of gathering the bones of saints, our elder
brothers, into our impoverished and devastated churches."[35]

While the transfer of relics from Rome to France provided holy places
scarred by civil war with a new legitimacy, it also served as a means to reinvigorate old rituals and to create new ones. The transfer of saintly remains
was generally accompanied by the creation of new holy feast days, which
served as a means to draw the faithful and unfaithful back into the Christian fold. Indeed, the transfer of the last set of Roman relics in the nineteenth century, those of Sainte Théodosie, to the site of Valence Cathedral in 1853 occasioned a great fête that celebrated both the Roman
Church and the regeneration of Catholic France.[36] In short, the newly discovered catacomb saints contributed to the rejuvenation of the French
Catholic Church and the propagation of Ultramontane piety, and they
were tangible reminders of the intense religious fervor associated with the
early Christian Church.

PHILOMÈNE'S FOLLOWING

If Sainte Philomène and other saints of the catacombs helped to legitimize the proselytizing efforts of the French Catholic Church and reflected the development of new forms of piety that were strongly encouraged by an Ultramontane clergy, her cult prospered because it attracted
a wide popular following. However, it must be said from the outset that it
is far more difficult to deduce the individual or collective meanings
which Philomène's rank-and-file followers gave her than it is to place her
cult within the political and ecclesiastical context of nineteenth-century
French Catholicism. Those who venerated Philomène came from a vari-

---

dans l'antiquité (Brussels, 1927). For non-Christian cults of relics, see P. Saintyves, Les reliques
et les images légendaires (Paris, 1912), pp. 56–83. For a discussion of meanings with which relics
have been invested through time, see Patrick J. Geary, Furta Sacra: Thefts of Relics in the Central Middle Ages (Princeton, N.J., 1990), esp. pp. 3–43.
[35] Guillaume Delmas, Vie de Mgr. Bouange, évêque de Langres, 2 vols. (Aurillac, 1885), quoted in
Boutry, "Les saints des catacombes," p. 909.
[36] Boutry, "Les saintes des catacombes," pp. 903–4.

ety of social and regional backgrounds. They included the aristocratic ladies of Bayeux and peasant and middle-class women who flocked to the parish of Ars. However, the place that Philomène occupied in their lives was shaped as much by common religious and cultural frames of reference as by divergent social experiences.

Philomène was undoubtedly venerated for her real or imagined thaumaturgic powers and complemented the cult of the Virgin Mary, which gained ground with the apparitions at La Salette, Pontmain, and Lourdes.[37] The difference between the cult of Sainte Philomène and that of the Virgin Mary, however, was the centrality of the saint's martyred and tortured body as a symbol of chastity and purity.

Martyrdom has acquired different meanings since the emergence of Christianity. The early saints of the Church who died violently at the hands of Roman authorities, were all, by definition, martyrs. The meaning of martyrdom expanded, however, with the changing nature of Christian society.[38] At times, a violent death was considered to be sufficient for martyrdom by the Catholic Church; at others, as in the case of Joan of Arc, a violent death was initially not enough for a victim to be considered a martyr. During the Reformation and Wars of Religion, some Catholics killed by Protestants were immediately declared martyrs, but many others were not.

Sainte Philomène's martyrdom—and that of other revolutionary and catacomb saints—raises questions about a specific model of female martyrdom. This form of martyrdom assumed a decidedly sexual form. Although sexual overtones are not absent from narratives surrounding other Christian martyrs, including saints Agnes, Agatha, and Angélique, the youth of the catacomb saints and the circumstances of their martyrdom merit careful reflection. Agnes was also martyred during the reign of the emperor Diocletian (at the age of 12) for refusing to become the wife of the son of a Roman prefect. Saint Agatha resisted the advances of the Roman magistrate Quinctianus and was tortured and killed. Sainte Angélique was martyred when she resisted the sexual overtures the son of the governor of Rome. She is alleged to have declared to him, "Remove

---

[37] For the cult of the Virgin Mary see Marina Warner, *Alone of All Her Sex: The Myth and Cult of the Virgin Mary* (London, 1985). For the cult in France, see Kselman, *Miracles and Prophecies in Nineteenth Century France*, pp. 89–112; Gibson, *A Social History of French Catholicism*, pp. 145–51; Harris, *Lourdes*; and Barbara Corrado Pope, "Immaculate and Powerful: The Marian Revival in the Nineteenth Century," in *Immaculate and Powerful: The Female in Sacred Image and Social Reality*, ed. Clarissa W. Atkinson, Constance H. Buchanan, and Margaret R. Miles (Boston, 1985), pp. 173–200.

[38] For a discussion of the varieties of martyrdom see Delooz, "Towards a Sociological Study of Sainthood," p. 206.

yourself from my sight, food of death, for I have given my heart to another husband! I love Jesus Christ: in loving him I remain chaste, in coming close to him, I am pure, in receiving him, I remain a virgin."[39] Her martyrdom assumed the form of sexual resistance. The female martyr was not a powerless victim, however, but rather a resolute defender of her body and her faith. Moreover, in narratives of female martyrdom surrounding the catacomb saints the figures representing physical and sexual aggression were those of secular authority. In the case of Sainte Philomène and Sainte Angélique, the young girls resisted sexual transgression by representatives of a prominent political authority in the persons of the emperor Diocletian and the son of the Roman governor.

While sexual renunciation was one of the obvious features of early Christianity and both male and female chastity a valued attribute since late antiquity, these virtues were given a new emphasis by the Catholic clergy and secular republicans alike at the end of the eighteenth century.[40] Boutry suggests that the chastity and youth of the Roman saints may have helped the Church to illustrate the brutality of their secular, pagan torturers and served a pedagogical purpose of encouraging the Christian virtues of purity and chastity, particularly among young women.[41] At the same time, Sainte Philomène in particular appears to have been embraced by French women with genuine enthusiasm. That enthusiasm had a great deal to do with the growing popularity of the female religious vocation. The story of Théodelinde Dubouché, who painted Philomène's martyrdom of the cathedral of Bayeux, is a case in point.

Théodelinde Dubouché was the daughter of an anticlerical government official from Périgord and a devout mother. She first became interested in painting in 1826 at the age of seventeen when she met Laure Girard, a successful female artist, who painted portraits of the British royal family. Girard introduced Dubouché to the painter Louis de Juinne in Paris, and she soon obtained permission to join his studio as an apprentice and assistant. By day she painted, helping de Juinne in a commission he executed for Louis Philippe in 1835. A lover of music, by night she went to the Théâtre des Italiens and the Opera. In 1840, two years after painting Sainte-Philomène, she exhibited two paintings in the Paris Salon. In 1841 and in 1844, she exhibited four more paintings.

---

[39] Quoted in Boutry, "Les saints des catacombes," p. 915.
[40] Outram, "*Le langage mâle de la vertu*," p. 125. The meaning attached to sexual renunciation in early Christianity is explored in Brown, *The Body and Society*.
[41] Boutry, "Les saints des catacombes."

According to Théodelinde's biographer, the "greatest influence in her life was the painting of the martyrdom of Sainte Philomène for the cathedral of Bayeux."[42] It marked a turning point in two respects. First, the painting of Philomène was her greatest artistic achievement and brought her to the attention of the public. Second, it marked the beginning of her vocation as a nun after having spent almost ten years as an artist in Paris. Théodelinde Dubouché went on to found one of the most successful of female religious congregations established in nineteenth-century France, the Congrégation des Soeurs de l'Adoration Perpetuelle.[43]

The story of Théodelinde Dubouché and that of other nuns illustrates the significance of the cult of Sainte Philomène in the lives of women religious during the course of the nineteenth century. Hazel Mills has argued that the Church began to lionize and legitimize the *femme forte*, the virtuous woman who played an active role in worldly affairs through charitable work.[44] Sainte Philomène embodied the other side of female virtue expressed both in the language of sexual renunciation and in sexual models of female martyrdom extolled in sermons, confraternities, and schools throughout the nineteenth century.

While the narrative of Philomène's martyrdom conflated chastity with female virtue and served as a lesson for young Catholic girls, it is intriguing because it mirrored many narratives of sexual danger surrounding the female martyrs of liberty during the Revolution. Indeed, the proliferation of narratives of sexual danger in the stories surrounding both the female saints of the catacombs and female martyrs of the Revolution is conspicuous.

Two of the most popular revolutionary martyrs of liberty, Perrine Dugué and Marie Martin, were praised in terms similar to those of Philomène, and their martyrdoms occurred in the context of resisting sexual defilement. Perrine Dugué was a nineteen-year-old girl from the Mayenne in the west of France who was martyred in 1796. Her brothers were fierce supporters of the French Revolution. On her way to see them, she was attacked by three *chouans* (counterrevolutionaries) and murdered. Her body was found the next day and buried in a nearby field. Contemporary ballads portrayed her as "a good Christian who preferred

---

[42] Marie-Thérèse, *Souvenirs d'une amie*, 2:7.
[43] Charles de Chergé, *Histoire des congrégations religieuses d'origine poitevine* (Poitiers, 1856), p. 225.
[44] Hazel Mills, "Negotiating the Divide: Women, Philanthropy and the 'Public Sphere' in Nineteenth-Century France," in *Religion, Society and Politics in France since 1789*, ed. Frank Tallett and Nicholas Atkin (London, 1991), pp. 29–54.

death to being raped."[45] Her murder seized the popular imagination, and
her tomb became a site of pilgrimage and miraculous healing. A chapel
was built in her name in 1797, and she was seen ascending to heaven with
tricolored wings. Unlike the male martyrs of liberty, this popular republican saint's martyrdom was defined in terms of resistance to sexual pollution, and her saintly quality resided in her purity. The same could be said
of the more famous Marie Martin, alias Sainte Pataude, who became a
popular saint after her murder in 1795. Martin, who sympathized with the
revolutionary cause, was seized by a group of *chouans*. They systematically
raped and tortured her by pulling out her nails, gouging her eyes and mu-
tilating her breasts.[46] They then hung her from a tree with only a shirt to
cover her. When Martin was discovered by villagers, they buried her at the
foot of the tree, which became an object of devotion and the site of miraculous healings.

The Revolutionary cults of saints reveal the extent to which Revolutionary ideology was grafted onto more traditional forms of Catholic devotion, but while Jacobin revolutionaries and Catholic peasants invested
their cults with different meanings, the sexual model of female martyrdom attached to them bore a very evident similarity to that of the catacomb saints. Articulations of virtue assumed a sexual form during the Revolution and suggest that narratives of sexual danger surrounding the
female martyrs of the Revolution were as much an inherent part of the
language of republican female virtue as they were a reflection of time-
honored Christian virtues of chastity and sexual renunciation. Indeed, the
cult of Sainte Philomène and that of the female Revolutionary saints were
a part of secular and religious discourses on the nature of female virtue in
the early nineteenth century.[47]

---

[45] Albert Soboul, "Popular Cults during the French Revolution," in *Saints and Their Cults:
Studies in Religious Sociology, Folklore, and History*, ed. Stephen Wilson (New York, 1983),
p. 220. Also see Abbé Augustin Ceuneau, *Un culte étrange pendant la Révolution: Perrine Dugué,
la sainte aux ailes tricolores, 1777–1796* (Laval, 1947); Georges Lefebvre, "Perrine Dugué, la
sainte patriote," *Annales historiques de la Révolution Française* (1949), p. 337; and Michel Lagrée and Jehanne Roche, *Tombes de mémoire: La dévotion populaire aux victimes de la Révolution
dans l'Ouest* (Paris, 1992), pp. 92–94.
[46] *Pataud* was the *chouan* term for a republican. Soboul, "Popular Cults during the French
Revolution," pp. 220–21. Also see Roger Joxe, "Encore une sainte patriote: Sainte Pataude,"
Annales historiques de la Révolution Française (1952), p. 91; and Lagrée and Roche, *Tombes de mémoire*, pp. 72–75.
[47] "Women's personal virtue (virtue = chastity) is equated with political virtue (virtue = putting state above personal interests), like Brutus, who executed his sons when they attempted
to betray the Roman republic. The continuum between the two senses carries a whole series
of messages: that female chastity is the prerequisite for political innovation undertaken in
the name of universal will. . . . 'Virtue' was in fact a two-edged word, which bisected the ap-

The symbolism of the martyred female body may also have reflected collective anxieties that assumed similar meanings among Catholics and the proponents of the Revolution. Just as narratives surrounding rape by enemy forces during war have often been transformed into images of a violated—and often feminine—national body, these narratives of sexual danger could become individual or collective metaphors of resistance.[48] Philomène, a member of the community of embattled Christians, died defending its values from attacks by pagan secular authorities, as died Marie Martin and Perrine Dugué defending the republic against the assaults of the counterrevolutionary *chouans*.

The anthropologist Mary Douglas has argued that the human body cannot be considered apart from the social system that gives it value, and indeed, that the body is often the very "symbol of society," and that the "powers and dangers credited to social structure" are often "reproduced in small on the human body":[49]

> I believe that some pollutions are used as analogies for expressing a general view of the social order. . . . I suggest that many ideas about sexual dangers are better interpreted as symbols of the relation between parts of society, as mirroring designs of hierarchy or symmetry which apply in the larger social system. . . . Sometimes bodily orifices seem to represent points of entry or exit to social units, or bodily perfection can symbolise an ideal theocracy.[50]

If the human body has often served as a symbol of society, its "boundaries can represent any boundaries that are threatened or precarious."[51] It is telling that the local inhabitants of Teillay in western France, where the cult of Sainte Pataude first emerged, now say that Marie Martin was shot

parently universalistic terminology of *le sovereign* [*souverain*] into two distinct political destinies, one male and the other female." Outram, "*Le langage mâle de la vertu*," p. 125. See Landes, *Women and the Public Sphere*; Scott, "French Feminists and the Rights of 'Man,' "; and Scott, " 'A Woman Who Has Only Paradoxes to Offer.' "

[48] Ruth Harris has argued that the actual rape of women by German soldiers during the First World War became a metaphor in public discourse for the violated national body during and immediately following the war. See Ruth Harris, "The 'Child of the Barbarian': Rape and Nationalism in France during the First World War," *Past and Present*, no. 141 (November 1993): 171–206.

[49] Mary Douglas, *Purity and Danger: An Analysis of Concepts of Pollution and Taboo* (London, 1966), p. 115.

[50] Ibid., pp. 3–4. Theresa Coletti suggests that medieval theological thinking saw in the openness of the female body a lack of boundary "analogous to its moral character." Coletti, "Purity and Danger: The Paradox of Mary's Body and the En-Gendering of Infancy Narrative in the English Mystery Cycles," in *Feminist Approaches to the Body in Medieval Literature*, ed. Linda Lomperis and Sarah Stanbury (Philadelphia, 1993), p. 69.

[51] Douglas, *Purity and Danger*, p. 115.

by the Germans for her role in resisting the Nazis during the Occupation.[52] Philomène became a symbol of the persecuted Roman Church, while Sainte Pataude became the embodiment of the besieged Revolutionary nation.

The pervasiveness of narratives of sexual threat and danger in stories surrounding the martyrdom of the catacomb and Revolutionary saints also raises tantalizing questions about the fear of and fascination with sexual violence in nineteenth-century French society. Philomène's martyrdom valorized virginity, but the punishment for sexual withholding was harsh and swift. Instead of viewing the cult of Sainte Philomène as an expression of sadomasochistic impulses and sexual repression, one might well consider it as a manifestation of the titillation and the real or feigned horror that sexual violence toward young girls inspired among the French public.

The Revolutionary decade certainly left the French countryside littered with human bodies. Rape, physical violence, and bodily mutilation were inherent parts of the Revolutionary interlude. The murder and alleged sexual mutilation of the princesse de Lamballe, for example, became a symbol of the Revolution's barbarity for counterrevolutionaries and an important part of royalist martyrology.[53] If many of these stories were apocryphal, the dread they occasioned and their narrative power survived into the nineteenth century.

Novelistic narratives of sexual danger and violence abounded in postrevolutionary novelistic literature and were integral parts of the "melodramatic mode" of the nineteenth century.[54] Richardson's *Clarissa* was translated on the continent and came to feed into an already rich claustral literature, which was such an important part of French Romanticism. The narrative of abuse—sexual and/or physical—also figured in a large number of real cases of young women who fled the *maison paternelle* for the religious life without parental consent in the nineteenth century. The Ministry of Religious Affairs sometimes cited evidence of abuse in cases in which it did not act to return the young women to their families.[55] Public preoccupation with the subject was manifested in the growing

---

[52] Gibson, *A Social History of French Catholicism*, p. 53.

[53] The princesse de Lamballe, who had been a close friend of Marie-Antoinette, was one of the many alleged victims of sexual violence during the September Days (1792). She was hacked to death and decapitated, and royalists claimed that her genitals were mutilated and paraded, along with her head, through the streets of Paris.

[54] See Brooks, *The Melodramatic Imagination*.

[55] Two such cases that came before the ministry in 1840–41 were those of Marie-Anne Pourchier and Marguerite Desirée Malherbe. For the Pourchier case, see AN F^{19}6312 and for the case of Marguerite Malherbe, see AN F^{19}6326.

number of abuse cases involving minors reported to legal authorities, and they ultimately shaped the framing of France's first law governing the abuse of minors in 1898.[56] While the narrative of sexual and/or physical danger surrounding Philomène's martyrdom gave the clergy a story with prescriptive value, it evidently found resonance among the nineteenth-century reading public, and it reflected anxieties about sexual and physical violence that were expressed in the early years of the July Monarchy.

PHILOMÈNE VS. THÉRÈSE

Sainte Philomène and the many other virgin saints of the catacombs served to reinvigorate Catholicism and were part of a larger drive among the French clergy to recuperate the fervor of the early Christian Church. Philomène's martyrdom, which took the form of resistance to sexual defilement at the hands of pagan unbelievers, ultimately became a symbol of an embattled French Church. Her life was also a lesson to a young, and particularly female, audience. It validated the growing number of female religious vocations and resonated among a reading public gripped by real and fictional tales of horror and sexual danger.

Philomène's star fell, however, almost as quickly as it rose. By the First World War the cult of Sainte Philomène had lost much of its popularity. The chapel devoted to Sainte Philomène in the Church of Saint-Gervais in Paris was, for example, rededicated to Saint Benoît Labre, and in 1961 the Vatican removed the by then largely forgotten Sainte Philomène from the calendar of saints.[57] Sainte Philomène's loss of favor must, above all, be linked to developments in the new science of archeology and to changes in Vatican policy. By the 1850s some clerics and laymen began to question the criteria used by the Vatican to determine whether of not tombs in the catacombs belonged to early Christian martyrs. Commentaries pointed out that epitaphs on the Roman tombs contained no mention of martyrs, that there was no evidence of the existence of these martyrs in the historical record, and that the so-called vial of blood found in the case of Philomène

---

[56] Statistical data indicate that between 1830 and 1890 reported cases of rape and other sexual crimes increased dramatically before beginning to decline toward the beginning of the twentieth century. An increasing number of these cases involved victims who were children or adolescents. The increase in the number of children and adolescents registered in the legal record reflects a growing societal concern about or response to the abuse of minors. Jean-Claude Chesnais, *Histoire de la violence en occident de 1800 à nos jours* (Paris, 1981), pp. 181–86.

[57] Stephen Wilson, "Cults of Saints in the Churches of Central Paris" in *Saints and Their Cults*, p. 240. For the cult of Saint Benoît Labre, see Jacques Gadille, "Autour de Saint Benoît Labre: Hagiographie et critique au XIXe siècle," *Revue d'Histoire de l'Eglise de France* 52 (1966): 113–26.

and other saints was not definitive proof of martyrdom.[58] As a result of these debates over the saints' authenticity they became a source of embarrassment rather than a fount of legitimacy. Official sponsorship of the cults began to slacken. By 1881, Pope Leo XIII sharply restricted access to the catacombs and banned any further exhumation of bodily remains from the underground graves. However, archeology and Vatican policy were not enough to send the cult of Sainte Philomène into a decline. She was eclipsed by two "real" young and virginal saints in the figures of Joan of Arc and Thérèse de Lisieux.[59] Joan of Arc, who was condemned as a heretic and burned at the stake defending king and country in 1431, was beatified quite late, in 1909, following a revival of interest in the female patriot during the early years of the Third Republic. She was canonized in 1920. Thérèse de Lisieux, who died in 1897 at the age of twenty-four, was beatified in 1923 and declared a saint in 1925. These saints shared Philomène's youth and chastity and came to be the favored saints of the French clergy. Indeed, the clergy encouraged devotion to them at the expense of Philomène. The transfer of clerical allegiance reflected both the changing tides of Vatican policy and the changing nature of clerical politics.

The Vatican encouraged the French clergy to embrace the republic and to renounce their resistance to the state during the period of *Ralliement* in the 1890s, and this olive branch that was proffered to the republic heralded the decline of the cult of Philomène as well. When the Dreyfus affair shattered this policy of appeasement, many in the Church found a home among the xenophobic, nationalistic New Right exemplified by the Action Française and the Ligue des Patriotes. While Ultramontanism was still a force among the lower clergy, many of its members had joined forces with a new nationalist Right represented by Charles Maurras and the Action Française.[60] Joan of Arc became the public chosen saint of those who linked throne and altar or who associated the Church with right-wing causes. As the Catholic Right became more nationalistic, Joan of Arc became a saint more suitable for public devotion. Many of those within the Church who did not necessarily share the right-wing convictions of the Ac-

---

[58] The controversy over the vial of blood was passionately debated after the publication of Edmond Le Blant's *La Question du vase du sang* (Paris, 1858). Boutry, "Les saints des catacombs," pp. 919–21.

[59] For the cult of Sainte Thérèse, see Guy Gaucher, *The Story of a Life: Sainte Thérèse de Lisieux*, trans. Sister Anne Marie Brennan (San Francisco, 1987). For the cult of Joan of Arc at the turn of the century, see Marina Warner, *Joan of Arc: The Image of Female Heroism* (Harmondsworth, 1983), pp. 255–75; and Gerd Krumeich, "Joan of Arc between Right and Left," in *Nationhood and Nationalism in France: From Boulangism to the Great War, 1889–1918*, ed. Robert Tombs (London, 1991), pp. 63–73.

[60] Eugen Weber, *The Nationalist Revival in France, 1905–1914* (Berkeley, Calif., 1959).

tion Française were embarrassed by the dubious status of the Roman saints and preferred the very "real" Thérèse de Lisieux, to whom Philomène is often compared.[61]

While Joan of Arc and Thérèse embodied some of the qualities belonging to the child saint Philomène—youth, chastity, and intense spirituality—the nature of Philomène's martyrdom was fundamentally different from the trials of Thérèse de Lisieux and Joan of Arc. The martyrdom to which Thérèse de Lisieux aspired was that of Christ himself, Saint Bartholomew, or Joan of Arc herself:

> *Martyrdom* was the dream of my youth and this dream has grown with me within Carmel's cloisters. But here again, I feel that my dream is a folly, for I cannot confine myself to desiring *one kind* of martyrdom. To satisfy me I need *all.* Like You, my Adorable Spouse, I would be scourged and crucified. I would die flayed like Saint Bartholomew. I would be plunged into boiling oil, like Saint John; I would undergo all the tortures inflicted upon the martyrs. With St. Agnes and St. Cecilia, I would present my neck to the sword, and like Joan of Arc, my dear sister, I would whisper at the stake Your Name, O Jesus.[62]

The actual form that Thérèse's suffering assumed, described in her own words in the posthumous publication of *Histoire d'une âme* (1898) was that of psychological pain and bodily sickness rather than that of sexual violence or aggression. Indeed, Sainte Thérèse, the Little Flower, acquired much of her popularity in the twentieth century among the wounded and disabled veterans of World War I. Philomène bore a greater resemblance to Thérèse's female saintly rival and "sister," Joan of Arc, who burned at the stake. However, Joan of Arc, though young and chaste, disguised herself as a man. She was an androgynous figure who bore little relation to the pale, angelic adolescent Sainte Philomènes that were painted for dozens of chapels, churches, and religious communities in France. Moreover, the narrative of sexual danger surrounding Philomène's martyred body was never associated with Joan of Arc, who came to represent martyred France and the lost provinces of Alsace and Lorraine. The young

---

[61] "Thérèse n'est-elle, à moins d'un siècle de distance, qu'une nouvelle Philomène?" Rosenbaum-Dondaine, *L'Image de piété en France, 1814–1914,* p. 175.

[62] *Story of a Soul: The Autobiography of Thérèse de Lisieux,* trans. John Clarke (Washington, D.C., 1976), p. 193. Thérèse visited the Roman catacombs in 1887, which left a "deep impression" on her, inspiring her to ask for the "grace" to become the first martyr of Jesus. During her visit she formed a special attachment to St. Cecilia, patroness of music. Philomène, who was so important to Théodelinde Dubouché, is conspicuously absent from her account. Ibid., p. 131.

FIGURE 6. *Thérèse de Lisieux (1873–97)* (c. 1895). Courtesy of Bridgeman Art Library, U.K.

and virginal French saints—Sainte Thérèse and Joan of Arc—supplanted Sainte Philomène, but their cults were invested with entirely different meanings.

The cult of Sainte Philomène was the reflection of a particular time and place. The decline in Philomène's popularity must be interpreted in the light of changes in the nature of clerical politics and patronage, but those changes do not fully explain the disappearance of her cult among her lay adherents. Her disappearance must be seen through the lens of other developments in French society. The new science of archeology called the authenticity of Sainte Philomène into question, as did the rise of secular values. Her earthly demise also had much to do with the fading of the violent memory of the French Revolution by the end of the nineteenth century; the decline in religious vocations by the beginning of the twentieth century; and the appeal of saints like Sainte Thérèse, whose suffering assumed psychological rather than physical forms.

Despite Philomène's fall from grace, tangible traces of her astonishing popularity survive in dozens of churches and religious houses throughout France. Not far from the Centre Georges Pompidou in Paris, an empty and unused chapel in the Church of Saint-Merri contains an altar painting and peeling frescoes of Philomène's martyrdom by the French "pre-Raphaelite" artist Eugène-Emmanuel Amaury Duval. One can also still find Théodelinde Dubouché's painting of the martyrdom of Sainte Philomène in a poorly lit chapel of Bayeux Cathedral.

Like the cults of the Sacred Heart and the newly invigorated devotion to the Virgin Mary, which the apparitions at Lourdes and La Salette encouraged, the cult of Sainte Philomène was one which was sanctioned by the Catholic Church in its struggle against anticlericalism and impiety. The language of female martyrdom, which was mirrored in the cults of revolutionary martyrs, revealed two sides of the same coin. While statues of Marianne were erected in public squares to represent the revolutionary nation, paintings and statues of the Virgin Mary were executed for churches throughout France.[63] Whether she was Marianne, Philomène, or Marie, the female image was at the symbolic center of the postrevolutionary struggle between the Catholic Church and a secularizing state.

---

[63] Maurice Agulhon makes this point in *Marianne into Battle: Republican Imagery and Symbolism in France, 1789–1880*, trans. Janet Lloyd (Cambridge, 1981).

CHAPTER 5

Madame de Guerry vs. Picpus: Religion, Property, and *Laïcité*

The Second Empire has generally been seen as the breeding ground for anticlericalism as a mature political ideology in the nineteenth century, and it set the stage for the rise of a new "positivist generation" of republicans who laicized the French state in the 1880s.[1] Their campaign in many ways marked the resolution of the century-long battle between Ultramontanism and Gallicanism, and it was also in part influenced by the republican defeat in 1848 and the Empire's initial proclerical policies. Indeed, from 1850 onwards the ties between the Church and the state were close and tight, just as they had been under the Bourbon Restoration.[2] In the space of seven years the budget allocated to the Catholic Church was raised from 39,518,544 francs in 1852 to 45,967,896 in 1859.[3] The Catholic hierarchy threw in its lot with the party of order and Louis Napoleon

---

[1] The adjective "anticlerical" was coined during this period. It first appeared in a report written by the prefect of the Nord in 1852, and it came to be used with increasing frequency in the 1860s. See Maurain, *La politique ecclésiastique du Second Empire*, p. 960; and Jacques Gadille, "On French Anticlericalism: Some Reflections," *European Studies Review* 13 (1983): 127.

[2] Katherine Auspitz argues that "in opposition to the power and privilege of the counterrevolutionary church—its exemption from laws restricting free association, its immunity from press censorship, its decisive control over education and public assistance—republicans developed what would now be called a counterculture." Auspitz, *The Radical Bourgeoisie: The Ligue de l'enseignement and the Origins of the Third Republic 1866–1885* (Cambridge, 1982), p. 18.

[3] Maurain, *La politique ecclésiastique du Second Empire*, p. 55.

soon after the Revolution of 1848 and the June days. It was rewarded with
the Falloux Law in 1850, which strengthened clerical control over education, and with lenient policies toward the formation of Catholic religious
orders and congregations. The Catholic Church regained power in the
public sphere. According to article 20 of the new constitution, for example, Catholic cardinals were allowed to sit in the Senate.

Louis Napoleon and many members of the propertied classes who supported him saw in the clergy a powerful potential ally and a force sustain-
ing moral and political order. The empire defended the interests of the
Church and the Church stood behind the empire. This alliance was expressed in a variety of different domains. The state tended to allow the
Church to adjudicate its own disputes, even in cases in which its members
might be found to violate civil law, and it protected the clergy from embarrassing publicity. If a priest were arrested for an offense, the state
often left the matter of punishment and discipline to the ecclesiastical hierarchy. In 1853, for example, four priests in the diocese of Versailles
were accused of acts of immorality and the abuse of children. The state allowed the bishop of Versailles to settle the matter and the incident was
hushed up.[4]

The Second Empire, in turn, often used the Church "as a kind of police
force" that placed higher education and society more generally under surveillance.[5] Soon after the founding of the Second Empire the "philosophical materialism" of the Paris medical faculty came under intense scrutiny.
It has become a truism to say that the "positivist generation" of French republicans who assumed the reins of government in the 1870s received
their political education and forged their political identity in opposition
to the proclerical Second Empire. The basis of their anticlericalism was
pointedly political as well as ideological and philosophical.[6] The nature of
the antagonism between these anticlerical positivist republicans and the
state was reflected, for example, in the state's 1865 ban on informal lectures given by Alexandre Axenfeld on Jean Wier, the sixteenth-century
physician who dared suggest during the European witch craze that many
women allegedly possessed were quite simply mentally ill. The ban was followed three years later by the empire's annulment of a medical degree

<hr/>

[4] Ibid., pp. 77–79.
[5] Adrien Dansette, *Religious History of Modern France*, trans. J. Dingle, vol. 1 (Freiburg, 1961),
p. 289.
[6] John Eros, "The Positivist Generation of French Republicanism," *Sociological Review* 3
(1955): 255–77; Louis Capéran, *Histoire contemporaine de la laïcité française: La crise du seize mai
et la revanche républicaine* (Paris, 1957), pp. 31–36; and Auspitz, *The Radical Bourgeoisie*,
pp. 22–31.

granted to one P.-J. Grenier by the Paris Faculty of Medicine as a result of pressure placed on the liberal-minded minister of education, Victor Duruy, by the Catholic Church. The contested thesis, "Etude médico-psychologique du libre arbitre humain," contained references to the positivist Auguste Comte, and Axenfeld made other offending remarks regarding the nonexistence of free will.[7] It was largely due to incidents such as these that anticlericalism experienced a "notable upsurge" in the second half of the nineteenth century, drawing mass support that was ultimately harnessed for political ends during the early Third Republic.[8]

Another perspective must be added, however. Anticlericalism was shaped by the continuing concern evoked by the impact that the growth of female religious communities and female piety had on family property and family relations. It was expressed in the public fascination with a number of cases of *captation*, or clerical kidnapping, the most famous of which, the Mortara affair, occurred in Italy during this period; and with cases of property disputes involving religious congregations.[9] These fears and anxieties came to be voiced by men associated with a number of political groups—including, ultimately, Bonapartists. Moreover, the laicizing impulse, which came from republicans, Orleanists, and in many cases Bonapartists, resulted in a clear shift in imperial policies toward female religious congregations before the advent of the Third Republic. Historians have acknowledged this shift, but they have generally argued that it must be attributed to the conflict engendered by France's involvement in war in the Italian peninsula in 1859, which was opposed by the pope and which sowed deep discord among Catholics in France. While the Italian question certainly created fissures among Catholics in France, particularly after the revolt of the papal province of Romagna, it must be emphasized that the shift in imperial policies occurred before the war in Italy broke out. In short, much of the anticlericalism attributed to positivist republicans excluded from power in the 1850s was embedded in the fabric of the Second Empire itself. The proliferation of a number of highly publicized

[7] Jan Goldstein, "The Hysteria Diagnosis and the Politics of Anticlericalism in Late Nineteenth-Century France," *Journal of Modern History* 54 (June 1982): 225–26.

[8] René Rémond, "Anticlericalism: Some Reflections by Way of Introduction," *European Studies Review* 13 (1983): 123–24. Alex Mellor notes that that there was a "renaissance" in anticlerical sentiment after 1859. Mellor, *Histoire de l'anticléricalisme français* (Tours, 1966), p. 290.

[9] René Rémond has argued that the kidnapping of one Jewish child in Italy did more for anticlericalism than the activities and gaffes of dozens of bishops and thousands of priests in a multitude of parishes. Rémond, *L'anticléricalisme en France de 1815 à nos jours* (Paris, 1976), p. 157.

scandals involving property disputes contributed to the virulence of anti-clerical sentiment, which increasingly focused on the famous "milliard," or hidden billions that female religious congregations allegedly pos-sessed.[10] One of the most notorious was that of the rebellious Sister Esther, who belonged to the order of Picpus in Paris.

RENEGADE NUN

On 5 June 1853 two French nuns were granted an audience with the pope in Rome to plead what was, in the opinion of one prelate, "one of the most difficult cases in ecclesiastical history."[11] They prostrated themselves before him, and the elder of the two women, madame de Guerry, or Soeur Esther, who was over seventy years old, declared her intention to leave the religious order of Perpetual Adoration of the Sacred Hearts of Jesus and Mary—more popularly known as Picpus, owing to its location in the rue de Picpus in Paris—and requested permission to form a new reli-gious community. She also demanded the restitution of the fortune that she had brought to the community when she joined it thirty-four years be-fore. While the pope agreed to allow her to leave Picpus in order to es-tablish a new community, he created a tribunal to adjudicate the matter of her property. Two years later, as the negotiations over the return of her property soured, madame de Guerry declared her intention to take the matter to a French civil court. The pope, who strongly opposed the inter-vention of secular authorities, responded by ordering that the case be closed and that she return to Picpus. She flatly refused and was, as a result, branded as a renegade by many in and outside of the Church.

Madame de Guerry, née de Grave, was born in 1783 and belonged to one of the oldest and wealthiest noble families in France. Her mother died in childbirth, and her father was killed at Quiberon during the French Revolution, fighting on the side of the defunct monarchy. Having spent most of her childhood as an émigré, she married the marquis de Guerry, who came from an equally wealthy and venerable noble family, at the age of twenty. Sixteen years later, after the death of her husband in battle as an officer, she became a childless widow and joined the commu-nity of Picpus as a nun at the age of thirty-six. Her lawyer described her as a woman who was "young, rich, surrounded by the advantages and charms

---

[10] Langlois, *Le catholicisme au féminin*, p. 344.

[11] *Affaire de Madame de Guerry contre la communauté de Picpus: Mémoire à consulter* (Paris, 1857), p. 8.

of life," and who renounced everything. It was for this reason she "asks once again for that which belongs to her."[12]

Like many of the religious communities in France at mid-century the order of Perpetual Adoration, or Picpus, was founded shortly after the end of the Revolution, in 1800, by a priest, Marie-Joseph Coudrin, who refused to take an oath to the Civil Constitution of the Clergy, and a noblewoman, madame Aymer de la Chevalrie.[13] Unlike many religious orders in France, it consisted of a male and a female component, each of which lived in separate quarters. It combined contemplative and active functions that included education, worship, and evangelical missions. Although the community was originally founded in Brittany in 1800, it moved to Paris when it bought a house in the rue de Picpus. While the pope authorized the community through a papal bull on 17 November 1817, it never requested and was not granted formal legal authorization by the French state.

The community of Picpus nonetheless became an important and visible part of the Parisian landscape. Jules Michelet explicitly mentioned the congregation in his 1845 diatribe against the Jesuits delivered in his now famous Collège de France lectures. Picpus also appears in the pages of Victor Hugo's *Les Misérables*. British travelers in Paris were brought to Picpus. Thomas William Allies noted in 1847 that Picpus counted more than twenty establishments throughout France and two in Chile. It is still a metro stop on the RATP, not far from the place de la Révolution.[14]

Madame de Guerry, now Soeur Esther, lived peaceably in the community of Picpus from the year she took her vows, in 1819, to 1837, when the spiritual director of the community, Coudrin, died and was replaced by Pierre-Dominique-Raphael Bonamie, the bishop of Chalcedon. Bonamie immediately tried to change the community's rule and governance, and it was over this issue that the trouble began. The main change concerned the authority of the superior general and the relationship between the male and female components of the order. Bonamie also attempted to establish clear differences between the *religieuses* and the *soeurs converses* (those who performed most of the domestic service). This was to be done by giving the two ranks different-colored habits. Finally, Bonamie wished

---

[12] Ibid., p. 133.
[13] Bernard Couronne, *Petite vie du Père Marie-Joseph Coudrin, fondateur de la congrégation des Sacrés-Coeurs* (Paris, 1997).
[14] Jules Michelet and Edgar Quinet, *Des jésuites*, 5th ed. (Paris, 1843). Hugo describes the nuns of Picpus as "pale and serious," noting that between 1825 and 1830, three went mad. Hugo, *Les Misérables*, vol. 1 (Paris, 1966), p. 173. Thomas William Allies, *Journal in France in 1845 and 1848* (London, 1849), pp. 210–14.

to require a minimum monetary amount to be brought to the congregation by all those wishing to enter it.[15]

While Picpus included nuns and priests, the order was one in which the former had a considerable degree of autonomy. The governance of the nuns belonged to the congregation's female general superior. The bishop of Chalcedon effectively proposed transferring that authority to himself by requiring nuns to vow their obedience to him and by insisting on approving the appointment of local superiors. He wanted, moreover, to change the procedures for the election of the female general superior from a system of "universal suffrage" to one of indirect election. Finally, he wished to require dowries of three thousand francs from all novices and to establish clear distinctions between the duties performed by nuns and lay sisters (*soeurs converses*) who resided in the convent. For de Guerry, the community's treasurer, and for the mother superior, madame de Viart, the usurpation of the superior's authority and the change of the congregation's rule represented an attempt to transform a "republic" into a community of "slaves."[16] By 1844, de Viart and de Guerry had successfully resisted all of the bishop's efforts to change the constitution of Picpus. They enlisted the support of the Gallican bishop of Chartres and the pope, and Pope Gregory XVI directed Bonamie not to change the community's rule.

Ultimately, however, the conflict came to divide the ecclesiastical hierarchy, which was already split into Gallican and Ultramontane camps. Pierre-Louis Parisis, the bishop of Arras, who was called upon to adjudicate the conflict in the early 1850s, sided with those who did not wish to change the order's rule, as did the Gallican Clausel de Montals, bishop of Chartres.[17] These prelates locked horns with Denys-Auguste Affre, the powerful archbishop of Paris, who was asked to investigate the matter in 1845. After an investigation by two of his *vicaires généraux*, he supported Bonamie's reforms, in spite of a stormy confrontation with Montals in the fall of 1845.[18] The issues surrounding the reform of Picpus remained unresolved at the time of Pope Gregory XVI's death in January of 1846. Six months later Clausel de Montals asked the new pope, Pius IX, to launch

[15] R. P. Remi Leriche, *Picpus et les constitutions de ses fondateurs* (Paris, 1856), pp. 73, 97.

[16] *Affaire de Madame de Guerry: Mémoire à consulter*, p. 18.

[17] For Parisis's role in the de Guerry case see Charles Guillemant, *Pierre-Louis Parisis, L'évêque d'Arras*, vol. 3 (Paris, 1924), pp. 347–53 and for that of Clausel de Montals, see Ernest Sévrin, *Mgr. Clausel de Montals, évêque de Chartres (1769–1857): Un évêque militant et gallican au XIX siècle*, vol. 2 (Paris, 1955), pp. 493–98.

[18] R. Limouzin-Lamothe, *Mgr. Denys-Auguste Affre, archévêque de Paris (1793–1848)* (Paris, 1971), pp. 258–59; At Affre's meeting with Montals, "tous deux Rouergats, d'un tempérament tenace, se heurtèrent violemment." (ibid., p. 260).

another investigation. In March of 1848, when Paris was in the midst of a revolution, Pius IX ruled that Bonamie was to remain in his position as superior general, but the pope stipulated that any change in the community's rule had to be submitted to Rome first.[19]

In 1850, madame de Viart, the general superior of the convent, died, and the marquise de Guerry was elected superior. She declined the honor, arguing that she was not in the best position to defend the congregation from the persistent attempts of Bonamie to change the community's rule, while he moved once again to change the rule of the community. This time he was successful in initiating some of the reforms he had long desired, and de Guerry decided to leave Picpus to found a religious community that adhered to the community's original principles of governance. It was this decision that ultimately led her to attempt to recover a part of the considerable fortune that she had brought into the community when she took her vows in August of 1819. Madame de Guerry was not the only one to protest the alteration of the congregation's rule. A male member of the order was expelled for disputing the proposed changes and published a book describing these changes and setting forth the original principles that had governed Picpus. He wrote in 1856 that the congregation had found itself divided into two camps for more than fifteen years. The "majority having obtained approbation from the pope" for changing the order's rule confronted a "minority afflicted by a change that it considers a calamity," and which wished to return to the original spirit of the order's constitution.[20]

PROPERTY, POWER, AND PUBLIC ORDER

The case that de Guerry brought to civil court against the community of Picpus was about many things. First and foremost, it was about money and property. It was about power and the role of women within the Catholic church. It was about the relationship between Church and state. But, even more fundamentally, it was about the rights of individuals and associations in a postrevolutionary world that had seen the disappearance of the corporate bodies and privileges of the Old Regime. While the plaintiff and defendants as well as their spokesmen had vastly different views of the general principles of the case, they both employed a language of right and contract. As the plaintiff was a woman, the debate over these rights was articulated in the context of broader discussions over the roles and status of women in postrevolutionary society and law.

[19] Ibid., pp. 261–62.
[20] Leriche, *Picpus et les constitutions de ses fondateurs*, pp. 3–4.

The community of Picpus was in a curious position because it had not asked for and had therefore not been granted legal recognition by the state. Governments of the Restoration, the July Monarchy, and, initially, the Second Empire, had all turned a blind eye to female religious associations that did not seek formal legal authorization, especially during the periods of the Bourbon Restoration and the early Second Empire. Indeed, during the Second Empire, female religious orders reached their apogee. The law of 31 January 1852 gave the state the power to authorize female religious associations by a simple imperial decree, and it came to do so with greater and greater frequency. Between 1852 and 1859 a total of 817 new female religious associations was authorized, which represented their most sustained growth since the French Revolution.[21]

Emile Ollivier (1825–1913), counsel for de Guerry, used Picpus's ambiguous status to argue that it had no legal right to exist and therefore no right to assume control of her fortune or that of anyone else. Counsel for the Church argued that because Picpus did not legally exist in the eyes of the state, the state had no right to apply its laws to the congregation's governance. Madame de Guerry's civil suit was first argued in great secrecy before the civil court in Paris in 1857, where she lost her case. She appealed the judgment, and the case then went to the imperial appeals court in February and March 1858. The proceedings there, unlike those a year earlier, had a great deal of publicity and attracted "a considerable crowd."[22] The sums involved in the case were immense. The French public was fascinated by the spectacle of a seventy-four-year-old nun from one of the oldest aristocratic families in France openly challenging the Catholic Church.

The case was argued by what was at first regarded as a striking pair. Picpus was represented by Pierre Antoine de Berryer (1790–1868), a lawyer with a reputation for impressive oratory who successfully defended Church interests in court for most of his career; de Guerry's advocate was the little known, but talented, Emile Ollivier, who was barely over thirty years old and who made a name for himself as a result of this case.[23] By all

[21] Maurain, *La politique ecclésiastique du Second Empire*, p. 216.
[22] *Gazette des Tribunaux*, 25 January 1858, p. 90. The court was filled with a large number of spectators. Also see ibid., 15–16 February 1858, p. 161; 22–23 February 1858, p. 185; 8–9 March 1858, p. 239. The final day of the trial, however, was not attended by nuns from Picpus or by the "dissident" followers of Sister Esther, though they had followed the previous proceedings assiduously.
[23] Despite the celebrity of the legal counsel for both sides and the remarkable nature of this case, no historical study of it has been published to date. Nonetheless, Claude Langlois cites the case in a chapter on the financial resources of congregations in his exhaustive study of the growth of female religious associations in nineteenth-century France. Langlois, *Le Catholicisme au féminin*, p. 368.

accounts, Ollivier was a remarkable orator, and the great liberal Catholic comte de Montalembert noted in his diary, after hearing him speak before parliament in 1858, "this young democrat will go far."[24] Emile Ollivier was a republican and a proponent of liberal empire soon to make his name as the chief architect of the transition from empire to republic on the eve of the Franco-Prussian War. The pairing up of the young liberal democrat and noble nun, who was intent on upholding her rights in the face of opposition from the Catholic Church, was astounding to all, to say the least.

Ollivier assumed a Gallican position, contending that religious associations must submit first and foremost to secular state authority for judicial, political, and economic reasons. Submission to secular authority was necessary for the maintenance of public order and for peaceful relations between Church and state. For this reason, unauthorized religious communities were by their very existence an affront to France's civil order. Moreover, he highlighted a fundamental contradiction in the first court's decision. On the one hand it had argued that unauthorized religious communities could not be sued because they had no formal legal existence, but on the other, it asserted that these communities existed in fact and could therefore make use of the property of their members under an implied contractual agreement.[25] He concluded that Picpus had no legal right to exist and therefore no right to assume control of de Guerry's fortune or that of anyone else.[26] But subtle legal distinctions concerning whether or not Picpus legally existed and could therefore be sued were not at the core of Ollivier's arguments. His broader claims concerning individual rights, the inviolability of individual private property, and the primacy of civil law over ecclesiastical law were most important.

---

[24] Theodore Zeldin, *The Political System of Napoleon III* (New York, 1958), p. 124. During the first trial, Ollivier wrote in his diary that his success surpassed what he had hoped for, but he came to see his performance in the appeals trial as even better. He ultimately received ten thousand francs from madame de Guerry for his services. Ollivier, *Journal*, vol. 1: *1846–1860* (Paris, 1961), pp. 263, 318, 322.

[25] See Ollivier, "Des congrégations religieuses non autorisées: Madame la marquise de Guerry contre la communauté de Picpus," *Revue pratique de droit français: Jurisprudence, doctrine, législation* 5 (1858): 97–131. The case generated considerable comment and debate in the French legal community. See, for example, M. Clamageran, cited by Ollivier in ibid., vol. 3; and Armand Ravelet, *Traité des congrégations religieuses: Commentaire des lois et de la jurisprudence* (Paris, 1869), pp. 341–64.

[26] "Les communautés existent pour prendre, ils n'existent pas pour rendre." Ollivier, "Des congrégations religieuses," p. 108. According to Ollivier, the first time that a congregation had used the defense of civil incapacity was in 1825. It involved the case of a religious congregation in Aix that had failed to pay for work undertaken at its request, arguing that it not liable for its actions because it did not formally exist. Ibid., p. 107.

The language that Emile Ollivier used to defend de Guerry's claims—his references to the community as a "republic" predicated on universal suffrage and the Church's attempts to turn it into a community of "slaves"—bore witness to a larger struggle between the Church and a liberal opposition during that period. The growing wealth of female religious communities contributed to the particularly venomous nature of French anticlericalism in the latter half of the Second Empire. Indeed, the case was used as ammunition by the state and anticlericals of all stripes.

One of the lawyers representing the Church declared that de Guerry (now aged seventy-five) had "one foot already in eternity" and was now in revolt against "all that she had sworn to respect [thus] giving the lie to her life of virtue." In short, the lawyer accused de Guerry and the twenty-five nuns who had left Picpus with her of throwing themselves into the arms of "parties who have a horror of convents and would make bonfires of joy on their ruins."[27] While de Guerry, like Jeanne Le Monnier, was attacked as a proud, insubordinate woman who vainly refused to submit to ecclesiastical authority and who, in her pride, sacrificed the interests of the Church, Ollivier declared, "There is a time to speak and a time to be silent. . . . she comes not only to claim her fortune, but also her honor as a nun and a Catholic woman."[28]

While the case of the renegade nun was an embarrassing scandal for the Church, it raised difficult legal questions regarding the relationship between secular and religious authority and civil and ecclesiastical law. It revealed, more particularly, the legal lacunae of the Napoleonic Code when it came to defining the property rights of women and the associational rights of religious congregations in postrevolutionary law. The labor movement also challenged revolutionary conceptions of individual property embodied in the Le Chapelier law of 1791 and the Napoleonic Code—which denied the right to free association—and the existence of large numbers of religious communities, many of which did not have legal recognition, also implicitly called that law and the Napoleonic Code into question.[29] As one jurist remarked in 1867, what characterized legislation governing religious congregations was "incoherence, together with the excessively large place that the obscurity and sometimes the silence of the texts leave to the discretion of judges. And, how could it be otherwise?,"

[27] "Plaidoirie de M. Dufaure," in *Affaire de Madame de Guerry contre la communauté de Picpus*, ed. J. Sabatier (Paris, 1858), p. 147.
[28] *Affaire de Madame de Guerry: Mémoire à consulter*, p. 9.
[29] See William H. Sewell Jr., *Work and Revolution in France: The Language of Labor from the Old Regime to 1848* (Cambridge, Mass., 1981), esp. chap. 6, "A Revolution in Property," pp. 114–42.

he asked, "every period has translated its thought into one or several laws . . . and all of these laws, which often contradict each other . . . await a powerful hand to bring them into harmony."[30]

As there was no real precedent for the case and no body of law that addressed the legal intricacies it posed, what determined its outcome was political conjuncture—specifically, a growing hostility of the state and its courts to the power of the Church; the court's assertion of the primacy of civil law over ecclesiastical law; and growing fears of the enormous hold that religion had on French women and the implications of that hold for property and family relations.

While the appeals court acknowledged that unauthorized congregations did not constitute "civil persons," it ruled that they nonetheless constituted social entities with responsibilities vis-à-vis their members.[31] To say otherwise would mean, ironically, that unauthorized congregations existing in defiance of the law would have legal immunity. Moreover, according to this judgment, the 1825 law governing female religious communities stipulated that unauthorized congregations could not acquire or possess goods, revenues, or properties. Although the judges reversed the first court's decision, they nonetheless limited the suit to the community of Picpus, instead of allowing Ollivier to extend the suit to specific individuals. Arguing that the actions of the nun were neither capricious nor worthy of blame, the imperial court decided in her favor. Taking into account the years she had lived in the community, she was awarded 475,000 francs.

Emile Ollivier declared that the case could not be decided otherwise, as it was a question of "public order," which was the foundation of civil society. As property and family were the bases for that order, the state was obliged to uphold madame de Guerry's rights to her property in the face of the Church's claim on it. In short, Ollivier used the interests of families in upholding madame de Guerry's property rights in making his case "on these bases, true under all regimes of government and all religions, the interest of families that one would wish to protect, the interest of nuns themselves that one would like to safeguard, against their own delusion and the

---

[30] Charles Jacquier, *De la condition légale des communautés religieuses en France* (Paris, 1869), p. 187.
[31] Ollivier was perhaps lucky to have C. A. Delangle (1797–1869)—a high magistrate in Paris and *procureur général* to the royal court of Paris at the end of the July Monarchy (1847–48)— preside over the case. As president of the municipal commission in Paris in 1856, he demonstrated himself to be hostile to congregations. See Maurain, *La politique ecclésiastique du Second Empire*, p. 215 n. 2.

seductions of the cloister [that are] so powerful in the midst of solitude."[32] How different this was from the case that de Guerry herself made before the pope. She had argued in terms of her individual rights and volition: "I will never consent to having my fortune and that of my family serve to sustain an endeavor different from that which I have chosen."[33]

Counsel for the community of Picpus, and by extension the Church, used contract theory and the principle of associational rights to make their case. As a result, both sides ignored or rejected appeals to the individual property rights of women religious in order to defend the family (in Ollivier's case) and protect the Church and its authority (in the case of the counsel of Picpus). De Guerry clearly asserted her rights as an individual under Napoleonic law, and the fact that she was a nun led to lively commentary. The counsel for Bishop Bonamie declared that the case undermined the Church by creating a scandal and "revealing to the world that there are also sorry secrets and odious passions" in convents.[34] Although Berryer argued that "this is the first time that such a claim has been raised by a nun against the congregation to which she belonged,"[35] the nineteenth century witnessed a number of instances of serious conflict between fiercely independent, strong-willed nuns or mother superiors and priests or bishops over questions of autonomy and authority. While many were not as highly publicized as the conflict between de Guerry and the Bishop Bonamie, these cases revealed the degree to which many women religious could defy their families, the state, the male hierarchy within the Catholic Church, as well as Rome.[36]

One of the earliest and most striking of such instances occurred in 1809. It has become a file available in the National Archives in Paris, entitled "Filles de la Charité résistantes et insoumises." The case involved a "revolt" among the Filles de la Charité following the replacement, under murky circumstances, of a popular mother superior by another nun, in flagrant violation of the rule and constitution of the order. In the midst of the Napoleonic wars, many of the Filles de la Charité, who staffed military hospitals throughout France, refused to recognize the authority of the new superior. By 1811, 274 of the congregation's 1,653 members were still in active rebellion against her. In this case, an exasperated Emperor

[32] *Affaire de Madame de Guerry: Mémoire à consulter*, p. 67.
[33] Ibid., p. 8.
[34] "Plaidoirie de M. Dufaure," in Sabatier, *Affaire de Madame de Guerry*, p. 147.
[35] Ibid., p. 120.
[36] See Turin, *Femmes et religieuses au XIXème siècle*, pp. 97–103, 125, for other instances of this kind.

Napoleon, who viewed this alleged disobedience as a threat to public order, wrote from St.-Cloud, "This scandal must end at once and the 22 houses [in which the rebellious nuns resided] must be closed."[37] The state's need for their obedient service in the midst of war largely determined the state's treatment of the incident.

There were many cases of this kind in subsequent years, which revealed the extent to which there were fissures within the Catholic Church, dividing a male clerical hierarchy and female religious congregations. The prefect of the Gironde, for example, reported to the minister of religious affairs in 1854 that the archbishop of Bordeaux had ordered the creation of an ecclesiastical commission on the 17th of November 1854 to begin an inquiry into the condition of the Sisters of Notre Dame of Bordeaux. For several years the archbishop and the superior had been locked in a battle over her refusal to ban the seclusion of nuns (*clôture*) in the community, as he wished to do. When the members of the commission arrived on the eighteenth, she refused to convoke the nuns and asked for an adjournment. In December the archbishop ordered that madame de Meilhac, the superior, be deposed, and appointed a provisional superior in her place. Instead of submitting to his decision, the nuns, led by de Meilhac, left the convent at Christmas with the effects of the community and moved to another house in Bordeaux. When asked to comply with the archbishop's decision, all but one nun continued, according to the prefect, their "revolt against diocesan authority." Moreover, madame de Meilhac announced before thirty people that she would appeal to the Sovereign Pontiff.[38] She continued to refuse to abandon her title as superior because she did not recognize the authority of the archbishop of Bordeaux to revoke it, but she relented by allowing the nuns to return to their former premises, and she urged them to recognize the authority of the provisional superior named by the archbishop.

In madame de Meilhac's case the state stepped in on the side of the archbishop. The departmental commission of the Gironde informed her that the boarding school (of forty-seven pupils) that she ran was not authorized and that the children had to be returned to their parents. She was also accused of financial improprieties. The *procureur impérial* of Bordeaux was ready to act against the recalcitrant nuns because they were in violation of article 291 of the penal code by behaving as an unauthorized society and teaching without diplomas. The state and judicial authorities were clearly unsympathetic to the plight of madame de Meilhac, and the

[37] 5 April 1812, AN F¹⁹6319.
[38] AN F¹⁹6313.

minister of religious affairs wrote to the archbishop that "the government will take all the necessary measures to have your authority respected" and enclosed a letter that he had sent to the prefect regarding "this deplorable affair."[39]

In contrast, madame de Guerry won her case, but it was far from over. Even though she got her money, left Picpus, and started a school with the other "renegade" nuns, she continued to be harassed by the archbishop of Paris who attempted to have the school she was running closed down by the prefect of police as late as 1862.[40]

FRANCE'S MORTARA AFFAIR

The growth in the number of cases involving the Church during the Second Empire galvanized the public's fears and provided grist for the anticlerical republican mill, but it also contributed to a shift in Bonapartist ecclesiastical policy toward religious orders and to their greater regulation by the state. This general reexamination of policy coincided with a changing of the guard in the Ministry of Education and Religious Affairs in 1856.

On 7 July 1856, H. N. H. Fortoul, who had been minister since the creation of the empire in 1852, died. Initially the emperor's choice, Paul Séverin Abbatucci, a Corsican hostile to legitimists and clericals alike, was chosen for the post. He turned down the powerful position on the grounds of his age and suggested an alternative in the figure of the *procureur général* of the court of appeals in Paris, Gustave Rouland.[41] In many respects the appointment of Rouland reflected a certain distancing from the clerical camp. Rouland was largely responsible for recasting imperial ecclesiastical policy before the deterioration of the relations between the Second Empire and the Vatican over French policy toward Italian unification. The Italian question merely crystallized and further justified initiatives assumed by Rouland as early as 1858. While Rouland was a practicing Catholic, he was an avowed Gallican, unlike his predecessor, and he set out to strengthen the authority of the state in religious affairs. Fe-

---

[39] Letter, n.d. AN F[19]6313; *Mémoire pour Madame de Meilhac, ancienne supérieure de la communauté de Notre Dame de Bordeaux, défendresse contre le sieur Guibert, cessionnaire de M. l'abbé Cassaigne, demandeur, en présence de M. Larré, avoué, nommé administrateur provisoire de la communauté de Notre Dame de Bordeaux, aussi défendeur* (Bordeaux, 1855).

[40] Letter to the Minister of Religious Affairs, 30 August 1862, AN F[19]6322.

[41] Rouland was born in 1806 and pursued a distinguished legal career. He was a Bonapartist and served as *procureur général* in a number of different courts. See Gustave Vapereau, *Dictionnaire universel des contemporaines* (Paris, 1880).

male religious orders were his battleground, and he became involved in a
number of publicized cases involving proselytism. He issued a circular to
all departments on 1 December 1861 on proselytism and the corruption
of minors in which he wrote that "I regret to state that in many circumstances religious communities ignore or neglect to apply the dispositions
of the law concerning the admission of minors into their establishments.
They seem to believe that their responsibility is sufficiently covered by
their pious motives or by the authorization of ecclesiastical superiors, and
they do not take into account enough the sentiment and the authority of
families."[42] He asserted that French legislation, "the wise and faithful expression of the ideas and principles of our time, has sovereignly constituted the rights of the family, and has required them to be respected by
all."[43] He instructed prefects to make it known to congregations that no
minor could be admitted into their establishments without the formal
consent of parents or guardians, or the congregations would be the subject of formal judicial prosecution. Indeed, a year later, Rouland encouraged the prosecution of the Redemptorists of Douai for encouraging a
minor to enter an establishment of the Clarisses without parental consent. This incident, which became, in the words of the *Courrier de Pas-de-
Calais*, a "petit drame claustral," was a lightning rod for Rouland's rather
stiff response to the nuns, as he also launched into a bitter invective
against the bishop of Arras in the Nord.[44] Rouland's letter to the bishop,
which was subsequently published in the *Moniteur Universel*, ended by his
asserting that "it is necessary, in order to insure the stability of families,
to repel, in the name of our national law, the exaggerated pretensions of
religious proselytism."[45]

As if these cases, which harked back to the period of the Restoration,
were not enough, the state received a number of complaints regarding
the forced conversion and/or incarceration of both Jewish and Protestant
children in a variety of religious establishments. These cases coincided
with the international sensation that was created by what seemed to be the
forced conversion of Edgardo Mortara, a six-year-old Jewish boy in Italy,
and his removal from his home against his parents' will.[46] France had its
own sensational case. In March of 1861 a Jewish child was baptized by a
priest from the Moselle, with the consent of the bishop, and placed in a

---

[42] AN F^{19}6313.
[43] Ibid.
[44] AN BB^{18}1602 and F^{19}6254.
[45] AN F^{19}6254.
[46] Kertzer, *The Kidnapping of Edgardo Mortara*.

Catholic family while his parents searched for him.[47] Another case involved a Jewish child, Sarah Linnerviel, who was placed with a wet nurse. When the parents stopped paying her fees the wet nurse raised the child as her own. When the wet nurse died in 1859, Sarah's father requested the return of his eighteen-year-old daughter, but the executor of the wet nurse's will, a Catholic, hid her with the Carmelites of Riom and with a pious Catholic woman. Rouland called for an investigation and two individuals were forced to pay damages.[48] Perhaps the international outcry over the Mortara affair heightened public sensitivity to the issue, but it was the prosecution of a fifty-four-year-old canon by the name of Napoléon-Célestin-Joseph Mallet, who was sentenced by the *cour d'assizes* of Douai to six years of confinement with hard labor—the maximum sentence allowed by the law—for *détournement des mineurs* or corruption of minors that galvanized the French public. This was France's Mortara affair.

The Bluth or Mallet affair involved a Catholic canon, several young Jewish women, and charges of *rapt*, and there were also insinuations of sexual impropriety. When the trial opened before the tribunal of the department of the Nord, many saw the case as having more than a point of contact with the Mortara affair. In the words of one commentator, "the department of the Nord believes itself to have its [own] Mortara affair."[49]

The young women involved in the case were daughters of Jacob Bluth, a schoolteacher from Weimar and the son of a rabbi. He and his wife, Sarah Levy, had eight children, six of whom were girls. The affair began when one of his daughters, Anna, went to Paris from Weimar to take up a post as teacher, in 1847. While in Paris, she came into contact with the abbé de Ratisbonne, a Jewish convert to Catholicism who headed the Maison de Notre Dame de Sion, whose main mission was the conversion of Jews. Anna was soon baptized and took the Christian name Marie-Siona. Her sister, Minchen, who was seventeen, followed her to Paris shortly thereafter, was also baptized, and was given the Christian name Gabrielle. In 1848, their father followed them to Paris, stayed in the Maison de Notre Dame de Sion for eight days, and was himself baptized. He ultimately left Germany and brought his other four daughters, who were in turn bap-

[47] AN BB³⁰1626. Also see Maurain, *La politique ecclésiastique du Second Empire*, pp. 575–76; and *Compte rendu du procès des enfants Baquol devant le tribunal civil de Strasbourg et le Cour Imperial de Strasbourg* (Strasbourg, 1858).
[48] AN BB³⁰386 and F¹⁹6253.
[49] *Cour d'Assises du Nord, Affaire du chanoine Mallet, compte-rendu des débats. Exposé de l'affaire. Acte d'accusation. Interrogatoire de l'accusé. Audition des témoins. Plaidoyers et répliques. Condamnation* (Douai, 1861), p. 1.

tized. Anna or Marie-Siona soon became a teacher in Cambrai where she met Canon Mallet. He took it upon himself to bring her brother Adolphe to the city in 1853 and placed him in the Maison des Missions Apostoliques, where he converted to Catholicism three months later.

Jacob Bluth's wife, Sarah, who ultimately followed her husband and daughters to Paris, viewed the conversion of her husband and children with considerable consternation. To guard against the conversion of the last of her children, her young son Isidore, she took him as well as one of her convert daughters, Elisabeth, to England, but Elisabeth was eventually returned to France, as Sarah bent to her husband's will. Husband and wife were finally reunited in Cambrai in 1854, when Sarah moved to that city, allegedly tired of domestic disputes. By this time Adolphe, who had converted to Catholicism, had become a German and English teacher in a Catholic school, and canon Mallet had set Minchen (Gabrielle) up in business by buying her a haberdashery. The Bluths placed their other son, Isidore, in an ecclesiastical college in Valenciennes, though he did not convert to Catholicism, and Elisabeth was taken in by the Bernardines of Cambrai. Two other daughters, Louise, baptized Philomène—indicating the currency of Sainte Philomène's name—and Thérèse, remained in Paris at the Maison de Notre Dame de Sion.

By 1854 a public scandal began to brew when Philomène (Louise) fell ill in Paris and returned to her parents in Cambrai. Canon Mallet told her that she should not stay in the household because her mother was Jewish. Moreover, it became clear to all that Anna Bluth, or Marie-Siona, was living with Mallet and there was public gossip about the nature of their relations. This situation, as well as complaints made by Gabrielle and Louise about the canon's liberal ways with them ("manières trop libres"), made Sarah Bluth leave Cambrai for Paris, where she was soon joined by her husband and Adolphe. The Bluth parents, now reunited, encouraged all of their children to return to the household in 1855. Briefly, Louise did so, but Ratisbonne encouraged her to leave the "maison paternelle" if she heard any word said against the Christian religion. Ultimately she fled, helped by Ratisbonne, and Mallet came to Paris in disguise to take her back to Cambrai. Upon her return to Cambrai, her sister, Marie-Siona, placed her in the convent of Sainte-Union in Douai, with the canon's help, where she was admitted under another name, Marie Delacroix. She stayed until her twenty-first birthday, but refused to become a nun, and left the convent to live in Mallet's household, where he made unwanted sexual advances toward her. As a result, she fled the house, worked for a time in Arras, and stayed in the Maison Notre Dame de Sion in Paris, before returning to her parents two and a half years later. All of their efforts to find her during this time were unsuccessful.

In 1856, Marie-Siona repeated the scenario with Elisabeth. She placed her in a convent in Belgium under the name Henriette LeGrand, and Elisabeth was then moved from convent to convent over a four-year period. Her parents were unable to trace her until she was committed to an asylum in 1860, afflicted by "mental disturbance characterized by religious exaltation." By law, the nuns were forced to inform the public authorities in such cases.[50]

Three of Bluth's daughters disappeared, then, having converted to Catholicism, and were subsequently placed in convents. Two of the daughters, Marie-Siona and Louise, eventually went mad, and the former had not recovered by the time of the trial. What compounded the seriousness of the charge filed against the canon was Mallet's sexual involvement with at least one of the daughters, and the fact that at the time of the trial, a fourth daughter, Sophie, had disappeared and was still missing.[51] It could only be guessed that she was in a convent in France or Belgium. Moreover, while Mallet was on trial, his actions were aided and abetted by dozens of nuns, who had accepted the young girls into their fold and had given them false names in order to prevent their parents from finding them. Rouland declared in a letter to the *procureur* associated with the case, a like-minded spirit whom he named to his post, "the laws of the country have been violated in an unworthy way, and it touches the principle of freedom of thought and the security of families from guilty attempts of a blind proselytism. It is for the guilty to respond to the scandal that they have provoked."[52]

In the wake of many such cases, Rouland set up a commission to study the status of female religious houses. He worried about the number of female religious communities authorized since 1852—their numbers had grown from 71 in 1852 to 137 in 1859. Among the questions the commission was charged to study was whether a further growth in their number might present dangers to the state and counter the interests that they ostensibly served. From 1858 onwards religious congregations could no longer count on a benevolent Ministry of Religious Affairs. One of Rouland's first

[50] Ibid., p. 5.
[51] Ibid., and AN F¹⁹5799 and 5842. It was suggested at the trial that Marie-Siona (Anna) was frequently inebriated, a habit that she acquired as a result of her association with Mallet. Her madness was linked to Mallet having taken her baby—to whom she allegedly gave birth though the baby was never in evidence at the trial—to avoid scandal.
[52] AN F¹⁹5842.

acts was to stop the practice of recommending the authorization of contemplative orders to the Conseil d'Etat. He was intent on checking the growth
and influence of female houses and allowed an increasingly hostile anticlerical press to help him by printing incidents of clerical waywardness. This was
the first step on the long road to laicization, which characterized much of
the period of the early Third Republic.

In 1861 Jules Michelet published another edition of *Du prêtre, de la
femme, de la famille,* and he wrote in the preface that his book had abun-
dant proof of clerical offenses. He thanked the justice system of France
for standing up for public morality, as reflected in hundreds of trials that
revealed the problems associated with clerical celibacy. And commenting
on the trials themselves, he wrote that most of these scandalous trials illu-
minated the political battles between civil authority and the clergy. One of
the most anticlerical of the polemicists of the Second Empire, Charles
Sauvestre, wrote *Les congrégations religieuses dévoilées* in which he asked, "are
there no laws . . . against this communism of celibates?"[53] Ironically, the
uproar over the behavior of those in religious communities provided an
argument against both the civil incapacity of women and for their equality. Sauvestre suggested that the remarkable growth in the number of congregations and in the women who entered them could be attributed to the
lack of professions that were sufficiently well paying for working-class
women: "women can only exceptionally make a living from their labor. In
the grip of misery, exposed to all the snares of vice, they search in the
cloisters, as during the centuries of invasion and barbarism, a refuge from
dishonor and hunger."[54] The convent, according to Sauvestre, offered security and dignity to women with ambition. The remedy, he believed, was
education and civil equality.

While imperial administrators did little to check the repressive weight
of clerical influence in France's universities, as the history of the Paris Faculty of Medicine suggests, the attempt to regulate religious congregations,
and the outcry that alleged abuses within them precipitated, suggest that
male bourgeois Bonapartists and republicans alike came to feel a clear dis-
taste for the power of female religious congregations and the influence of
the Church in the private sphere of the family. It is therefore not surprising that during the final years of the Second Empire the clash of Church
and state centered on the issue of the laicization of women's secondary ed-

---

[53] Charles Sauvestre, *Les congrégations religieuses dévoilées,* 4th ed. (Paris, 1879), p. iii. Charles
Sauvestre was in contact with government officials and on 22 February 1867 sent the minister of justice and religious affairs one of his books "en souvenir du bon accueil que vous avez
bien voulu faire à l'auteur." AN 6254.
[54] Ibid., p. 7.

ucation—before the great laicizing crusade of the early Third Republic. Although Rouland's successor, Victor Duruy, did not formally oppose the clerical party that attacked the Paris Faculty of Medicine for its philosophical materialism in 1868, he did oppose the Catholic Church by investing much of his time and effort in the creation of a secular system of secondary education for women.[55] To this extent the state could be said to have practiced policies of differentiated and gendered anticlericalism during this period.

OUTCOMES

These cases, which stimulated a shift in imperial policy, stirred up the public at large. They came to highlight the arbitrary power of the Catholic Church in civil society, the alleged defenselessness of women in the face of it, and religious difference in the family (the devout wife and the atheist husband), which undermined society as a whole. These views were not confined to a single class or political camp. Throughout the nineteenth century petitions demanded that the legal age of women entering religious congregations without parental consent be raised, and legislatures continued to discuss laws that would limit the amount of property that women could bring to these communities. Many a politician pointed out that stricter requirements governed marriage vows than religious vows and should, therefore, certainly be applied to the latter. In 1856, for example, the comte de Rochemur, whose daughter had entered a religious order without his consent at the age of twenty-four, petitioned the Senate, demanding that the 1825 law governing religious congregations be modified so that women who had reached the age of majority conformed to the same laws as women taking marriage vows. The *rapporteur* of the proposed legislation argued that "one should not overturn the natural order of ideas, to establish the legal presumption in favor of children against their parents!," while Senator Tourangin noted with irony that it was in the name of unlimited liberty that the perpetual loss of liberty (in assuming a religious vow) was demanded.[56]

On 25 March 1860, almost four years after the Senate reviewed Rochemur's petition—and almost forty years after the Loveday affair—the Senate was again asked to consider legislation that called for the limita-

[55] Duruy replaced Rouland as minister of education in 1863. Goldstein, "The Hysteria Diagnosis and the Politics of Anticlericalism," p. 226–28; and Jean Rohr, *Victor Duruy, ministre de Napoleon III: Essai sur la politique de l'instruction publique au temps de l'empire libéral* (Paris, 1967), pp. 165–71.

[56] AN F^196313, Procès verbal, Sénat, 3 April 1856, p. 39.

tion of the property rights of women who entered religious communities. The *rapporteur* of the proposed legislation was Charles Dupin, the brother of André Dupin, Loveday's lawyer in 1821. In the case of the comte de Rochemur and the marquise de Guerry the loftiest aristocratic families in France squared off against the Catholic Church—and the central issue in each case was one of paternal right and of property, respectively. But the power of unregulated female religious orders could affect other elements in society as well, as in the case of a woman by the name of Antoinette Laprete, whose mother required her help in old age. Unregulated religious congregations, particularly those which were unauthorized, and therefore had no formal legal existence, could, by existing on the margins of the law, acquire and hold property and persons at will. Moreover, the control that these orders had over the education of young women at the primary and secondary levels only added to their alleged insidious power.

Complaints by the comte de Rochemur and the marquise de Guerry struck a deep chord in French republicans and Bonapartists alike because they began to see that female religious communities could call family patrimony into question. By 1858 the imperial administration and judicial authorities began to closely monitor cases in which these communities were at issue. Indeed, it was more the threat that the Church posed to the integrity of the family than to the public arena of international political affairs that inspired a newly invigorated anticlericalism. Moreover, the emergence of this form of anticlericalism during this period demonstrates that the seeds of the anticlerical laws of the 1880s were not simply or always planted in reaction to a proclerical Second Empire; many of them were already deep in the soil of the empire itself.

In short, the unfolding of these cases before the advent of the Italian question demonstrates that neither anticlericalism nor the concept of *laïcité* was the exclusive property of a positivist generation of French republicans excluded from political power, or a simple product of the conflict between Gallicanism and Ultramontanism. Nonetheless, in fundamental ways, public and republican reaction to a recognized form of feminized Catholicism contributed to making *laïcité* an essential constituent element and distinguishing feature of male bourgeois political culture in the late nineteenth century, even if *laïcité* was primarily associated with French Republicanism and a motor force behind the anticlerical campaign of the early Third Republic.

Finally, the de Guerry case also ironically revealed the threat that the existence of female religious communities could pose for the male hierarchy within the Catholic Church itself. Cases like hers led both the Church and the state to argue for the limitation of women's property rights, even though the legal and ideological bases of their arguments could not have been more different. While the ambiguities of the law persisted, however, they gave the rapidly rising number of women who entered religious associations during the nineteenth century the ability to challenge the authority of family, Church, and state in ways that would have been unimaginable for their secular counterparts.

Gender, Religion and *Laïcité*

The advent of the Third Republic in 1871, following the demise of the Second Empire and the Franco-Prussian war, brought a new, republican political leadership to France. Much of the succeeding thirty years was taken up by a pitched battle between the Catholic Church and the republic. Gambetta's battle cry, "cléricalisme, voilà l'ennemi," was translated into specific legislation designed to attack the temporal and spiritual power of the Catholic Church.[1]

While much of this legislation was bound up with the politics of the Left and the Right in the late nineteenth century, it also marked the culmination of a century-long debate surrounding the feminization of religion and female religiosity more generally. That debate began in the seventeenth century and was subsequently transformed by the experience of the Revolution. The politics of the Catholic Church and its relationship to each successive regime—First Empire, Bourbon Restoration, July Monarchy, Second Republic, Second Empire, and Third Republic—in a century of turbulent revolution, helped to shape the rhetoric of that conflict. The Gallican-Ultramontane divide, which pitted proponents of a more independent national Church against those who turned to Rome for directives, further complicated the way in which the conflict played out.

---

[1] See Lalouette, *La libre pensée en France*, pp. 282–93; Auspitz, *The Radical Bourgeoisie*, pp. 123–60; and Nord, *The Republican Moment*.

Fueled by the views of the proponents of the Ligue de l'Enseignement, which was founded in the 1860s, republicans began to focus their attention on the status of religious congregations and educational reform. Legislative assaults on the Church came in two waves. The first was launched in 1879 and the second in 1901; the latter, which followed close on the heels of the Dreyfus affair, culminating in the Separation of Church and State in 1905.

Jules Ferry, a prominent republican opponent of the Second Empire, played a leadership role as minister of education in this assault and is intimately associated with the early stages of laicizing France's educational institutions. Shaped by positivism, freemasonry, and liberal republicanism, the educational and secular laws that were put in place were also ones that had the goal of republicanizing the French countryside in order to ensure the stability of the republic. In 1879, Jules Ferry supported a bill that prohibited Catholic schools from issuing degrees, and that contained an article that banned religious orders from teaching in public and private schools. While this article was defeated in the Senate, by 1886 legislation was passed that only allowed Catholic orders to teach in public schools for five more years. A law banning religious instruction in schools became a keystone of the new educational system that was constructed in France. The new republican regime also created a free, compulsory, universal system of education at the primary level.

A second anticlerical campaign followed close on the heels of the Dreyfus affair, which divided the country into two opposing camps and brought a rabidly anticlerical majority to power. It was presided over by the fierce anticlerical Emile Combes, who had once trained for the priesthood before leaving the seminary, and René Waldeck-Rousseau, a lawyer from Nantes. One of the government's concerns was to put the Church, which had appeared to threaten the legitimacy of the Republic during the Dreyfus affair, in check. This was achieved through a Law on Associations, one of the keystones of the early Third Republic's anticlerical campaign. The bill that Waldeck-Rousseau proposed would require all congregations to be authorized by the Conseil d'Etat and to accept the jurisdictional authority of bishops. The bill, in an altered from, became law on 1 July 1901. In many ways the new bill was tougher than the initial formulation in stipulating that all congregations had to seek authorization from parliament, not from a legal court, and that they had three months to do so or they would be dissolved. In addition, no member of an unauthorized religious congregation would be permitted to teach. In the hands of a hostile parliament, the law gave the new government an instrument through which to disband religious orders entirely. Because of the confusion surrounding it, a great many congregations did not seek authorization. Some believed that they were in conformity with the law by having received recognition under previous regimes, and others chose not to seek authorization because they wished to remain independent of diocesan authority. In all, 215 out of 830 congregations did not seek authorization.[2]

After the elections of 1902, which brought Combes to power, a new government was formed and the Law on Associations began to be applied ruthlessly. Only a few orders that were useful to the republic for their missionary activity in the colonies were given authorization, and the government began to embark on an endeavor to close all schools run by unauthorized religious houses. As the majority of congregations in France were female, they were most affected by the measures. By October of 1903 more than ten thousand schools run by congregations were closed, and nuns were forcibly expelled from them.[3]

Chapters in this book have examined the constituent elements of both a pro-Catholic, and more especially, anti-Catholic rhetoric regarding the relationship between the Catholic Church and civil society that came to inform many of the debates that led to these outcomes. During the French Revolution religion became associated with the sphere of the feminine as the Catholic Church came increasingly to be linked to the forces of counterrevolution. The figure of the "femme fanatique" emerged as the defender of tradition, the monarchy, and the Old Regime even before the First Republic was established in 1792. The bitter anticlerical sentiment that surfaced during this period, and the war waged against the Catholic Church, had lasting consequences for the relationship between Church and state, men and women, and civil society at large. Napoleon I, in claiming to complete the Revolution on the principles with which it began, wished to stand by the religious legislation passed during the 1790s. That legislation disbanded all religious orders and congregations, but many of the orders and congregations that had sprung up under the Directory and in the Napoleonic years were gradually given legal recognition for pragmatic reasons. The state, which had no established system of education or medical care, could well use their services. Nonetheless, the concerns raised by religious divisions and the religious divide between men and women that had surfaced during the French Revolution did continue to shape public debates about the role of religion in the family and civil society. This became evident in the early years of the Restoration, at the

[2] Adrien Dansette, *Histoire religieuse de la France contemporaine* (Paris, 1965), p. 571.
[3] See Nicholas Atkin, "The Politics of Legality: The Religious Orders in France, 1901–45," in Tallett and Atkin, *Religion, Society and Politics in France since 1789*, pp. 149–65.

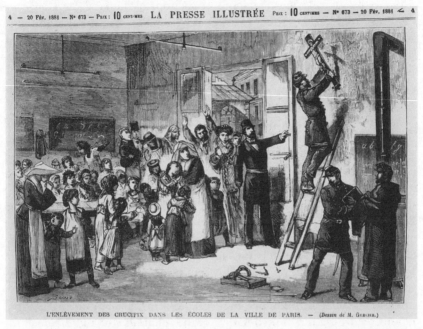

4 — 20 Fév. 1881 — N° 673 — Prix: 10 centimes LA PRESSE ILLUSTRÉE Prix: 10 centimes — N° 673 — 20 Fév. 1881 — 4

L'ENLÈVEMENT DES CRUCIFIX DANS LES ÉCOLES DE LA VILLE DE PARIS. — *(Dessin de M. Gerlier.)*

FIGURE 7. "The Removal of Crucifixes from Schools in Paris," from *La Presse Illustrée,* 20 February 1881. Engraving by Gerlier, private collection. Courtesy of Bridgeman Art Library, U.K.

height of the great missions that were established to rechristianize society after the "godless" Revolution of 1789. Anticlerical rioters who took to the streets during this period accused the clergy, and particularly the Jesuits, of undermining the family, and even went so far as to accuse them of crimes of rape, incest, false testimony, and bestiality.[4] However, it was the sway that priests had over women that generated some of the most emotional invective, particularly against Jesuits. The Loveday case of 1821 was one of the most highly contested examples of these concerns because of the attention that it received in the Chamber of Peers and in the press, but the charge of spiritual seduction was rife throughout the country during this period, and continued to occupy the public's attention until the Third Republic. Many of these complaints did not reach the courts, but traces remain in the form of petitions in the governmental archives. The anticlerical Restoration newspaper *Le Constitutionnel* and the *Gazette des Tribunaux,* a newly created newspaper devoted to legal affairs, both moni-

[4] Kroen, *Politics and Theater,* p. 206.

tored cases of *captation* (religious seduction). What the Loveday case demonstrated was the extent to which religious divisions in the family, and indeed religious conversion to Catholicism, could strike at the heart of the principle of paternal authority and public order enshrined in postrevolutionary law. While the rights of women were sharply limited in Napoleonic law, the religious domain opened a loophole, which legislators never fully resolved until female religious congregations and orders began to be dismantled during the Third Republic. The case also revealed the ironic consequences of the affair as right-wing legitimists argued for Emily Loveday's individual rights and liberals argued for the principle of paternal authority.

The language used in discussions of *captation* and seduction played an important role in creating the social imagery of religious conflict and French anticlericalism more generally. This was reflected in the theme of claustration, which ran through a number of literary texts of the period, as well as through many debates about the legitimacy of religious orders in France. Indeed, it emerged very powerfully in the great parliamentary debates of 1824–25, which centered on the general legislation and guidelines for the authorization of female religious orders in France. The stipulations regarding the limited nature of the religious vow and the need for parental consent were at the heart of those guidelines, as were dispositions regarding property.

If, however, the close association of women with Catholicism helped to fuel the virulent anticlericalism that characterized much of the nineteenth century, the way in which the legal status of congregations came to be defined in light of this sentiment had tremendous consequences for women religious. In the case of the marquise de Guerry, the lack of clarity in French law regarding the property rights of women religious afforded her perhaps more freedom to dispose of her person and property than might otherwise have been possible in civil society. Her defiance of Church authority, while not necessarily representative of most nuns in France, suggests that French women religious were not the pawns of a masculine ecclesiastical hierarchy, as the anticlerical rhetoric of the century argued, and that the hierarchy was itself deeply divided. To make a claim for some sort of "féminisme en religion," however, would be misplaced. As Ruth Harris has argued, this was a "largely secular creed associated with the emancipation of women."[5] While feminism, and particularly drives for the political emancipation of women, were relatively weak in France, ironically many women religious—Emily Loveday, Françoise Le

[5] Harris, *Lourdes*, p. 361.

Monnier, and the marquise de Guerry, to name only a few—did use a postrevolutionary language of individual rights rather than religious arguments to press their claims for freedom of conscience, freedom of movement, and freedom to dispose of their property.[6] "Familialism" was central to French political culture in the nineteenth and twentieth centuries, but it is striking that the language of individual rights had permeated the dark recesses of the cloister.

The secular culture of republicanism that emerged in France during the course of the nineteenth century was guided by the belief that "he who holds woman holds all." In addition to Jules Michelet, two generations of politicians, jurists, and writers had commented on the religious divide between men and women. Free government came to be seen as reliant on the support of women. Edgar Quinet wrote that "men make laws," but "women shall make the mores."[7]

Female religious congregations and female religiosity posed a similar threat to the state and the family in the nineteenth century, though, ironically, this threat was used as an argument both for denying women political rights and for arguing in favor of their political and civil emancipation. In 1907, Georges Clemenceau, Radical prime minister of the Third Republic, published a pamphlet in which he argued that "if the right to vote were given to women tomorrow, France would all of a sudden jump backwards to the Middle Ages."[8] This argument persisted among many French men until French women finally received the vote after the Second World War. It proved to be more persuasive than its alternative, which linked women's involvement with religion and the resulting divisions within the family and in society to their very lack of civil equality and political rights. This sentiment was voiced by the time of the early Third Republic by Ernest Legouvé in his *Moral History of Women*: "Convents have always been regarded as prisons for women, and no institution has been more accused of unhappiness and inspiring legitimate cries of revolt; nevertheless women have never been free except within their walls, for only there have they been free to show what they are capable of." He added that "whoever would rightly estimate women should read the histories of the great religious institutions," where one found them managing prop-

---

[6] See Hause and Kenny, *Women's Suffrage and Social Politics in the French Third Republic;* and Karen Offen, "Depopulation, Nationalism, and Feminism in the Fin-de-Siècle," *American Historical Review* 89 (1984):648–76, for a discussion of the nature of the women's movement in France.

[7] Quoted in Auspitz, *The Radical Bourgeoisie*, p. 39.

[8] Clemenceau, *La "justice" du sexe fort* (Paris, 1907). Cited in McMillan, "Religion and Gender in Modern France," p. 56.

erty, running communities, establishing rules, going on journeys, carrying on lawsuits, and drawing up wills.[9] Legouvé argued that "to re-attach women to France, it is necessary to create not only rights for them, but duties as well."[10] The emancipation of women, for him, would lead to the "perfection of the family," and, by implication, to the perfection of the state and civil society.[11]

To a large extent, the campaign waged against the perceived stranglehold that the Catholic Church held on women and education during the early Third Republic was successful. The removal of religious personnel from state schools subsequently made religious recruitment difficult. The laicization of the teaching and nursing professions opened up new opportunities for women that had not existed previously, and many women chose to pursue them.[12] By 1914 the century that belonged to a particular form of feminized Catholicism was over. The beginning of the twentieth century also heralded a religious revival among men, the appearance of new Catholic women's organizations, and new discussions concerning women, religion, and sexuality.[13] This does not mean that women ceased to be central to Catholic life, and that they were not therefore still suspect to many republicans, socialists, and communists. The specter of the religious divide and divided houses continued to haunt the public sphere in France, but houses were no longer divided in quite the same way.

The secular culture of republicanism, which was intimately linked to the religious culture of Catholicism in the nineteenth century, survived into the twentieth century. This was observable as late as 1989, the year of the bicentennial of the French Revolution, when the expulsion of three young Muslim girls from a school set off a debate that touched a number of chords relating to the question of women's agency; the status of Islam in France; the assimilation of immigrants, particularly those from former colonies in North Africa; the problem of *insecurité* (the fear of urban crime); and the issue of French national identity itself. One historian has

---

[9] Ernest Legouvé, *The Moral History of Women*, trans. J. W. Palmer (New York, 1860), pp. 328–29.

[10] Ibid., p. 334.

[11] Ibid., p. 342.

[12] Katrin Schultheiss, *Bodies and Souls: Politics and the Professionalization of Nursing in France, 1880–1922* (Cambridge, Mass., 2001).

[13] The decade prior to the First World War witnessed a religious revival among men, particularly in intellectual circles, which is documented by Roger Martin du Gard in his novel *Jean Barois*. New converts included Charles Péguy, Léon Bloy, Paul Claudel, and Joris-Karl Huysmans. See Agathon, *Les jeunes gens aujourd'hui* (Paris, 1913). Also see Annette Becker, *War and Faith: The Religious Imagination in France, 1914–1930*, trans. Helen McPhail (New York, 1998); and Martine Sevegrand, *Les enfants du bon Dieu: Les catholiques français et la procréation au XXe siècle* (Paris, 1995).

argued, comparing controversies over the wearing of Islamic headscarves in French classrooms and the existence of Catholic crucifixes in Bavarian ones in the 1990s, that the debates over religious symbols are symptoms of crises of national identity and sovereignty in contemporary European states.[14] Others regard the French debate as a symptom of France's inability to come to terms with its colonial past.[15] While the furor created by the wearing of scarves, veils, chadors or *hijabs* is not unique to France, nowhere in Europe has it been more intense and more divisive.[16] Issues of sovereignty, colonialism, immigration, fear of Islamic fundamentalism, and the rise in anti-Semitic violence in France are all important to understanding the specific late twentieth-century context of the controversy over headscarves, but it is nonetheless significant that the principle of *laïcité* and the religious or cultural behavior of girls are at issue. In many respects, the distinctive nature of the debate over the wearing of headscarves by Muslims is also linked to the way in which *laïcité* came to be articulated in the Republic's struggle with another religion, Catholicism, and with a feminized Catholic Church in the century following the French Revolution. It is significant that the term *foulard* (scarf) is used interchangeably with *voile* (veil), which harks back to the religious veils worn by Catholic women in the nineteenth century. While the incident of the expulsion of the three girls involved the Muslim religion and issues surrounding immigration, the rhetoric of the debate recalls that of the nineteenth and early twentieth centuries when the religious bifurcation between men and women had left France so deeply divided.[17]

As Françoise Gaspard and Farhad Khosrokhavar have argued, the wearing of the "veil" had several meanings that struck a chord with the French public.[18] Crucifixes and religious symbols had long ago been removed from classrooms. The wearing of any religious insignia was an affront to the principle of *laïcité* enshrined in the Republic's schools since the 1880s.

---

[14] Leora Auslander, "Bavarian Crucifixes and French Headscarves: Religious Signs and the Postmodern European State," *Cultural Dynamics* 12 (3), 2000: 283–309.

[15] Jocelyne Cesari, "The Re-Islamicization of Muslim Immigration in Europe," in *Islam, Modernism and the West: Cultural and Political Relations at the End of the Millennium*, ed. Gema Martin Munoz (London, 1999), p. 219.

[16] There are echoes of this debate in Turkey. Nilufer Göle, *The Forbidden Modern: Veiling and Civilization* (Ann Arbor, 1996). The city of Berlin has, moreover, recently banned the wearing of visible religious insignia in the public sector. "A Berlin, les signes religieux interdits dans la fonction publique," *Le Monde*, 3 April 2004.

[17] Beriss, "Scarves, Schools and Segregation"; and Gaspard and Khosrokhavar, *Le foulard et la république*.

[18] Also see Göle, *The Forbidden Modern*, for a discussion of the way in which so-called "veiling" by the young in present day Turkey, which really consists of the wearing of headscarves by, in many cases, educated and upwardly mobile women, has galvanized politicians and the Turkish public in ways that are similar to France.

The "veil" has also become a cultural symbol of immigrant France, and a refusal to accept the notion of cultural unity that was embodied in republican universalism as it came to be defined in the century following the French Revolution. The fact that the "veils" were being worn by young women conjured up, among other things, the image of feminine oppression that Catholicism had once represented in the nineteenth century. This challenged the very basis of republican democracy.[19] For some, a supposed pluralism. or *le droit à la différence*, would lead to American style ghettoization and further inequality, to a kind of "affirmative exclusion."[20] Alain Finkielkraut, Elisabeth Badinter, and Régis Debray wrote in a letter to the French magazine *Le Nouvel Observateur* that in allowing a young woman to wear a Muslim headscarf, Education Minister Lionel Jospin would be saying that the emancipatory space of the school could be violated.[21] The wearing of scarves was thus viewed as a divisive force that undermined French national identity and the Republic itself. As David Beriss has argued, the wearing of scarves represented a kind of capitulation to "Islam, *a fortiori* to fundamentalist Islam, and second to those who would subjugate women."[22]

The matter of the wearing of "veils," which seemed to subsume all other debates for months in 1989, was finally resolved by the Conseil d'Etat, which ordered that the wearing of religious symbols in school was legal, if it did not impinge on the religious freedom of others, and if these symbols were not worn in a provocative or proselytizing way. This judgment did not entirely dispose of the matter, however. In recent years the debate has been reignited, even as the number of disputes arising in schools fell since Hanifa Chérifi was appointed mediator of national education in 1994. The climate in France also changed after the events of 11 September 2001, and new incidents have brought the matter to the attention of the public once more. For example, Dallila Tahri, a young woman who worked for a telemarketing firm, lost her position for wearing a headscarf, only to be reinstated in December of 2002. In July of 2003, Nadjet Ben Abdullah, who worked in the public service sector, was suspended for fifteen days for wearing a scarf, and her case was brought before the ad-

[19] Gaspard and Khosrokhavar, *Le foulard et la république*, pp. 34–69.
[20] Jean-Pierre Chevènement, minister of defense in 1989, stated that "those who, for fifteen years, have wished to sell the 'right to difference' boast the charms of the 'American model.' But it is not the United States that they prepare us for—supposing that that is desirable—it is quite simply Lebanon." Quoted in Beriss, "Scarves, Schools and Segregation," p. 8 (my translation). Also See Jean-Loup Amselle, *Affirmative Exclusion: Cultural Pluralism and the Rule of Custom in France*, trans. Jane Marie Todd (Ithaca, N.Y., 2003).
[21] Beriss, "Scarves, Schools and Segregation," p. 7.
[22] Ibid., p. 5.

ministrative tribunal in Lyon.[23] President Jacques Chirac finally created a "mission d'information sur la question des signes religieux à l'école" in the summer of 2003. The result was four proposals designed to ban headscarves. Many school officials, who had argued that expelling girls from school for wearing headscarves would only lead to further isolation and to "particularism," stepped back from this position. And some saw a crisis looming in the ranks of the French Left, with certain of its representatives expressing the belief that they had gone too far in defending "le droit à la différence." While in 1989, the head of the antiracist organization SOS-Racisme, Harlem Désir, defended the rights of the three young girls who wore their headscarves to school, now the organization has come out against it. Figures such as Jack Lang, former Socialist minister of education, and the popular philosopher Bernard-Henri Lévy, author of the blatantly Islamophobic *Who Killed Daniel Pearl?* have declared themselves to have been naïve on the matter.[24]

One of the arguments in favor of setting up the commission to study such questions was that this was fitting and necessary in that France would soon celebrate the centenary of the 1905 legislation on the Separation of Church and State. In establishing the commission, Jacques Chirac saw its work as one which would give French people a more concrete sense regarding the exigencies of the principle of *laïcité*, which consisted of "the neutrality of public service, respect for pluralism, religious liberty, and liberty of expression, but also the reinforcement of cohesion and fraternity among citizens, equal opportunity, the rejection of discrimination, equality between the sexes, and the dignity of women."[25] The commission consisted of a broad cross-section of France's academic and administrative elites including the prominent academic figures Jean Baubérot, of the Centre National de Recherche Scientifique, a specialist on Protestantism in France; Patrick Weil, who had drafted legislation regarding immigration under the Socialist government that preceded France's current government; and Gilles Kepel, author of *Banlieues de l'islam.*[26] The positions

[23] "Le foulard de la discorde," *Le Monde: Les clés de l'info,* July–August 2003, p. 2.
[24] Ibid.
[25] Commission de Réflexion sur l'Application du Principe de Laïcité dans la République, *Rapport au Président de la République, remis le 11 décembre 2003.*
[26] The other members were Mohammed Arkoun, emeritus professor of the history of Islamic thought at the Sorbonne; Hanifa Cherifi, mediator for the Ministry of Education; Jacqueline Costa-Lascoux, director of research at the CNRS and former president of the Ligue de l'Enseignement; Régis Debray, philosopher and professor; Michel Delebarre, Socialist deputy mayor from the Nord; Nicole Guedj, lawyer; Ghislaine Hudson, principal of a lycée; Marceau Long, honorary vice president of the Conseil d'Etat; Nelly Olin, senator and mayor; Henri Pena-Ruiz, philosopher and author of books on *laïcité*; Gaye Petek, a specialist on the integration of Turks; Maurice Quenet, *recteur* of the Academy; René Rémond, profes-

taken mirrored those assumed early in the wake of the debacle during the 1989 debate, with perhaps more noise made about the way in which girls were oppressed by mullahs or their male relatives and forced into wearing the "veil." Interviews took place, and ultimately the thrust of the commission's report centered on the role of the school as an avenue of social and cultural assimilation. In essence, what became clear was that through the scarf, the state was trying to address all kinds of other issues such as crime and other problems in North African neighborhoods, social inequality, terrorism, anti-Semitism, and the threat of fundamentalism. The report presented by Bernard Stasi, who had been named to the council of ministers in 1998, to Jacques Chirac advised that "the principle of *laïcité*, fundamental to national unity, be recognized and respected by all those who live on our territory."[27] What were the recommendations presented to the president of the republic on 11 December 2003? First, all "conspicuous" religious symbols should be banned from public schools—scarves, yarmulkes, crucifixes, Muslim crescents—and then a hair-splitting discussion ensued about what was "conspicuous" or not, or to use the French terminology, what was "visible," "ostensible," or "ostentatoire." Crucifixes had been removed from school walls in the 1880s, so discussions now centered on measuring the size of crosses worn around the neck. Most recently, the discussion of the ban has had new twists, with a former minister of education, Luc Ferry, suggesting that even beards or facial hair, if they are deemed to be an expression of religion, should be banned. The commission also recommended—inspired, in this case, by Patrick Weil—that as a concession, the state create two new holidays—one Jewish and one Muslim—and the commission made further proposals regarding dietary restrictions in school cafeteria. Chirac ultimately accepted the first recommendation but not the rest. The National Assembly and Senate voted into law the ban on dress and ostentatious insignia of a religious nature in public schools, which took effect in the fall of 2004.[28]

In the meantime, France's first Muslim high school opened its doors in the town of Lille in northern France in September 2003. The aim of the school is to give Muslims an alternative to state schools. The school, named after the twelfth-century Spanish-Arab philosopher Averroës (Ibn Rushd), consists of no more than three classrooms and an unequipped

---

sor and specialist on the history of religion in France, Raymond Soubie, ex-*conseiller social* for Jacques Chirac; Alain Touraine, sociologist; and Rémy Schwartz, *conseiller d'Etat.*
[27] Commission de Reflexion sur l'Application du Principe de Laïcité dans la République, *Rapport au Président de la République,* p. 1.
[28] Luc Bronner, "François Fillon propose une version clarifiée de sa circulaire sur le voile," *Le Monde,* 3 May 2004, p. 13.

science laboratory on the third floor of the Al-Imane Mosque. Tuition is about eleven hundred dollars per year. On the day of the school's opening, not only did the school's female students wear scarves, but the Lycée Averroès's headmistress, Sylvie Taleb, a French-born convert to Islam and an expert on the French author Gustave Flaubert, wore one of her own.[29] Amar Lasfar, the director of the mosque that houses the school, said that the Lycée Averroès is a "general education high school, except that it exists in a Muslim culture and with a Muslim sensibility," calling the school's opening "a great day for secularism" and "a great day for Islam in France."[30] At the same time, Jean Baubérot, a member of Chirac's commission, has noted that when he travels abroad, he is asked why there is a "scarf affair" at all, and why such a fuss is made over it. In France, on the other hand, he is asked whether he is for or against women wearing headscarves.[31] The difference in perspective is significant in revealing the extent to which the anxieties engendered by alleged attacks on *laïcité* in France reflect a longer and still unfinished debate about the meaning of female religiosity and the relationship between women and religion in a modern secular society. It must be acknowledged, however, that the debate over the *foulard* is complicated by the legacy of colonialism. For many in France today, expressions of cultural and religious difference like the wearing of a headscarf by Muslim women threaten to destroy not only the core of the Republic but the heart of the nation itself. The wearing of such "symbols" appears, for many in metropolitan France, to be "part of an intimidation strategy," even a provocation against the republic. And the state, in the view of one prominent contemporary writer, should continue to intervene forcefully, without showing any compromise, tolerance, or compassion.[32]

---

[29] Elaine Sciolino, "Muslim Lycée Opens in Secular France, Raising Eyebrows," *New York Times*, 9 September 2003. Germany embarked on its own debate when a high court ruled on 24 September 2003 that a Muslim teacher could not be barred from wearing a headscarf in a public school. The teacher in question, the daughter of an Afghan diplomat, said that she had no plans to indoctrinate her students. Mark Landler, "A German Court Accepts Teacher's Head Scarf," *New York Times*, 25 September 2003.
[30] Quoted in Sciolino, "Muslim Lycée Opens in Secular France."
[31] Jean Baubérot, "Nous ne voilons pas les yeux," *Libération*, 4 July 2003, p. 5.
[32] "Il faut légiférer. L'argument de l'effet pervers constitue l'argument réactionnaire par excellence, c'est à dire celui qui autorise à ne rien faire. Aujourd'hui, il ne s'agit plus seulement de droits de l'homme ou de morale, mais de politique. Le port du foulard fait partie d'une stratégie d'intimidation face à laquelle l'Etat doit intervenir de façon non irénique." Interview with Pierre-André Taguieff by Renaud Dely, "L'evènement," *Libération*, 14 July 2003, p. 4.

SELECTED BIBLIOGRAPHY

ARCHIVAL SOURCES

Archives Nationales, Paris

Series BB^{30} (Justice)
BB^{30}194 Religious affairs
BB^{30}386 Reports of procureurs généraux, Rennes, Riom
BB^{30}436 Religious affairs

Series F^{19} (Religious Affairs)
F^{19}5799, 5842 Mallet affair
F^{19}6253 Second Empire, Dupin report to the Senate
F^{19}6254 Congregations of the Nord (1856–65)
F^{19}6310 Female religious congregations—laws, reports, observations
F^{19}6311 Female religious congregations—general documents
F^{19}6312 Female religious congregations—Conseil d'Etat, reports, jurisprudence
F^{19}6313 Female religious congregations—authorization requests, statutes, parental
   complaints, *détournements des mineurs*
F^{19}6314 Female religious congregations—judicial matters
F^{19}6315–6328 Female religious congregations—alphabetical classification
F^{19}6427 Diverse religious associations

NEWSPAPERS

Le Constitutionnel
La Gazette de France
La Gazette des Tribunaux

Le Journal des débats
Le Siècle

CONTEMPORARY PRINTED WORKS

Affaire de Dame Jeanne-Françoise Le Monnier contre dame Marie Le Caplain, Dame Caroline de St.-Séverin, Dame Reine Jourdain, et Dame Renée-Charlotte Le Chasseur. Caen: Charles Woinez, 1845.

Affaire de Madame de Guerry contre la communauté de Picpus. Paris: Schiller, 1857.

Allies, Thomas William. *Journal in France in 1845 and 1848.* London: Longman, 1849.

Bert, Paul. *Le cléricalisme: Questions d'éducation nationale.* Paris: Armand Colin, 1900.

Billecocq, Jean-Baptiste-Louis-Joseph. *Du clergé de France en 1825.* Paris: Gosselin, 1825.

Le bon sens, ou entretien d'un fermier avec ses enfants, sur miss Emily Loveday par M. Ferdinand S.-L. Paris: Plancher, 1822.

Bressoles, M. G. "De la reconaissance légale des communautés religieuses de femmes et des effets civils qu'elles produisent." *Revue critique de la législation et de jurisprudence* 5 (1854): 332–51.

Calmette, A. *Traité de l'administration temporelle des congrégations et communautés.* Paris: Durand, 1857.

Cayla, J.-M. *Le diable: Sa grandeur et sa décadence.* Paris: Dentu, 1860.

——. *Plus de couvents!* Paris: Dentu, 1861.

——. *Le 89 du clergé.* Paris: Dentu, 1861.

——. *La conspiration cléricale.* Paris: Dentu, 1862.

Chambre de pairs de France: Session de 1824. Séance du mardi 13 juillet 1824. Opinion de M. le Vicomte de Bonald sur le projet de loi relatif aux communautés religieuses de femmes. Paris: Didot ainé, 1824.

Charrier, L.-L. *Commentaire sur la loi des congrégations religieuses des femmes.* Paris: J. L. Chanson, 1825.

Chavlin, E. *De l'état civil des religieux en France.* Paris: Adrien Le Clerc, 1880.

Cour d'Assises du Nord. *Affaire du chanoine Mallet, compte-rendu des débats. Exposé de l'affaire. Acte d'accusation. Interrogatoire d'accusé. Audition des témoins. Plaidoyers et répliques. Condamnation.* Douai: Adam, 1861.

D'Adhémar, Mme. *La jeune et parfaite demoiselle: Manuel de conduite, de morale et de religion offert aux jeunes personnes.* Paris: Maumus, 1836.

D'Agoult, Marie, comtesse. *Mes souvenirs, 1806–1833.* Paris: Calmann Lévy, 1877.

Daminois. Adèle. *Le cloître au XIXe siècle.* Paris: Werdet, 1836.

Denantes, M. E. *Dissertation sur la position que la loi du 24 mai 1825 a fait aux associations religieuses de femmes non autorisées.* Grenoble: Vellot, 1858.

Dulaure, J.-A. *Histoire de la Restauration.* Vol. 3. Paris: Degorce-Cadot, 1870.

Dupanloup, abbé. *Des associations religieuses: Véritable état de la question.* Paris: Lecoffre, 1845.

——. *Femmes savantes et femmes studieuses.* Paris: Charles Douniol, 1867.

——. *La femme chrétienne et française: Dernière réponse à M. Duruy et à ses défenseurs.* Paris: Charles Douniol, 1868.

Dupin, André. *Mémoires de M. Dupin,* vol. 1: *Souvenirs du barreau.* Paris: Plon, 1855.

Fouilland. *Sainte-Philomène ou le triomphe de la virginité: Tragédie en cinq actes*. Lyon: Girard et Josserand, 1852.

Histoire des missionaires dans le Midi de la France: Lettres d'un marin à un hussard. Paris: Plancher, 1819.

Instruction paternelle du docteur D., ministre de la religion anglicane, à Miss Emily Loveday. Translated by Charles-Lazare Laumier. Paris, n.p., 1822.

Jacquier, Charles. *De la condition légale des communautés religieuses en France*. Paris: Boucherel, 1869.

La Harpe, Jean-François de. *Du fanatisme de la langue révolutionnaire ou de la persecution suscitée par les barbares du XVIIIe siècle*. Paris: Chaumerot, 1821.

Lambert. *Les congrégations de femmes en France de 1825 à 1901*. Paris: Henri Jouve, 1905.

Legouvé, Ernest. *The Moral History of Women*. Translated by J. W. Palmer. New York: Rudd and Carleton, 1860.

———. *Les pères et les enfants au XIX siècle*, vol. 2: *La Jeunesse*. Paris: Hetzel, 1866.

Leriche, R. P., Remi. *Picpus et les constitutions de ses fondateurs*. Paris: Carré-Michels, 1856.

Loveday, Douglas. *Pétition à la Chambre des Députés par M. Douglas Loveday, anglais et protestant, se plaignant de rapt de séduction operé sur ses deux filles et sur sa nièce*. Paris: Baudoin, 1821.

———. *Pétition à la Chambre des Pairs par M. Douglas Loveday, anglais et il les avait placées à Paris*. Paris: Baudoin, 1821.

———. *Bittschrift an die Deputierten-Kammer, von Hrn. Douglas Loveday, Engländer und Protestant . . . aus dem französischen*. Strasbourg: H. H. Heitz, 1822.

———. *Pétition ampliative à la Chambre des Députés par M. Douglas Loveday, anglais et protestant, avec les pièces justificatives de son contenu et des observations additionelles*. Paris: Baudoin, 1822.

———. *Pétition à la Chambre des Deputés par M. Douglas Loveday, anglais et protestant, se plaignant de rapt de séduction opéré sur ses deux filles et sur sa nièce*. 2d ed. Paris: Corréard, 1822.

———. *Pétition à la Chambre des Pairs par M. Douglas Loveday, anglais et Protestant, se plaignant de rapt de séduction opéré sur ses deux filles et sur sa nièce*. 2d ed. Paris: Corréard, 1822.

Loveday, Emily. *Réponse de Miss Emily Loveday à la pétition présentée au nom de son père à la Chambre des Pairs*. Paris: Delaunay, 1822.

Mabillon, Jean. *Réflexions sur les prisons des ordres religieux*. Caen: Charles Woinez, 1845.

Martin du Gard, Roger. *Jean Barois*. 2d ed. Paris: Nouvelle Revue Française, 1913.

Mémoire pour Madame de Meilhac, ancienne supérieure de la communauté de Notre Dame de Bordeaux, défendresse contre le sieur Guibert, cessionnaire de M. l'abbé Cassaigne, demandeur, en presence de M. Larré, avoué, nommé administrateur provisoire de la communauté de Notre Dame de Bordeaux, aussi défendeur. Bordeaux: Delmas, 1855.

Michelet, Jules. *Du prêtre, de la femme, de la famille*. Paris: Hachette, 1845.

———. *Du prêtre, de la femme, de la famille*. 7th ed. Paris: Chambérot, 1861.

Michon, J. H. *La femme et la famille dans le catholicisme: Conférences*. Paris: Charles Borrani, 1845.

Morel, abbé Jules. *Souvenirs d'une amie sur la vie de Théodelinde Dubouché: Par une religieuse ursuline.* 2 vols. Paris: Casterman, 1882.

Ollivier, Emile. "Des congrégations religieuses non autorisées: Madame la marquise de Guerry contre la communauté de Picpus," *Revue pratique de droit français: Jurisprudence, droit, législation* 5 (1858): 97–131.

——. *Journal,* vol. 1: *1846–1860.* Paris: Julliard, 1961.

Plaidoyer prononcé par M. Cazeneuve devant le cour royale d'Agen pour Dame Bernarde-Emilie Lecomte, ex religieuse, habitante de Toulouse, contre le sieur Sainte-Colombe, prêtre, son ancien confesseur, habitant de Montrède (Gers), pour rapt de séduction. Toulouse: Dupin, 1844.

Poujoulat, M. *Les associations ou congrégations religieuses: seconde lettre à M. Dupin.* Paris: Charles Douniol, 1860.

Poumiès de la Siboutie, François-Louis. *Souvenirs d'un médecin de Paris.* 3d ed. Paris: Plon, 1910.

Quelques mots clairs et distincts addressés à Mlle Reboul par M. Loveday fils (William Lockyer), protestant éclairé à l'âge de dix-sept ans. Paris: Delauney, 1822.

Ravelet, Armand. *Traité des congrégations religieuses: Commentaire des lois et de la jurisprudence.* Paris: Palme, 1869.

Reboul, Ernestine. *Réponse de Mlle. Reboul aux imputations dirigées contre elle dans une pétition présentée aux deux Chambres par M. Loveday.* Paris: Lamy, 1822.

——. *Nouvelle réponse de Mlle Reboul, provoquée par la pétition ampliative de M. Loveday.* Paris: Lamy, 1822.

Richer, Léon. *Le confesseur de ma femme.* 2d ed. Paris: Gobet Jeune, 1880.

Sauvestre, Charles. *Sur les genoux de l'église.* Paris: Dentu, 1869.

——. *Les congrégations religieuses dévoilées: Enquête par Charles Sauvestre.* 4th ed. Paris: E. Dentu, 1879.

Simon, Jules. *La famille.* Paris: Degorce-Cadot, 1869.

Simon, Jules, and Gustave Simon. *La femme au XIXe siècle.* 13th ed. Paris: Calmann Lévy, 1892.

Soeur Sainte-Marie, Bénédictine. Récits par elle-même. Mémoire, débat judiciaire, comptes rendus et jugement. 2d ed. Caen: Charles Woinez, 1845.

Soeur Sainte-Marie Bénédictine. Récits par elle-même. La procédure. Les enquêtes. La prévue. Orgeuil et placement au B.-S. Caen: B. de Laporte, 1846.

Taxil, Léo. *Les livres secrets des confesseurs dévoilés aux pères de famille.* Paris: Taxil, 1883.

Tillard, Léon. *Réflexions sur les prisons des ordres religieux.* Caen: Charles Woinez, 1845.

Vapereau, Gustave. *Dictionnaire universel des contemporaines.* Paris: Hachette, 1880.

Véron, Dr. Louis Désiré. *Mémoires d'un bourgeois de Paris.* 6 vols. Paris: G. de Gonet, 1853–55.

Voilquin, Suzanne. *Souvenirs d'une fille du peuple ou le Saint-Simonienne en Egypte, 1834–1836.* Paris: Sauzet, 1866.

Vuillefroy, A. *Traité de l'administration du culte catholique: Principes et règles d'administration.* Paris: Joubert, 1842.

SECONDARY WORKS

Agulhon, Maurice. *Marianne into Battle: Republican Imagery and Symbolism in France, 1789–1880.* Translated by Janet Lloyd. Cambridge: Cambridge University Press, 1981.

Albert, Jean-Pierre. *Odeurs de sainteté: La mythologie chrétienne des aromates.* Paris: Editions de l'EHESS, 1990.

——. *Le sang et le ciel: Les saints mystiques dans le monde chrétien.* Paris: Aubier, 1997.

Allen, James Smith. *Popular French Romanticism: Authors, Readers, and Books in the Nineteenth Century.* Syracuse, N.Y.: Syracuse University Press, 1981.

Amselle, Jean-Loup. *Affirmative Exclusion: Cultural Pluralism and the Rule of Custom in France.* Translated by Jane Marie Todd. Ithaca: Cornell University Press, 2003.

Arnold, Odile. *Le corps et l'âme: La vie des religieuses au XIX siècle.* Paris: Seuil, 1984.

Atkin, Nicholas. "The Politics of Legality: The Religious Orders in France, 1901–45." In *Religion, Society and Politics in France since 1789,* ed. Frank Tallett and Nicholas Atkin, pp. 149–65. London: Hambledon, 1991.

Aulard, Alphonse. *La révolution française et les congrégations: Exposé historique et documents.* Paris: Cornély, 1903.

Auslander, Leora. "Bavarian Crucifixes and French Headscarves: Religious Signs and the Postmodern European State." *Cultural Dynamics* 12, no. 3 (2000): 283–309.

Auspitz, Katherine. *The Radical Bourgeoisie: The Ligue de l'Enseignement and the Origins of the Third Republic 1866–1885.* Cambridge: Cambridge University Press, 1982.

Baczko, Bronislaw. *Les imaginaires sociaux: Mémoires et espoirs collectifs.* Paris: Payot, 1984.

Baubérot, Jean. *La morale laïque contre l'ordre moral.* Paris: Seuil, 1997.

Baubérot, Jean, and Valentine Zuber. *Une haine oubliée: L'antiprotestantisme avant le "pacte laïque" (1870–1905).* Paris: Albin Michel, 2000.

Becker, Annette. *War and Faith: The Religious Imagination in France, 1914–1930.* Translated by Helen McPhail. New York: Berg, 1998.

Beebee, Thomas O. *Clarissa on the Continent: Translation and Seduction.* University Park: Pennsylvania State University Press, 1990.

Beriss, David. "Scarves, Schools and Segregation: The Foulard Affair." *French Politics and Society* 8, no. 1 (Winter 1990): 1–13.

Blackbourn, David. *Marpingen: Apparitions of the Virgin Mary in Bismarckian Germany.* Oxford: Oxford University Press, 1993.

Boutry, Philippe. "Un sanctuaire et son saint: Jean-Marie Vianney, curé d'Ars." *Annales, économies, sociétés, civilisations* 36 (1980): 353–79.

Brémond, Henri. *Histoire littéraire du sentiment religieux en France depuis la fin des guerres de religion jusqu'à nos jours.* 11 volumes. Paris, 1916–33.

Brinton, Crane. *French Revolutionary Legislation on Illegitimacy 1789–1804.* Harvard Historical Monographs, vol. 9. Cambridge, Mass.: Harvard University Press, 1936.

Brooks, Peter. *The Melodramatic Imagination: Balzac, Henry James, Melodrama, and the Mode of Excess.* New Haven, Conn.: Yale University Press, 1976.

——. *Reading for the Plot: Design and Intention in Narrative.* New York, 1984.

——. "The Law as Narrative and Rhetoric." In *Law's Stories: Narrative and Rhetoric in the Law*, ed. Peter Brooks and Paul Gewirtz, pp. 14–22. New Haven, Conn.: Yale University Press, 1996.

Brown, Peter. *The Cult of Saints.* Chicago: University of Chicago Press, 1981.

——. *Society and the Holy in Late Antiquity.* Berkeley: University of California Press, 1982.

——. *The Body and Society: Men, Women, and Sexual Renunciation in Early Christianity.* New York: Columbia University Press, 1988.

Buffault, Anne Vincent. *A History of Tears: Sensibility and Sentimentality in France.* London: Macmillan, 1991.

Bynum, Caroline Walker. *Holy Feast and Holy Fast: The Religious Significance of Food to Medieval Women.* Berkeley: University of California Press, 1987.

——. *Fragmentation and Redemption: Essays on Gender and the Human Body in Medieval Religion.* New York: Zone Books, 1992.

Cabanis, José. *Michelet, le prêtre et la femme.* Paris: Gallimard, 1978.

Cameron, Vivian. "Political Exposures: Sexuality and Caricature during the French Revolution." In *Eroticism and the Body Politic*, Ed. Lynn Hunt, pp. 90–107. Baltimore: Johns Hopkins University Press, 1991.

Carroll, Michael P. *The Cult of the Virgin Mary: Psychological Origins.* Princeton, N.J.: Princeton University Press, 1986.

Cesari, Jocelyne. "The Re-Islamicization of Muslim Immigration in Europe." *Islam, Modernism and the West: Cultural and Political Relations at the End of the Millennium*, ed. Gema Martin Munoz, pp. 211–23. London: I. B. Tauris, 1999.

Chadwick, Owen. *The Secularization of the European Mind.* Cambridge: Cambridge University Press, 1975.

Chambers, Ross. *Story and Situation: Narrative Seduction and the Power of Fiction.* Minneapolis: University of Minnesota Press, 1984.

Chesnais, Jean-Claude. *Histoire de la violence en Occident de 1800 à nos jours.* Paris: Laffont, 1982.

Choudhury, Mita. "Despotic Habits: The Critique of Power and Its Abuses in an Eighteenth-Century Convent," *French Historical Studies* 23, no. 1 (Winter 2000): 33–65.

——. *Convents and Nuns in Eighteenth-Century French Politics and Culture.* Ithaca, N.Y.: Cornell University Press, 2004.

Christian, William A., Jr. *Person and God in a Spanish Valley.* Princeton, N.J.: Princeton University Press, 1989.

Corbin, Alain. *The Village of Cannibals: Rage and Murder in France, 1870.* Translated by Arthur Goldhammer. Cambridge, Mass.: Harvard University Press, 1992.

——. *Village Bells: Sound and Meaning in the Nineteenth-Century French Countryside.* Translated by Martin Thom. New York: Columbia University Press, 1998.

Couronne, Bernard. *Petite vie du Père Marie-Joseph Coudrin: Fondateur de la Congrégation des Sacrés-Coeurs.* Paris: Desclée de Brouwer, 1997.

Cubitt, Geoffrey. *The Jesuit Myth: Conspiracy Theory and Politics in Nineteenth-Century France.* Oxford: Clarendon Press, 1993.

Curtis, Sarah. *Educating the Faithful: Religion, Schooling, and Society in Nineteenth-Century France.* DeKalb: Northern Illinois University Press, 2000.

Dansette, Adrien. *Histoire religieuse de la France contemporaine.* 2 vols. Paris, Flammarion, 1948–85.

Darnton, Robert. *The Great Cat Massacre and Other Episodes in French Cultural History.* New York: Vintage, 1985.

David, René, and Henry De Vries. *The French Legal System: An Introduction to the Civil Law System.* Paris: Oceana, 1958.

Davidoff, Lenore, and Catherine Hall. *Family Fortunes: Men and Women of the English Middle Class.* Chicago: University of Chicago Press, 1987.

Davis, Natalie Zemon. *Society and Culture in Early Modern France.* Stanford, Calif.: Stanford University Press, 1975.

De Certeau, Michel. *La possession de Loudun.* Paris: Juilliard, 1970.

Delumeau, Jean, and Daniel Roche. *Histoire des pères et de paternité.* Paris: Larousse, 1990.

Denby, David. *Sentimental Narrative and Social Order in France, 1760–1820.* Cambridge: Cambridge University Press, 1994.

Desan, Suzanne. *Reclaiming the Sacred: Lay Religion and Popular Politics in Revolutionary France.* Ithaca: Cornell University Press, 1990.

——. "The Family as Cultural Battleground: Religion vs. The Republic under the Terror." in *The French Revolution and the Creation of Modern Political Culture,* vol. 4: The Terror, ed. Keith Baker, pp. 177–93. New York: Pergamon, 1994.

Diefendorf, Barbara B. "Give Us Back Our Children: Patriarchal Authority and Parental Consent to Religious Vocations in Early Counter-Reformation France." *Journal of Modern History* 68, no. 2 (June 1996): 265–307.

Donzelot, Jacques. *The Policing of Families.* Translated by Robert Hurley. London: Hutchinson, 1970.

Douglas, Ann. *The Feminization of American Culture.* New York: Knopf, 1977.

Edelman, Nicole. *Voyantes, guérisseuses et visionnaires en France 1785–1914.* Paris: Albin Michel, 1995.

Fayet-Scribe, Sylvie. *Associations féminines et catholicisme, XIXe–XXe siècles.* Paris: Editions Ouvrières, 1990.

Ford, Caroline. *Creating the Nation in Provincial France: Religion and Political Identity in Brittany.* Princeton, N.J.: Princeton University Press, 1993.

——. "Religion and Popular Culture in Modern Europe." *Journal of Modern History* 65 (March 1993): 152–75.

Garaud, Marcel. *Histoire générale du droit privé français (de 1789 à 1804): La révolution et l'égalité civile.* Paris: Sirey, 1953.

Gaspard, Françoise, and Farhad Khosrokhavar. *Le foulard et la République.* Paris: Editions La Découverte, 1995.

Gauchet, Marcel. *La religion dans la démocratie: Parcours de la laïcité.* Paris: Gallimard, 1998.

Gibson, Ralph. *A Social History of French Catholicism, 1789–1914.* London: Routledge, 1989.

——. "Why Republicans and Catholics Couldn't Stand Each Other in the Nineteenth Century." In *Religion, Society and Politics in France since 1789,* ed. Frank Tallett and Nicholas Atkin, pp. 107–20. London: Hambledon Press, 1991.

——. "Le catholicisme et les femmes en France au XIXe siècle." *Revue d'histoire de l'Eglise de France* 49 (1993): 63–93.

Ginzburg, Carlo. "Microhistory: Two or Three Things I Know About It," *Critical Inquiry* 20 (Autumn 1993): 10–35.

Godineau, Dominique. *Citoyennes tricoteuses: Les femmes du peuple à Paris pendant la Révolution française.* Paris: Alinea, 1988.

Goldstein, Jan. "The Hysteria Diagnosis and the Politics of Anticlericalism in Late Nineteenth-Century France." *Journal of Modern History* 54, no. 2 (June 1982): 209–39.

——. *Console and Classify: The French Psychiatric Profession in the Nineteenth Century.* Cambridge: Cambridge University Press, 1987.

Göle, Nilüfer. *The Forbidden Modern: Civilization and Veiling.* Ann Arbor: University of Michigan Press, 1996.

Goncourt, Edmond de, and Jules de Goncourt. *La femme au dix-huitième siècle.* Paris: Flammarion, 1982.

Grimaud, Louis. *Histoire de la liberté d'enseignement en France,* vol. 5: *La Restauration.* Paris: Rousseau, 1956.

Guillemant, Charles. *Pierre-Louis Parisis, l'évêque d'Arras.* Vol. 3. Paris, 1924.

Guitton, Jean. *La conversion de Ratisbonne.* Paris: Wesmael-Charlier, 1964.

Hanley, Sarah. "Social Sites of Political Practice in France: Lawsuits, Civil Rights, and the Separation of Powers in Domestic and State Government, 1500–1800." *American Historical Review* 102 (Fall 1997): 27–52.

Harris, Ruth. *Lourdes: Body and Spirit in the Secular Age.* London: Allen Lane, 1999.

Hartman, Mary. "The Sacrilege Law of 1825 in France: A Study in Anticlericalism and Mythmaking," *Journal of Modern History* 44 (1972): 21–37.

Hause, Steven C., and Anne R. Kenney. *Women's Suffrage and Social Politics in the French Third Republic.* Princeton, N.J.: Princeton University Press, 1984.

Hayden, J. Michael, "States, Estates and Orders: The Qualité of the Female Clergy in Early Modern France" *French History* 8, no. 1 (Spring 1994): 51–76.

Herzog, Dagmar. *Intimacy and Exclusion: Religious Politics in Pre-Revolutionary Baden.* Princeton, N.J.: Princeton University Press, 1996.

Hudson, Nora E. *Ultra-Royalism and the French Revolution.* New York: Octagon, 1973.

Hufton, Olwen. "The Reconstruction of the Church, 1796–1801." In *Beyond the Terror: Essays in French Regional and Social History,* ed. Gwynne Lewis and Colin Lucas, pp. 21–52. Cambridge: Cambridge University Press, 1982.

——. *Women and the Limits of Citizenship in The French Revolution.* Toronto: University of Toronto Press, 1992.

——. *The Prospect before Her: A History of Women in Western Europe 1500–1800.* London: Harper Collins, 1995.

Hufton, Olwen, and Frank Tallett, "Communities of Women, the Religious Life, and Public Service in Eighteenth-Century France." In *Connecting Spheres: Women in the Western World, 1500 to the Present,* ed. Marilyn Boxer and Jean Quaetert, pp. 75–85. Oxford: Oxford University Press, 1987.

Hugo, Victor, *Les misérables.* Vols. 1 and 2. Paris: Editions Rencontres, 1966.

Hunt, Lynn. *The Family Romance of the French Revolution.* Berkeley: University of California Press, 1992.

Jonas, Raymond. *France and the Cult of the Sacred Heart: An Epic Tale for Modern Times.* Berkeley: University of California Press, 2000.

Kelley, Donald R. *Historians and the Law in Postrevolutionary France.* Princeton, N.J.: Princeton University Press, 1984.

Kertzer, David I. *The Kidnapping of Edgardo Mortara.* New York: Knopf, 1997.

Kniebiehler, Yvonne. *Les pères aussi ont une histoire.* Paris: Hachette, 1987.

Kroen, Sheryl. *Politics and Theater: The Crisis of Legitimacy in Restoration France, 1815–1830.* Berkeley: University of California Press, 2000.

Kselman, Thomas. *Miracles and Prophecies in Nineteenth-Century France.* New Brunswick, N.J.: Rutgers University Press, 1983.

Lalouette, Jacqueline, *La libre pensée en France, 1848–1940.* Paris: Albin Michel, 1997.

———. *La république anticléricale, XIXe–XXe siècles.* Paris: Seuil, 2002.

Landes, Joan. *Women and the Public Sphere in the Age of the French Revolution.* Ithaca: Cornell University Press, 1988.

Langlois, Claude. *Le catholicisme au féminin: Les congrégations françaises à supérieure générale au XIX siècle.* Paris: Cerf, 1984.

Le Goff, Jacques, and René Rémond, eds. *Histoire de la France religieuse,* vol. 3: *Du roi très chrétien à la laïcité républicaine.* Paris: Seuil, 1991.

Léonard, Jacques. "Femmes, religion, et médecine: Les religieuses qui soignent en France au XIXe siècle." *Annales, économies, sociétés, civilisations* 32 (1977): 887–907.

Limouzin-Lamothe, Roger. *Mgr. Denys-Auguste Affre, Archévêque de Paris (1793–1848).* Paris: Vrin, 1971.

Mack, Phyllis. *Visionary Women: Ecstatic Prophecy in Seventeenth-Century England.* Berkeley: University of California Press, 1992.

Maître, Jacques. *L'orpheline de la Bérésina: Thérèse de Lisieux (1873–1897).* Paris: Cerf, 1996.

———. *Mystique et fémininité: Essai de psychanalyse sociohistorique.* Paris: Cerf, 1997.

Maurain, Jean. *La politique ecclésiastique du Second Empire de 1852 à 1869.* Paris: Felix Alcan, 1930.

Mayeur, Françoise, and Jacques Gadille, eds. *Education et images de la femme chrétienne en France au début du XXème siècle.* Lyon: Hermès, 1980.

Maza, Sarah. "Le Tribunal de la nation: Les mémoires judiciaires et l'opinion publique à la fin de l'ancien régime." *Annales, économies, sociétés, civilisations* 42 (January 1987): 75–90.

———. *Private Lives and Public Affairs: The Causes Célèbres of Prerevolutionary France.* Berkeley: University of California Press, 1993.

———. "Stories in History: Cultural Narratives in Recent Works in European History." *American Historical Review* 101 (December 1996): 1493–1515.

McCleod, Hugh. "Weibliche Frömmigkeit—männlicher Unglaube?" In *Bürgerrinen und Bürger: Geschlechterverhältnis im 19. Jahrhundert,* ed. Ute Frevert, pp. 134–56. Göttingen, 1988.

McMillan, James F. "Religion and Gender in Modern France: Some Reflections." In *Religion, Society and Politics in France since 1789,* ed. Frank Tallett and Nicholas Atkin, pp. 55–66. London: Hambledon Press, 1991.

Mellor, Alec. *Histoire de l'anticléricalisme français.* Tours: Mame, 1966.

Mills, Hazel. "Negotiating the Divide: Women, Philanthropy and the 'Public Sphere' in Nineteenth-Century France." in *Religion, Society and Politics in France since 1789*, ed. Frank Tallett and Nicholas Atkin, pp. 29–54. London: Hambledon Press, 1991.

Nettement, Alfred. *Histoire de la littérature française sous la Restauration.* 2d ed. Vol. 2. Paris: LeCoffre, 1858.

Nord, Philip. *The Republican Moment: Struggles for Democracy in Nineteenth-Century France.* Cambridge, Mass.: Harvard University Press, 1995.

Nourrisson, Paul. *Histoire légale des congrégations religieuses en France depuis 1789.* 2 vols. Paris: Sirey, 1928.

Outram, Dorinda. "*Le langage mâle de la vertu:* Women and the Discourse of the French Revolution." In *The Social History of Language,* ed. Peter Burke and Roy Porter, pp. 120–35. Cambridge: Cambridge University Press, 1987.

Owen, Alex. *The Darkened Room: Women, Power, and Spiritualism in Late Victorian England.* Philadelphia: University of Pennsylvania Press, 1987.

Ponton, Jeanne. *La religieuse dans la littérature française.* Laval: Presses de l'Université de Laval, 1969.

Pindle, Karen, "A Bas les couvents!" Anticlerical Sentiment in French Opera in 1790." *Music Review* 42 (1981).

Rapley, Elizabeth. *The Dévotes: Women and the Church in Seventeenth-Century France.* Montreal: McGill University Press, 1990

Rebérioux, Madeleine. "Ruptures et figures contemporaines." In *Histoire de la France: Les formes de la culture,* ed. André Burguière and Jacques Revel, 397–420. Paris: Seuil, 1993.

Rémond, René. *L'anticléricalisme en France, 1815 à nos jours.* Paris: Fayard, 1976.

Revel, Jacques, ed. *Jeux d'échelles: La micro-analyse à l'expérience.* Paris: Gallimard, 1996.

Rogers, Rebecca. "Retrograde or Modern? Unveiling the Teaching Nun in Nineteenth-Century France." *Social History* 23 (May 1998): 146–64.

Ronsin, François. *Le contrat sentimental: Débats sur le mariage, l'amour, le divorce, de l'ancien régime à la Restauration.* Paris: Aubier, 1990.

Sabean, David Warren. *Power in the Blood: Popular Culture and Village Discontent in Early Modern Germany.* Cambridge: Cambridge University Press, 1984.

Saupin, Guy, ed. *Tolérance et intolerance de l'édit de Nantes à nos jours.* Rennes: Presses universitaires de Rennes, 1998.

Savart, Claude, *L'abbé Jean-Hipplolyte Michon, 1806–1881: Contribution à l'étude du libéralisme au XIXe siècle.* Paris: Belles Lettres, 1971.

——. *Les catholiques en France au XIXe siècle: Le témoignage du livre religieux.* Paris: Beauchesne, 1985.

Schultheiss, Katrin. *Bodies and Souls: Politics and the Professionalization of Nursing in France, 1880–1922* Cambridge, Mass.: Harvard University Press, 2000.

Scott, Joan W. "French Feminists and the Rights of 'Man': Olympe de Gouges's Declarations." *History Workshop* 28 (Autumn 1989): 1–21.

——. "'A Woman Who Has Only Paradoxes to Offer': Olympe de Gouges Claims Rights for Women." In *Rebel Daughters: Women and the French Revolution,* ed. Sara E. Melzer and Leslie Rabine, pp. 102–20. Oxford: Oxford University Press, 1992.

——. *Only Paradoxes to Offer: French Feminists and the Rights of Man.* Cambridge, Mass.: Harvard University Press, 1996.

Seeley, Paul. "*O Sainte Mère:* Liberalism and the Socialization of Catholic Men in Nineteenth-Century France." *Journal of Modern History* 70, no. 4 (December 1998): 862–91.

Sévrin, Ernest. *Les missions religieuses en France sous la Restauration.* 2 vols. Saint-Mandé: Procure des prêtres de la Miséricorde, 1948–59.

——. *Mgr. Clausel de Montals, évêque de Chartres (1769–1857): Un évêque militant et gallican au XIXe siècle.* 2 vols. Paris: Vrin, 1955.

Smith, Bonnie G. *Ladies of the Leisure Class: The Bourgeoises of Northern France in the Nineteenth Century.* Princeton, N.J.: Princeton University Press, 1981.

Tackett, Timothy. *Religion, Revolution, and Regional Culture in Eighteenth-Century France: The Ecclesiastical Oath of 1791.* Princeton, N.J.: Princeton University Press, 1986.

——. "Women and Men in Counterrevolution: The Sommières Riot of 1791." *Journal of Modern History* 59 (December 1987): 680–704.

Taylor, Katherine Fischer. *In the Theatre of Criminal Justice: The Palais de Justice in Second Empire Paris.* Princeton, N.J.: Princeton University Press, 1993.

Tetu, Jean-François. "Remarques sur le statut juridique de la femme au XIXe siècle." In *La femme au XIXe siècle: Littérature et idéologie,* ed. R. Bellet, pp. 5–17. Lyon: Presses universitaires de Lyon, 1979.

Théry, Irène, and Christian Biet, eds. *La famille, la loi, l'état, de la Révolution au Code Civil.* Paris: Imprimerie Nationale, 1989.

Timmermans, Linda. *L'accès des femmes à la culture (1598–1715).* Paris: Honoré Champion, 1993.

Traer, James F. *Marriage and the Family in Eighteenth-Century France.* Ithaca: Cornell University Press, 1980.

Tristan, Flora. *The Worker's Union.* Translated by Beverly Livingston. Urbana: University of Illinois Press, 1983.

Trumbach, Randolph. *The Rise of the Egalitarian Family: Aristocratic Kinship and Domestic Relations in Eighteenth-Century England.* New York: Academic Press, 1978.

Turgeon, Charles. *Le féminisme français: Emancipation individuelle et sociale de la femme.* Paris: Larose, 1902.

Turin, Yvonne. *Femmes et religieuses au XIXe siècle: Le féminisme "en religion."* Paris: Nouvelle Cité, 1989.

Turmann, Max. *La conquête de l'âme féminine: Institutions post-scolaire "laïques" et oeuvres chrétiennes.* Paris: Lecoffre, 1966.

Turquan, Joseph. *Les femmes de l'émigration, 1789–1815.* 4th ed. Paris: Emile Paul, 1911.

Valenze, Deborah. *Prophetic Sons and Daughters: Female Preaching and Popular Religion in Industrial England.* Princeton, N.J.: Princeton University Press, 1985.

Voilquin, Suzanne. "Recollections of a Daughter of the People." In *The French Worker: Autobiographies from the Early Industrial Era,* ed. Mark Traugott, pp. 92–115. Berkeley: University of California Press, 1993.

Welter, Barbara. "The Feminization of American Religion, 1800–1860." In *Clio's Consciousness Raised,* ed. Mary S. Hartman and Lois Banner, pp. 137–57. New York: Octagon Books, 1974.

Zeldin, Theodore. *The Political System of Napoleon III.* New York: Norton, 1958.

———. "The Conflict of Moralities: Confession, Sin and Pleasure in the Nineteenth Century." In *Conflicts in French Society: Anticlericalism, Education and Morals in the Nineteenth Century*, ed. Theodore Zeldin, pp. 13–50. London: George Allen and Unwin, 1970.

———. *France, 1848–1945: Politics and Anger* (Oxford: Oxford University Press, 1979.

INDEX

Page numbers in italics refer to figures.